A MINGLED MEASURE

A Mingled Measure

DIARIES, 1953–1972

James Lees-Milne

JOHN MURRAY
Albemarle Street, London

To my step-great-grandson
KANE
a writer

Frontispiece: '. . . with A. and me walking self-consciously down the lime alley'.

Friday, 5 May 1972

© James Lees-Milne 1994

First published in 1994
by John Murray (Publishers) Ltd.,
50 Albemarle Street, London W1X 4BD

Reprinted in 1994, 1995, 1998

The moral right of the author has been asserted

A catalogue record for this book is available from the British Library

ISBN 0–7195–5362 8

Typeset in 11.5/13 Bembo by Pure Tech Corporation, Pondicherry, India
Printed and bound in Great Britain by
The University Press, Cambridge

Contents

Preface

The last volume of my published diaries ended with the year 1949. It was entitled *Midway on the Waves*. And little did I suppose at the age of 43 that I had exactly reached midway in breasting the waves of my lifespan in so far as it was to be allotted me.

Alvilde and I were married in November 1951. At the time she was domiciled in France. During the ensuing decade she was resident for three-quarters of the year at La Meridienne on the edge of the old mountain village of Roquebrune in the Alpes Maritimes. Roquebrune was a thousand feet above the Mediterranean and three miles from the Italian border. It was well away from the Riviera coast, that resort of good-timers dubbed 'the septic belt', which neither of us much relished.

La Meridienne was a very small house, indeed an old cottage or peasants' cabin which had been charmingly converted into something little larger than a hermit's cell, with one minute dependency. In due course we added another detached room for a bed and grand piano. The house was approached only by a narrow footpath along which all luggage had to be carried. Cars had to park in 'la place' at the entrance to the village from the Grande Corniche. At La Meridienne Alvilde made an enchanted garden out of a series of descending vine terraces, on the top one of which the house perched.

I had a London flat at no. 20 Thurloe Square, South Kensington, which I rented in Geoffrey Houghton-Brown's house. There Alvilde would join me as long as her passport permitted. I was still working on the staff of the National Trust but in a part-time capacity until 1966 when I retired, thereafter serving on one or two of the Trust's committees. In the 1950s we also travelled a good deal in England, France, Italy, Spain and Germany, either separately or together.

In 1961 we put a term to our Box and Cox existence. Alvilde sold La Meridienne and gave up her French domicile. We also left

Thurloe Square. That autumn we bought and moved into Alderley Grange, two miles from Wotton-under-Edge in Gloucestershire. Alderley at the foot of the Cotswolds is no more than a hamlet with a church. The Grange has an elegant mid-Georgian front of silvery stone tacked on to a simple Jacobean block at the rear. We made it our only dwelling and intended to live there for ever.

For three years after 1949 I kept no diary at all. From 1953 to 1971 I resumed it very intermittently indeed. A lot I destroyed one day in revulsion. In the following pages I include some excerpts from what has survived from those years. These I have carefully headed Roquebrune, Thurloe Square, Alderley or wherever they were written so as to minimize the reader's confusion.

The volume continues with a regular resumption in July 1971, to conclude in December 1972.

My motives in resuming the diaries were various and are touched upon in some entries. As for my temerity or folly in publishing a fresh volume I really can offer no explanation.

If I have inadvertently wounded a friend I am sorry and suggest that he looks in the index to see if there is another reference to him. He may find that on the next day I laud him to the skies. After all, a diary is a register of spontaneous impressions which, I am bound to admit, sometimes contradict one another.

I am especially grateful to my old friend Burnet Pavitt for ploughing through the rough and ready typescript and proffering his advice; and to Grant McIntyre and Gail Pirkis of John Murray's for seeing it into print.

J. L.-M.

The shadow of the dome of pleasure
Floated midway on the waves;
Where was heard the mingled measure
From the fountain and the caves.

S. T. Coleridge, 'Kubla Khan'

1953

Willie [Somerset] Maugham who dined with Alvilde and me to-night in Monte Carlo talked of Rudyard Kipling 'not being quite a gent'. Kipling once lunched with Willie in the Villa Mauresque at Cap Ferrat and the name of a mutual friend was mentioned. 'He's a white man,' exclaimed Kipling. Willie thought, 'This is characteristic. How I wish, in order to fulfil my preconceptions of him, he would say he was a pukka sahib.' 'He's a pukka sahib all right,' continued Kipling. I said how friendly and intelligent I found Mrs Bambridge* last summer when I lunched with her at Wimpole. 'Yes,' Willie said, 'she can be, but she is also a demon.' Everyone says the same of her so I suppose she really must be. We took Willie and Alan Searle† to the Dutch Ballet which was pretty bad. They were like cheeses rolling around, A. observed. Between the acts Willie went to be photographed with the *corps de ballet*. Alan then said he noticed great changes in Willie. He was ageing. 'He is no longer very happy, hates being alone, sleeps little and with his door open, and is inclined to weep.' But he *is* old and will be 79 tomorrow; and his face is like a nutcracker, carelessly wrapped in parchment.

Tuesday, 27th January

The Graham Sutherlands‡ to dine. A. finds he too has aged since last year. He is 50, but very good-looking and still youthful in figure. He has a slow, deliberate way of speaking and never says a foolish thing. I should say he is not an intellectual, but a most intelligent man. He gives a wrong impression of simplicity. This and his natural charm make him thoroughly disarming without his setting out to be so. She has raven black hair as smooth as a

---

* Elsie Bambridge, 1894–1976, daughter of Rudyard Kipling. Married 1924 George Bambridge.
† Alan Searle, Somerset Maugham's confidential secretary and friend.
‡ Graham Sutherland, OM, 1903–80, artist. Married 1927 Katharine (Kathie) Barry.

gramophone record, and is pretty, foolish, catty but fanatically
devoted to him and jealous of his reputation. In her own right she
is an excellent draughtsman and does the liveliest caricatures. She
is quite satisfied that he is the world's greatest painter. They are
devoted to one another. I said to Graham that I did not understand
why so many artists today bothered to travel miles from England
to, say, Naples, or Marrakesh in order to paint a petrol pump
which they could as easily have painted in the Fulham Road. He
said this was a point of view that had not occurred to him and he
could not share. Delightful though he is conversation is made
difficult by her always wanting to assert herself. When one is
talking to him she invariably butts in. When talking to her she does
not concentrate.

The Sutherlands both knew Denton Welch.* A. and I are deeply
interested in him having greatly enjoyed his journals and his *Voice
through a Cloud*. Graham said he was not a nice character and had
no friends; was self-centred, querulous and cissyish. She said he
was yellow and ugly; that he liked attracting sailors and toughs and
then would spurn them when they became familiar. He hated
being touched.

It is strange, in correcting the typescript of my book, to see
Eddie Marsh's† astringent pencil marks and notes in the first two
chapters, and realize that that mind, so active a month ago, has
disappeared overnight. I never cared deeply for Eddie. Intellectu-
ally he was aloof, and dismissive; had favourites; also was inaudible; talked through his teeth. I never felt comfortable with
him. He dined with us on Christmas Day and we thought then we
might not see him again. That was an awful day for me. I had
received a letter from him that he could not continue correcting
my book: the type was so faint it hurt his eyes; besides he said I
was a *bad* writer. My use of words was odd. I could not express
myself. For two days I was miserable; then on reading through his
corrections and the book again I realized he was absolutely right.
Apart from having made a fool of myself – this worried me because
he must have told many people – I was no longer the least hurt. I
truly believe I can improve my style on the lines he has shown me:

---

* Denton Welch, 1915–48, writer and painter.
† Sir Edward Marsh, 1872–1953, civil servant, scholar and patron of the arts
and literature.

i.e. to be natural. So I am grateful to the poor old deceased to that very real extent.

I well remember my first meeting with Eddie in the early 1930s while staying at Cumberland Lodge (Windsor Park) with the old FitzAlans.* Why they had invited me I just can't understand. The other guests were ancients – Lord and Lady Salisbury,† Mrs Belloc Lowndes,‡ General Sir F. and Lady Isobel Gathorne-Hardy (terribly boring and stuffy),§ Abbot Sir David Hunter-Blair,¶ the Stanley Baldwins,‖ and Eddie Marsh. They are all now dead except me. I am alive. It was in the summer. We changed clothes ceaselessly – for church (at least the Protestants did), for luncheon, for walking after luncheon, for tea, for dinner. I went before breakfast for a walk round the Copper Horse with Mr Baldwin who was then Prime Minister, followed closely by two detectives in bowler hats, looking absurdly out of place and hot. Mr Baldwin lit his pipe during dessert while peeling an apple at the dinner table. I thought it odd. Tea took place under a lime tree on the lawn, carried there on silver trays by footmen. The women held sunshades and wore fluffy dresses and gossiped like refined sparrows. What I remember of my talks with Baldwin was his adoration of Worcestershire which conveyed to him the same ineffably cosy, remote, hay-meadow, apple-orchard, hop-garden nostalgia which it does to me – the very mention of the word – and his pleasant memories of croquet parties before 1914 at Ribbesford with my grandparents. Eddie had a room next to mine – we were the bachelors – and he sat in collarless shirt and dressing-gown on the end of my bed before we said goodnight. A brass stud bobbled up and down his Adam's apple. Next morning I confided in

---

* 1st Viscount FitzAlan, KG, 1855–1947, statesman, and leading Roman Catholic layman; and his wife Lady Mary C. Bertie.
† 4th Marquess of Salisbury, 1861–1947, Leader of the House of Lords; and his wife Lady Alice Gore.
‡ Marie Belloc Lowndes, novelist, d. 1947. Sister of Hilaire Belloc.
§ The Hon. Sir Francis Gathorne-Hardy, 1874–1949, General and GOC-in-Chief; and his wife Lady Isobel Stanley.
¶ Right Revd Sir David Hunter-Blair, 5th Bt., 1853–1939, Abbot of Fort Augustus, OSB.
‖ Stanley Baldwin, 1867–1947, Prime Minister, created Earl Baldwin of Bewdley 1937; and his wife Lucy Ridsdale.

Mr Baldwin my misery at Reuters, and took his advice, which was to send in my notice at once, before I was sacked.

Monday, 2nd February

We dined at Somerset Maugham's to meet the Kenneth Clarks who are staying with him. The Graham Sutherlands there. I sat between Jane and K. She is not a little tiresome like most proud wives of distinguished husbands, and full of pretensions; but she is affable. Has just recovered from a second bad operation. K. always terrifies me because he is about the cleverest man I know. His gracious manner puts men properly in their place but evidently raises women to his own high estate. He is finishing his book on the Nude which Jane says will be the best he has written. I asked him how many portraits there were by Leonardo of Ginevra Benci. He said only the Lichtenstein one in the National Gallery. So I told him the story of Inigo Jones unpacking the one sent to Charles I which I.J. pronounced to be of Ginevra Benci because of the G and B inscribed on her breast; and K. said the Lichtenstein portrait had been cut down and he did not know whether it had been in Charles I's collection or not.

Monday, 9th February

Last week the bell at the gate pealed loudly and a very chic motor-cyclist, wearing a white helmet and armed cap-à-pie appeared, saluted smartly and handed me two letters in heavily embossed envelopes. Alvilde had warned me that Pierre [de Monaco]* mentioned that we were to be invited to luncheon at the Palace to meet the Duff Coopers.† At first I resolutely refused to go, but seeing how much she wanted to accept, relented. Also agreed that perhaps the Ruritanian experience ought not to be missed. One of the letters was addressed to the Norwiches, the other to us. I gave back the Norwich invite since we didn't know

---

* Prince Pierre de Monaco (né Prince Pierre de Polignac), 1895–1964, father of the reigning Prince of Monaco.
† Duff Cooper, 1st Viscount Norwich, 1890–1954, diplomatist, politician, ambassador, author; and his wife Lady Diana Cooper.

where they were staying and they were after all to be the principal guests.

Today was the occasion. I wore my dark grey flannel suit, the most sombre suit I have here, and A. put on her best dress. We went to the Hôtel de Paris where we left Mama who had already arranged to spend the afternoon with the Jack Muirs* now staying in Monte Carlo. There we joined Duff and Diana. Today I liked both more than I had done hitherto. He is not easy to talk to. She says whatever comes into her head and is very funny. The four of us then packed into the *Topolino*, our tiny 3-horsepower Fiat, and went roaring up to Monaco. The Palace guards in their striped sentry boxes were so surprised and shocked by the insignificance of the vehicle that they stopped us before allowing us to enter the courtyard. This compelled me to go into bottom gear before starting off again. So we passed uphill through the gatehouse making a deafening din. Duff clambered out, crumpled and creased, and shut the door on Diana who yelled at him, 'Papa, let me out!' By this time the servants and soldiers ranged on the steps were bewildered. There seemed to be hundreds of them, soldiers in medieval helmets and soldiers holding pikes, major-domos in chains, on every step of the hotel-like marble staircase. We were given table-cards and ushered into a pretty Louis XV room of gilded *boiserie* overlooking the outer court. We were received by aides-de-camp and an American Monsignore. The British Consul was the next to arrive. Then the Monégasque Minister of Finance. No one else. The other guests we were told had succumbed to influenza.

We stood on one foot and then another until a far door opened, and in walked shyly a good-looking young man, plump but not gross, in a dark serge suit and monk's shoes with buckles in place of straps. He [Prince Rainier] has a head somewhat like Napoleon's, an olive complexion and dark hair with one streak of grey in the front. I liked his face. Each was presented in turn. Alvilde curtsied and I bowed. He then led the way to the large dining-room after we had been handed cocktails. Since there were more men than women I sat with an aide-de-camp on my left: the dull old Dame du Palais on my right, between me and the Prince, to

---

* John B. Muir, b. 1876, of Kiftsgate Court, Glos.; and his wife Heather (née Muir).

whom I didn't pass a word the whole afternoon. Although the Palace was quite cold I did not dare drink the several wines which A. said afterwards were better than the food. This was not good and looked and tasted as though it had been brought from outside, and not cooked in the Palace. I believe the Prince does not live in the Palace but with a film star in a villa at Beaulieu. What a suitable young man we thought for Clarissa [Chaplin, my stepdaughter] to marry. His sister Princess Antoinette was there too. Rather pretty and has recently married a tennis professional with whom she has lived for several years and by whom she has several illegitimate children.

Duff and Diana came back with us to the Meridienne afterwards. She is still extremely beautiful; melting ice-blue eyes. Manner warmer than her appearance. I wish I could see more of her to know her better. Her appeal is in the open way of saying exactly what she is thinking: and sometimes even before she has properly thought.

Friday, 13th February

We have taken Mama back to Nice. From the departure terrace I watched her climb into the aeroplane. It rose briskly into the air and vanished into a thundery sky.

Mama stayed with us for ten days and the visit was not a success. Alvilde was intensely irritated and although correct in her manner never friendly and at times quite snubbing. I too have been intensely irritated and yet sad indeed that I could not be nicer. For me the visit was a conflict of emotions. It is the first time for years that I have been with Mama for a comparatively long period. She has become extremely affected, gushing and unnatural. Her conversation is confined to the Haineses,[15] Lottie her maid, and herself. Nothing, nothing else interests her. She brings every sentence round to herself. 'Don't you think I am rather wonderful to walk up these steps?' 'Of course I had a bad headache this morning, but I managed to conceal it from you.' 'Don't bother about me. I don't need any dinner.' Then abuse of her children and children-in-law. A. says she has never in her born days met anyone more difficult, unless it was her first mother-in-law. I have

---

* Norris Haines, my parents' old chauffeur for sixty years, and his wife.

to face up to the terrible truth that I have grown miles and miles apart from her. I dare not look at her for fear she will say something so silly that I shall be driven to snap. Then I feel bitterly, miserably penitent. And who the hell am I to dare judge her, my mother? And why do I fail every time to give her what she wants, confidence, flattery and oceans of sympathy, since deeply, deeply down I do love her? I cannot, however hard I try. O glory!

Thursday, 19th February

We were asked to meet Colette* at luncheon today by Daisy Fellowes.† A. said we must accept: that Colette was 80 and a person of the greatest importance in the literary world of the twentieth century. But since I haven't read a word of hers and because of my indifferent French I didn't want to go in the least. However I did go, needless to say, and my misgivings were realized. I was able to contribute nothing. We met Daisy in the hall of the Hôtel de Paris, went to the bar and were joined by Colette's husband, a nice, kind, attentive man of about 58 I should judge. Then Colette was wheeled up in a chair. There were no other guests. There was a procession to the dining-room and as we followed the chair a wash of heads turned in our direction. Then a ripple of comments. I sat on her right. Under a fuzz of thin, greyish hair she has an oval, piquante little face: very pretty. Large eyes, expressive and beautiful and mascara'd. The skin round the right eye bruised black like a 'black eye' caused by a blow. Neatly shaped little nose; plump, expressive, pretty hands like the bronze letter-weight hand which lies beside me on my table as I write (and which I bought in the Nice junk market), and two large amethyst rings on the little and next finger of the left hand. She wore a blue blouse on which was pinned the new order she was awarded at the Palace today, and over it a pretty deep blue coatee with gold braid and blue-embroidered border.

Daisy was absolutely wonderful with Colette, for she told her fanciful little stories and laughed in the most affectionate way about the things she chose to eat; and she pandered to every whim. The luncheon ordered was exquisite, but Colette would have none of it,

---

* Colette, 1873–1954, French novelist.
† Marguerite (Daisy), 1890–1962, wife of the Hon. Reginald Fellowes, daughter of 4th Duc Decazes, and widow of Prince Jean de Broglie.

and asked for radishes, on which she sprinkled salt, and then an artichoke. Then she ordered China tea, and cheese. She is very frail and touchingly childlike, yet sharp still, and came out with pertinent little phrases and rather poetic expressions in a deep Burgundian voice. Her speech, like her whole style of writing, is clipped, economical and exact. She took a long time to warm up to conversation, and even so conversation did not exactly flow. She kept interrupting us with little bird-like cries of complaint about the spoon, or the salt, while looking bewildered and muddled. She told a story, which I have somewhere read before, of her only visit to England. She stayed in the country with an Anglo-Indian Colonel Manson who kept a dog. To her surprise he always addressed the dog in execrable French. (He never spoke to anyone but the dog.) The reason being that the only book he had ever read was a French one picked up at his club in Quetta when he had nothing better to do. She talked of fish and the superior intelligence of the pike. Her mother, she said, had a tortoise called Charlotte, which slept throughout the winter. There came a day every year when she heard her mother call out: '*Charlotte s'éveille. C'est le printemps!*'

She reminded me not a little of Gertie Millar[*] when I met her staying with Patsy Ward.[†] The same candour, suppressed bitchiness, lack of society nonsense, gaiety, generosity – in fact the old music-hall qualities; like someone left behind in an empty ballroom, someone to whom the muted echoes of outdated music and song are still clinging. The ghost in fact from a departed *belle époque* more idyllic, yet more earthy than our own.

It was quite touching to watch Willie [Maugham], who was lunching nearby, trot up to her and embrace her while she stroked his arm. A flirtation took place between the two octogenarian novelists.

Friday, 27th February

This evening before dark went for a short walk along the Gorbio mountain path and on my return heard the familiar tinkle-clang of the goats being folded. There they all were on the path returning

---

[*] Gertrude Millar, d. 1952, Gaiety or Gibson Girl. Married 1924 2nd Earl of Dudley.
[†] Lady Patricia Ward, 1924–64, stepdaughter of the above.

home to bed. The little black dog came bounding up to me, then resumed his duty. The old goats are so wise and patient, but irritable at times and snap silently at the black dog, who wags his tail. There seems to be an instinctive understanding between them. As the path is narrow and precipitous I couldn't pass the goats for a long time so I walked with the sullen young goatherd and was determined to talk to him. Although his clothes are unromantic – he wears old tweed trousers, a slouch hat and carries a long stick but no flute – he nevertheless cuts a pastoral or rather bucolic figure. He has that quiet, philosophic, almost cynical, unsurprised air of the real peasant. Tells me that in May he goes off to the mountains with his goats until November. In the winter he sleeps in Roquebrune village, God knows where. In a barn? But in the summer on the bare hills as far as I can make out. Says he is Italian, but speaks a better French than most of the inhabitants of the village. Says this place – quietly waving his stick around – was Italy until quite lately and is now France. You don't know where you are from one moment to the next. Tells me the name of the village across the valley which I mean to walk to; but has never heard of La Mórtola* which I point out to him across the water. I much admire the detached, indifferent but infinitely court-eous way in which he says goodnight. He is very well bred.

Saturday, 28th February

The last days of February are cloudless and still and the sun is almost scorching. A. and Joan Moore[†] drop me on the Riviera road just past Antibes this afternoon. They go on by car to Cannes. I walk into the hinterland to the Glenconners,[‡] La Baumette. To start with the road is not pretty, but after two miles the hideous Riviera strip of villas is left behind. Why are French suburban roads crueller and less person-alized than English ones? There are no hedges. Barbed wire is attached to rickety posts. The scenery and all nature are behind the barbed wire. But today it was not me who was the prisoner, but the

---

* Capo Mórtola, or the Hanbury Garden, near San Remo, on the Italian Riviera.
† Joan Carr, pianist, wife of Garrett, Viscount Moore, later 11th Earl of Drogheda. Both d. 1989.
‡ Christopher Tennant, 1899–1983, and Elizabeth Powell, 2nd Lord and Lady Glenconner.

distant Chinese mountain tops, the olives and the woman bending over the soapsuds so that her skirt at the back disappeared into her waist. Then the telegraph posts here are so makeshift and hoisted into the air on insecure-looking iron stilts to prevent the ants eating the wood. It is all so untidy and tasteless. The little houses by the roadside have no gardens or boundary walls. Barbed wire again and that hard, clinkery earth. There is nothing lush about the undergrowth of the pine-tree wood when I get to it. The cistus, the oak scrub, the toe-stubbing boulders are prickly, arid and uncomfortable. It is curious that they should be haymaking in February. In an olive grove was a hay-cart and a man throwing the dry grass up to another man on the top of the stack. A horrid old yellow lorry passed me; it had a sprig of fresh mimosa tied to the bonnet. Just before the Glenconners' turning there is the only pretty pylon I have ever seen. It has delicate dunce caps and drooping finials like tired hands and the framework is a pattern of diamonds.

Sunday, 1st March

Janie Bussy said we might buy some of her father, Simon Bussy's* pictures, so this evening we went to look through them at Le Souco. Simon and Madame B, 'Olivia', have gone to England, the old man to be put in a home – on the site of Bedlam Janie explained caustically – for incontinence and senile forgetfulness. Last year when we saw him he was merely quiet and reserved, replying to questions in a deep, gruff but not disagreeable voice. He looked like an old railway porter. We scanned the paintings carefully. They vary greatly in merit and the early ones are the best, still influenced by the Impressionists. We finally chose a lemur, very finely done, with a halo of fur, and a delicate pastel of distant Mentone seen through olives, done years ago from my favourite chapel corner beyond our village, before the view towards the town was spoilt; and a tiny sketch called *Paysage Anglais*, which resembles a scene sketch by Inigo Jones for the masque *Luminalia*. A. has given it to me.

---

* Simon Bussy, French painter, and his wife Dorothea (m. 1903), sister of Lytton Strachey and authoress of *Olivia*.

Stalin is dead. Thank God! I have finished my Inigo Jones book after very hard work on it since 23rd January and reduced its length by 16,000 words, not 20,000 as I was asked to do. I pray Batsford won't tell me to cut it down still further, for I am sick of it. Whenever I believe I have come to the end of a book I never have; there is always something extra to be done. If not returned for further cutting there are still the preface, the bibliography and the index to be tackled. I like to think this book is the best I have so far written. But it is less readable than the others.

Joan Moore has taken the two manuscript notebooks to London for me, via Paris. It was with much apprehension that I watched the aeroplane containing them (and dear Joan) dart into the blue sky this morning at Nice. It had hardly risen into the air before it disappeared.

After luncheon I changed into my dirtiest shirt and went for a mammoth walk to Castellare, the village I have long seen as a mirage floating above Mentone, and determined to visit. I had to go via Mentone. Soon got away from the civilized strip and was among the peasant women carrying long sheaves of silver olive branches on their shoulders, and peasant men with baggy trousers, patched and filthy. So filthy that I dared not look too close. The *vallons* or coombs behind Mentone are crammed with disused mills with vast wooden water-wheels and runnels of swift water from one wheel into another. In one of the mill-houses which had been nastily modernized and concreted Alvilde found a dwelling for the Sutherlands, which they are delighted with. Castellare is so embowered in olives that it can be seen only from a distance on its own level. I clambered through terraced groves. Under the gnarled old trees grew thin green grass or wheat, interspersed with violets and grape hyacinths. The village is quite unspoilt. On reaching it I discovered to my surprise that it was on a peak and not on the slope of the Roc d'Ormea as I had supposed. This huge iodine cliff stands like a drop scene sheer behind it. At the end of the narrow main street, cobbled, a little domed building has a wrought-iron balcony with bookrest – Bible, Missal? – to enable the preacher to read from it in the open air. I drank lemon water seated in the sun behind the café overlooking the distant sea.

In spite of the natural beauty on all sides my attention was distracted by the oratory of a bourgeois French shopkeeper at the next table with only his frowsty wife and an obsequious daughter for audience. The substance of his talk mere gossip about their relations, Oncle Josef, Tante Marianne, Cousine Bette. O so boring. This sort of Frenchman wonderfully insensitive to feelings of neighbouring tables.

Entered the tiny shrine at Castellare and was glad to be a Papist, a participant in the universality, I suppose. It would be impossible to remain a Protestant if living in a Catholic country. Yet it is not disagreeable being a Catholic in a Protestant country. How is this?

Tuesday, 10th March

Met the goatherd on the Gorbio path this evening. He was smellier, more affable and less shy, and positively greeted me; then talked for five minutes while the black dog and goats rambled off on their own. I noticed that his handsome little face was covered with ghastly livid spots and blackheads, and under the right eye was a large swelling caused by a boil. Inadequate food I daresay, poor thing. I was surprised however when he told me he was only 17 for he already has a wispy, bristly black moustache. He says the sea air gives him spots and he always feels better in the summer months up in the mountains and away from the sea. He finds it *ennuyeux* being alone all day long with no one to talk to and hopes that one day he may work in Mentone. When I asked him what he thought about by himself on the hills the reply was '*J'n'ai pas de temps pour penser.*'

I left the path and climbed the steep slope looking for wild flowers. Found several hepatica, little blue stars with white rays; they grow in the long grass where there is much leaf mould and I doubt if they would thrive in our garden. Also picked primroses, a scabious and one *Scylla italica*, very delicate and Gothic. Alas, there are few flowers on these slopes. I fear all dug up since Moggridge wrote his *Flowers of Menton* or all eaten by goats. When I came home before 7 the sea was deep mauve and the sky over the Tête du Chien custard – not pretty.

Saturday, 14th March

A. and I set off for Italy at 8 o'clock. We changed cars at Mentone and travelled in the Plymouth. Stopped at Albenga on the Riviera where indeed few of the old towns are worth visiting. Here we looked at the octagonal baptistery of very early date. The most remarkable feature the windows with fairly delicate stone tracery, too small for alabaster fillings, and I suppose always were un-glazed.

We were asked by Quentin Crewe[*] to stay the night at Gli Scaffari near Lerici. He is companion and reader to Percy Lub-bock,[†] the owner. It is exactly twenty years since I stayed in this villa with the George Lloyds[‡] who rented it. We all bathed. It was August or September and I had arrived from Corsica where I had ridden across the island on muleback. I was dressed as near as I dared be to a Corsican bandit in sky-blue trousers and a wide red bandana round my waist and striped sailor jersey. Absurdly preten-tious and silly I must have appeared to the staid Lloyds.

Mr Lubbock is 73, purblind and groping about; charming, gentle, with a sort of sardonic, deprecatory chuckle. Deeply read and academic. We instantly liked him; and he was very welcom-ing. His sympathies are wholly left-wing. Dismisses all social standards and gossip. He and Quentin make a rather touching couple, each with his physical disability. Quentin aged 28 is crippled with an incurable muscular disease and moves in a stiff, ungainly gait, ugly to watch. He is a very intelligent young man. The garden is divine: a grove of terraced olives above a rocky escarpment on the sea. Jonquils, irises, and hyacinths are growing under the olives among the dry grass.

Sunday, 15th March

Poor A. very bored (but good) with my desire to see the duomo and piazza at Leghorn. The cathedral destroyed in the war is being rebuilt on the old lines, for what that is worth; the piazza on modernistic lines mostly, but one side on the old recognizable lines of round-headed arcades and *piano nobile* and attic storey above. What Inigo Jones presumably saw, and what influenced his Covent Garden piazza.

---

[*] Quentin Crewe, b. 1926, journalist, traveller, writer and half-brother of Mary (Midi) Gascoigne.
[†] Percy Lubbock, 1879–1965, writer.
[‡] George, 1st Lord Lloyd of Dolobran, 1879–1941, statesman and proconsul, and his wife Blanche Lascelles.

Our visit to Rome was on account of the next book on my agenda. I have chosen the subjects: essays on Ancient Roman, Early Christian, medieval, Renaissance, baroque and rococo monuments of each period. I mean them to be poetical and free, not to be guide-booky or too factual, but representative of each historical and architectural context. I mean to explain what great buildings signify aesthetically and associatively. This will be a test of my limited powers. Maybe I shall fail. Goodness knows who will publish them.

We saw a lot of the Beits* in Rome. I am extremely fond of both. Alfred highly intelligent, determined, has broad interests. Clementine always sunshine, is likewise very well informed. She takes immense pains to see all she can and as thoroughly as possible. Won't waste a moment while sight-seeing. What I like.

Sunday, 29th March (Palm Sunday)

Back at Roquebrune. Walterine our maid called us with two palms she bought at the village shop, beautifully plaited; mine in shape of a Maltese cross, A.'s of a star, and both with tails. At church all the children came *endimanchés* and carrying the most elaborate plaited palm branches hung with sweets in coloured papers and small witch-balls. The Curé carried a thin, long palm branch like a pheasant's tail, waving; the old people large branches of flowering laurel, orange blossom or plain olive to be blessed. The scene in church was very gay. Here they do such things with éclat. They are not shy about religious festivals and processions. The Curé gave three tremendous knocks on the outside of the door before he was allowed admittance. Then Mass.

Pierre de Monaco, pompous and correct, pays us an unexpected call. Peals the bell by the gate. From an upstairs window Walterine screams, '*J'arrive! J'arrive!*' And then as though that were not enough, '*Madame est au water!*' Pierre vastly amused. But A. obliged later to instruct W. in more delicate ways of excusing her mistress's dilatoriness in receiving a guest.

I haven't yet heard from Batsford's whether my Inigo Jones manuscript is definitely accepted. There is much I want to get

* Sir Alfred Beit, 2nd Bt., 1903–94, MP; and his wife Clementine Mitford.

down to now. First, the Rome book; then the Jacobean book of
essays on three or four characters, Anne of Denmark or James I,
Lord Pembroke and Francis Bacon. Then a life of Lord Burlington; then a dictionary of country houses.

Good Friday, 3rd April

Roquebrune village still observes a long-cherished tradition on
Good Friday evenings. At 8.30 there are Stations of the Cross in
the church of which the interior is draped with black curtains, a
valance of white stars at the top and silver tears falling below; altar
covered with arum lilies. At 9.30 takes place the procession. This
consists of villagers only. First come four Roman centurions wearing helmets and breastplates over yellow tunics, breeches and laced
boots. They carry spears. Four bearers wearing white surplices and
oriental turbans carry on a bier a figure of the dead Christ covered
with a fine net sheet. Two male figures carry a long shroud. A
veiled woman carries St Veronica's towel with the face of Our
Lord imprinted on it. More Roman soldiers, not so important,
mere boys. Then a long trail of women wearing orange garments
and black shawls, or black dresses and orange shawls, their faces
almost covered, and holding candles in parchment lanterns. A man
with a drum which he beats at intervals. Behind them all the nice
quizzical *curé* hugging a monstrance. The procession begins at the
high altar, preceded by a surpliced figure bearing a high wooden
crucifix. He is followed by those visitors come to watch, on a circuit
of the village. The Roman centurions, who are the electrician, the
plumber and the man at the *épicerie* – these I recognize – bear flaming
torches. The procession takes place in great earnestness. There is no
giggling or sniggering. The performers never recognize their friends
in passing. The veiled women recite the Rosary and the men intone
on the march.

The village is lit up for the occasion. Each house puts out snail
shells filled with oil round doors and windows and up steps and
staircases. This is charming and pretty. Princess Ottoboni who
lives in a large villa outside the village gives prizes for the best
illuminated houses which some people deplore because it makes
the villagers mercenary. On the other hand this tradition might die
out altogether. In spite of the sightseers the whole affair is quite
unsophisticated and thoroughly bucolic. The participants bump

into each other, trip up, drop their torches and look for all the world what they are – peasants.

Lennox [Berkeley]* who is staying with us accompanied me into the church and followed the stations with a sort of dumb reverence. He is come to finish a concerto he is composing, to be performed on the Third Programme in Coronation week, and from his pavilion piano I hear emerge occasional dissonant noises, but nothing consecutive. I much wonder how good a composer he is. I am incapable of judging. I admire his exceptionally good and utterly childlike nature. Deeply earnest and remote in his own world, which is not mine and into which I cannot penetrate. He has much humility and simplicity of heart. The little I have heard of his music strikes me as chill. He doesn't play the piano very well and it is odd to hear him say he cannot perform his own compositions because he hasn't got the score with him. When he has got it he stumbles, goes back again and says such and such passages are too difficult for him.

Monday, 6th April

I go back to England this evening by the Blue Train from Monte Carlo. We came out here on a Monday, exactly three months ago. I have been happier here this winter than the last. Yet I am glad to be leaving. I have been long enough away from England and my interests. Yet I somewhat dread returning to the National Trust. I know I ought to leave it altogether for my presence there is redundant, even embarassing. Robin [Fedden]† doesn't now need me. In many ways he is better at the job than I was. It is awkward for him when I am about. It is always a mistake to hang around when one has resigned from a post. Yet what am I to do? I can't leave England altogether and give up the £700 a year which the Trust still pays me. Without it I have no regular income at all.

I am fond of my little pavilion in the garden at Roquebrune where I am writing at the moon-shaped table in the window. Beside me my lamp with blue shade and at its foot three blue mustard-liner glasses in Ritzy-Louis Quinze containers of ormolu, and the bronze hand letter-weight and the paper-clip of a duck's

---

* Sir Lennox Berkeley, 1903–90, composer.
† Robin Fedden, 1909–77, writer, secretary of Historic Buildings Committee, National Trust, 1951–74.

head in pewter in which I keep my letters. On a corner shelf the figure of Our Lady with Child, all in white biscuit, once belonging to a church no doubt, on a plinth of angel heads, bought by me in the Nice flea market. My Jump & Vuilliamy travelling clock which strikes the hours and quarters, tells the date, day of the week, and phases of the moon. I have to take it with me because if it runs down how can I ever set it properly again? Alas I have the minimum of reference books; there is no room. The pavilion is the size of a wagon-lit, just large enough to contain emergency bed, chest of drawers, two chairs and a niche for clothes, plus minute wash-basin.

20 Thurloe Square, SW7   *Thursday, 16th April*

At Brooks's I overhear Sir John Coke, Queen Mary's Comptroller, telling another member how terribly sad he is made by her death, and how he and all her Household adored her. He said she never altered her mind once she had made it up; that she had never been known to be late once in her life; that now she was gone there was no member of the royal family to keep the rest of them up to the mark; no one now to prevent the Queen from having meals with people like the Douglas Fairbankses, from motoring in a jeep without wearing a hat, etc. He said Queen Mary knew she was dying. She died on a Monday. The previous Saturday before leaving for the weekend Coke said goodbye to her with the words, 'I shall see you on Monday, ma'am.' Queen Mary's reply was, 'I think you will not.'

Once only I met her. I conducted her round an exhibition I organized in Cheyne Walk at the very beginning of the war. It was in aid of the Finns. She was extremely stiff, formal and rather ungracious. Very knowledgeable and informative, about furniture and bibelots of a royal sort, and contradictory: but splendid and awful. I had the greatest reverence for her and when I learnt of her death while I was in Rome, felt really bereft of the past which I did not feel when the late King George VI died. The Palace had far more telegrams on her death than on the King's. Her death truly is the end of a spent era. The last breath.

Yesterday I was at Petworth with Robin putting finishing touches to the house which is to be opened in May. The furniture is poor; the pictures on the other hand outstanding. Sculpture not up to much; and the architecture highly esteemed by the academic, because of the seventeenth-century French flavour. Whiffs of the Sun King. Some truly wonderful rooms of a rare period. And the carvings. And Turner.

Monday, 20th April

One of the strange things of the present age is listening to the voices of dead friends. This evening at the end of the first act of an opera the announcer of the Third Programme said we were about to hear a repeat performance. It was a conversation recorded in the '40s between Margaret Jourdain[*] and Ivy Compton-Burnett[†] about Ivy's novels. Margaret's familiar, governessy voice was as natural as if she were in the room, talking to Ivy who of course is alive – just. A still stranger thing perhaps was my turning off the wireless in the middle of the talk because I had something else to do. Now if any one of us had been told in 1923 that he could hear a friend, who had died two years previously, conversing with another friend he would have hung on every word, marvelling. Instead I today rather blasé-ly hung up.

When Rosamond [Lehmann][‡] dined with me last week she said I was unusual in my blending of the masculine with the feminine; that for a male man I had a very female sensibility. She said she had as many women as men friends and, if anything, preferred their society, yet she admitted there were few women with whom she could talk about fundamental things. Ros has a strong femininity with which I feel at times impatient. I am sure she does not expect or want a gesture of love from me, but I am occasionally made uncomfortable in suspecting that she would welcome the pretence of one. In other words a very close friendship with a woman, not so much older than oneself, can seldom be quite as straightforward as with a man.

After I wrote to Paul Latham[§] inviting myself to stay at Herstmonceux last Friday he telephoned while I was out. I was rather

---

[*] Margaret Jourdain, 1876–1951, authority on English furniture and decoration.
[†] Dame Ivy Compton-Burnett, 1884–1969, novelist.
[‡] Rosamond Lehmann, 1901–90, novelist.
[§] Sir Paul Latham, 2nd Bt., 1905–55, MP.

touched that, even ten years after he left prison, he would not give his name to Emily [my housekeeper], who I am sure is totally unaware of his past misdemeanours with youths while an MP. Somewhat amused she told me that a friend had telephoned: 'Tell him that Paul expects him to dinner on Friday.' Poor Paul has become a worse bore than ever. Incessant, absolutely inarticulate talk about himself. He said with candour and, I am sure, truth that he had nearly died so often, once when he tried to commit suicide on a motor-bike, that he had no fear of death and rather longed for it.

Friday, 8th May

Got back in time for dinner after touring Cheshire. Motored from Charlie Brocklehurst's* at Hare Hill, near Macclesfield, where I stayed two nights, by way of Ilam and the Dove valley which I had never seen before. Ilam Hall, half pulled down by the National Trust, has one of the loveliest English settings; views over a pastoral foreground, with church (nineteenth century) to sloping downs and a mountain, probably a hill only, like the Sugar Loaf. But it is scale, not height, which makes a mole-heap as impressive as Everest. Behind the house an amphitheatre of beech trees athwart a sickle of a meadow, all sunny in yellow greenness and freshness, one tree piled on top of another. And at the base the brown Dove river, I suppose, into which bubbles of current well from the ground, a subterranean tributary.

The day before was full of some beautiful moments: one while climbing to the top of Beeston Castle which has a splendid site, surely unique for England but common in the Rhine valley. The ruins are perched precariously on a projecting rock over a plumb-line drop. Below, pasture and comfortable farmsteads of the 1840s and '50s. I can think of nothing in landscape more thrilling than abrupt contrast between nature savage and nature refined by man within a narrow compass. Another moment was examining the 1527 grisaille Renaissance panels on the screen of Bunbury church with Charlie and the young vicar: black hair, silver over the ears only, sallow skin and eyes like a gazelle's. I have never seen eyes of

---

* Charles Phillips-Brocklehurst, b. 1904. National Trust representative for Cheshire, and silver expert.

comparable depth not radiating anything but absorbing greedily like quagmires the objects focused upon. A nice vicar, and educated too, which for these days is remarkable, and so keen an archaeologist. His name is Ridgeway and he had written me a charming letter after reading my Tudor book to inform me of the existence of these panels of which hitherto I knew nothing. Another moment: Chatsworth floodlit. Charlie insisted on 'running me over', as he expressed it, after dinner. It took one and a half hours each way across the Pennine chain. We had felt so worn on our return to Hare Hill before dinner after a long day that we drank two whiskies and soda and half a bottle of red wine each – he more than this. In consequence we were drunkish in the car, reaching Chatsworth a little before 11 o'clock, just in time to pay 2/6 and dash round the gardens before closure. The Talman block was illuminated with a pink light which at first I misliked, then approved for giving life to the sombre stone. Seen across the park in a rising mist the great mass, detached from the nineteenth-century additions, seemed to be sailing across the sky. The fountain plumes were lit with white light, the willow tree with green. Spectacular visions. Water emerges from a cupola on the dome of the cascade temple, falls down the front of it into a basin and then slides like satin down steps into a lower basin. The dome made to look as though liquifying with fire.

At 11.30 we called on Andrew,[*] Debo being away at Lismore. Cagey Charlie is clearly a little in love with handsome Andrew, tall, willowy and rather too thin, inclined to stoop, who has dark thick hair which he sweeps his hand through so that it stands on end and is always tousled. Mouth very expressive, and curve of lip between nose and mouth reflective of that of chin. I have always admired his appearance, the fragility of steel. He is terribly nervous. Talks in a fast, clipped manner peculiar to Cecils [his mother was one] and throws himself about when speaking. This nervousness and quick-silverness are the disconcerting things about him. Another is his extreme courtesy. Does it, like the French sort, mask disdain? He is a very public-spirited man and I should think very good. An extrovert and loves women. Must be popular in the country round about for he is always appearing at public functions, has no shyness

---

[*] Andrew Cavendish, 11th Duke of Devonshire, b. 1920, and his wife the Hon. Deborah Mitford.

and is fearless in saying what he says, treating all human beings in the same frank manner. Charlie is right. A young, immensely clever duke is a rarity to cherish. And then, lucky man, there is Debo, beautiful and desirable.

I love my country tours more and more as I grow older and become more and more fascinated by persons, places and things. I am a later developer than most men of my generation and in some respects still quite adolescent, an opsimath indeed. Other scenes and incidents of these few days will stick in my mind. The wild yellow wallflowers growing out of the crevices of Beeston Castle and throwing out chunks of scent – the vicar on all fours before the panels in Bunbury church, tracing with finger the outline of a Renaissance figure and asking excitedly, 'Are these knees or bosoms?' Another is a typical commentary on the universal depreciation of quality. Dining next to my table in the hotel at Stafford were two youths of about 18. They were ordering dinner and choosing a pudding. 'Sherry, trifle and cream – real cream, sir?' asked the old waiter, bending both knees like a caricature by Phiz in *The Pickwick Papers*. 'No, we don't like the new-fangled sort of cream,' said one of the youths, 'we prefer the artificial.'

Sunday, 10th May

The Duke of Alba is blessed (or inconvenienced) with an immensely outsized member. His valet told the Londonderrys' butler, who told the gardener, who told the garden boy, who told Richard Rumbold,* who told me yesterday, as we sat in the sun drinking tea in a river garden by a weir outside Bath. And how came the garden boy to impart this astonishing fact to Richard in a punt on the lake at Mount Stewart?

Yesterday I had to go to Stourhead and took Richard with me. A divine day, the country bursting with vigour and green shoots. Every wayside garden crammed with sweet-smelling shrubs and flowers. I wanted to see Dodington Park, the Codringtons' near Bath. It is disappointing. Late eighteenth-century houses must be kept up. They do not decay well. Their material is often shoddy.

---

* Richard Rumbold, 1913–61, journalist and writer. Committed suicide.

Richard is a new old friend. That is to say I met him before the war with Harold Nicolson. Then hiatus. Now he has become – outwardly at least – calm and philosophic after a phase in a Zen monastery. But he is still rather wild underneath, a smouldering personality, weird, more than a fraction unbalanced. Perhaps handsome and a little theanthropic. Has a physique like a flawed Greek sculpture: big head like a magnified Praxiteles. Straight nose not the least Roman, but Greek, descending from brow across a shallow bridge. Low eyebrows and piercing blue eyes in which lunacy may be perceived. A cleft chin like Byron's. A serious fault is the central upper teeth which project, imparting a slightly rabbity air. He is one of those people whom one wants to make laugh because when he does laugh, sharply after a dawning illumination of features, the shadows flee away and gaiety and serenity irradiate him for a quick moment. He is absolutely uninhibited and finds me buttoned-up and contemptibly strait-laced. He is a dedicated writer. His autobiography *My Father's Son* is a fine piece of writing. You can discuss anything with him for he listens, considers and then advises. There is an innate wisdom about him such as simple people (and God knows he is complex) often display. Out of the mouths of babes and sucklings, *and* village idiots. He never thinks ill of anyone. And yet in an awful way he revolts me.

Sunday, 24th May

All last week I spent with Eardley* motoring round Cornwall and Devon. It was our West Country spring week which we always contrive to take together at this glorious time of year. It poured with rain every day but one, and blew a gale every day. Yet it didn't altogether matter. Devon has a character quite its own – the most lush of all our counties, its valleys more verdant, its beech trees more glossy green, its lanes more flowery than any other's. We motored down miles of tunnelled lanes indecently clothed with bluebells, mauve campions and white starry stitchwort. Cornwall has its special character which I don't quite capture, but felt this time a little. The bit between Penzance and St Ives is, I imagine, the real Cornwall of Tristan and Isolde – a country wild and wide under a cloudy, swiftly

---

* Eardley Knollys, 1902–91. Painter and National Trust representative in south-west counties.

flying sky; fields divided by walls so overgrown with grass and turf that they become banks; gorse in full curry bloom, boggy weedy pools and weird rock formations, primeval and whether natural or prehistoric man-made one can't determine. Lanyon Quoit we stopped to look at like an old giant's tripod table standing on the moor alone; bluebells again glowing out of dried-up bracken, fern denoting the appalling rainfall, and cement-grouted cottage roofs, the incessant gales, and bluest alkanet.

St Michael's Mount we visited on Tuesday. Very romantic indeed and a landmark new to me but part of every Cornishman's vision, I presume. Lord St Levan* was waiting for us on his quay as our – or rather, his – motor-boat plodded across the sound. He is tall, weak-chinned, distinguished and probably clever in that English way which disconcerts and misleads foreign diplomats. Must have been attractive to women as a young man, with reservation (the chin). He took us all round the house. Some pretty Strawberry Hill Gothic rooms painted blue and white. Most of the castle now Victorian but jolly good too. The Victorians generally, and Piers St Aubyn [architect] in particular, had a fine sense of the picturesque. The silhouette of St Michael's Mount was very carefully bettered by him. It seems casual enough but is really deliberately balanced and thought out. Unfortunately the quality of the Victorian work here is coarse. The Chevy Chase hall is very good rough Jacobean work, Gothicized in the eighteenth and nineteenth centuries very feelingly.

The eccentricity of people living in large English country houses is almost certain. But the houses must be large and the owners – they must be owners – must live in them all the year round. Evidently the owners need not necessarily be representatives of old families, or even county families, for eccentricity catches on like burrs. (Another book I have long had in mind is about eccentric owners. This I hope soon to start collecting notes for.) In fine the houses must be large enough to sustain the eccentricity.

On Thursday we went to Bickleigh Castle near Tiverton. We were told the owner Colonel Henson wished to sell; and the Trust has a legacy of £25,000 with which to buy a house in the West Country. Colonel Henson who is 70 was very agreeable – comes from Manchester, I think – is never happy without tinkering with

---

* Francis Cecil St Aubyn, 3rd Lord St Levan, 1895–1978.

the old place and has accordingly spoilt it with injudicious, amateurish and bad taste improvements. Yet has made the old place
pretty enough, but not good enough for our purposes – too old in
fact. He would *not* get to, or if he did get to it, stick to the point.
But rambled on and on with an irrelevant disquisition about the
good and bad qualities of the married couples he and his wife had
engaged since the war. Mrs Henson, clad in an overall, for which
she unnecessarily apologized, belongs to the sort of woman who
invites pity for the tremendous amount of housework she is
obliged by her husband to do.

She was very different to Mrs Philip Tilden* whom we came
across on Friday. I had told Eardley I must see a house near
Holworthy called Dunsland where I believed there to be a John
Webb-like ceiling. So we drove unannounced through dilipidated
lodge gates down a long, sad track to this wonderful house. Front
door wide open, so I went up the steps. In the hall an old woman
with shawl over her head was talking distractedly to the district
nurse. 'Oh doctor, doctor, thank God you've come!' she turned to
me. No, I said, I was sorry not to be the doctor. I added on the
spur of the moment that I had heard the house was in danger of
demolition, and wanted to find out. She was very voluble, invited
us both in – I beckoned to Eardley – and showed us round for two
hours. We saw everything except the one ceiling I had wished to
see. In fact her breathless volubility drove it out of my mind. She
told us she was over 80. She had lovely crystal-blue eyes. Spoke
with a broken accent. Explained that she lived in the house alone
apart from her husband ('If you can count him.') Philip Tilden, the
architect, who was in bed paralysed by a stroke, almost *non compos*,
and dying. By the way, she reminded us, she was expecting the
doctor any minute. Instead of showing what you might call concern for her husband's condition she was astonishingly egocentric,
and vain. '*I* never get tired because my bones are so strong.' She
cooks and does all the housework like Mrs Henson of Bickleigh.
The house is far too big for her. She made Tilden buy it four years
ago because *she* had had a dream that they would have this very
house. She described the dream in detail, the drive overgrown
with trees and the house at the end of it, exactly as Dunsland

---

* Philip Tilden, 1887–1956, architect, chiefly of country houses. Married
1914 Caroline Brodin.

turned out to be. She explained how on emerging from the drive she found a horizon stormy and threatening. That, she went on, was the augury of events, her husband's present condition. *She* must now sell up. She bored us with an elaboration of her story for a further half hour as we stood in a little room upstairs. Then we heard a plaintive cry from downstairs. 'I think Mr Tilden needs you,' we ventured, edging our way to the front door and freedom.

Instantly E. and I realized that Dunsland was the house which the National Trust must buy with the legacy money.* It is amazingly unspoilt. Has a Charles II front tacked on to a Tudor block in the rear. Evidently the drawing-room where Mr Tilden lay moaning has the fine plaster ceiling, a rib circlet of flowers suspended on copper wires. The handsome stairs were copied from the original in 1830 – after a fire? Charles II classical doorways and wainscot marble-grained. Poignancy lies in the fact that the tiresome old woman simply adores her stricken husband, so John Betjeman assured me last night; and that Tilden is a genius, like Lutyens.

John said that he and Penelope had to leave their pretty house at Farnborough for their present plain one in Wantage because he suffered persecution mania in the village. In the end he couldn't go down the village street for anxiety lest he forgot the names of neighbours and thereby caused hurt feelings. Wantage town is big enough for it not to matter whom he forgets by name. I can well understand this and in a lesser way suffer the same worry in Roquebrune village.

Sunday, 31st May

I am at Wickhamford with my mother who has confided in me that she is thinking of marrying a neighbour. I tell her that on the whole I favour it because she will have companionship with a man who is eminently decent and intelligent. But – she protests – he uses such dreadful expressions, darling. I tell her that doesn't matter in the least so long as he hasn't got habits that irritate. She says he has not, beyond saying ' 'phone' and 'going to town' which strike me as fairly venial, and I tell her she can train him to drop them. The worst disadvantage I gather is his children. Mama will have four or five stepchildren, to say nothing of stepgrandchildren

---

* It did buy it. And Dunsland House was burnt to the ground in 1967.

which he will undoubtedly want to have to stay, in addition to her own. This, I agree with her, is enough to kill anyone stone dead. The prospective bridegroom is well educated (which is more than my mother is) and well read and, I find, very companionable. How he can put up with my mother's sillinesses and repetitions I can't imagine.

On Friday Alvilde, Clarissa and I went to the Abbey dress rehearsal of the Coronation. We were in our seats by 8 a.m. They were in the first range built over the entrance to the north transept. Thus we looked across to Poets' Corner and over the theatre in the middle of which was set the Queen's throne on steps. The seats are hung with sky-blue damask hangings embroidered with crowns and insignia. The floor is covered with golden yellow carpet, plain. I could just see King Edward's chair on my left but not the throne of state or the altar. A magnificent spectacle. Proceedings lasted until 1 o'clock. The ushers were dressed in black velvet court dress with silver buckles and silver hilted swords, and knee breeches. Their uniform handsomer than the scarlet dress uniform of the Brigade of Guards, or the overdressed Highland uniform with too much jabot and too many daggers and horn bugles. Our usher was George Howard* of Castle Howard whose scarlet uniform was very bedraggled. His belt kept slipping down. He is an uncouth creature. The music was only rather beautiful, not very. I thought Walton's *Te Deum* had vigour but Vaughan Williams's *Credo* boring. The Duchess of Norfolk deputized for the Queen and was excellent. She wore the Queen's robes and carried the regalia. Her cloth of gold robe and rich imperial crown unforgettable. The weight of orb and sceptre carried in either hand called for much balancing and physical strength. The little pages' silk coats were of sky-blue, saffron and maroon; their breeches of white satin. Each followed close behind his peer. The peers' coronets were very absurd and looked like washstand basins with feet sticking up in the air. I saw Gerry Wellington[†] under his, worn at a scornful tilt like an old dowager's toque. David

---

[*] George Howard of Castle Howard, Yorks., 1920–84, created Lord Henderskelfe (life peerage).
[†] Gerald Wellesley, 7th Duke of Wellington, KG, 1885–1972. Architect and connoisseur.

Crawford* looked roguish in his. In truth the robes and uniforms with their depth of colour and glitter of gold were far too splendid for most of the wearers. Nearly all the males were bald. The strong arc lights were unkind to faces and pates, though flattering to the robes. The most striking figure was the Dowager Duchess of Devonshire in red velvet, wearing an enormous diamond tiara and small coronet, a heavy train of infinite length, and long white gloves. Fortune Euston† was one of the Queen's ladies, dressed like Rhine maidens. The history of England epitomized in this glamorous ceremony.

Tuesday, 2nd June (Coronation Day)

A. called me at 5 this morning at which I was very cross for it seemed unnecessarily early. So having slept little all the night I dozed on till 5.30. Then started getting up. Did not put on morning dress but my best blue suit. Clarissa had already gone to her seat with her young man by the time I was drinking coffee in the kitchen. A. dressed in black with her diamonds and the prettiest striped turban hat. There was a queue at South Kensington station but we eventually got into a train, jammed like sardines. At Green Park station got out and in our finery had to walk up the escalator which for some reason wasn't working. Had no difficulty getting to Brooks's where was a vast concourse of members and friends. Hardly a seat to sit on. It was bitterly cold with the windows all out and steps up to balconies erected against the façade. We were perished and sat before a fire in the morning-room wearing overcoats. We read or talked to friends, chiefly the young Meade-Fetherstonhaughs,‡ and watched the Abbey ceremony on the television. It was very moving, the young Queen so calm, grave and sure of every movement, and so palpably serious

---

* David Lindsay, 28th Earl of Crawford, 1900–75, chairman of National Trust, 1945–65.

† Fortune Smith, wife of Hugh FitzRoy, Earl of Euston, and Lady of the Bedchamber to the Queen. In 1970 they became Duke and Duchess of Grafton.

‡ Richard Meade-Fetherstonhaugh and his wife Jean Falkner (m. 1948) of Uppark, Sussex.

and intent. Certain scenes specially memorable: her entry to the theatre with arms dropped over her skirt in token of humility; and when the Archbishop walked to the four sides of the Abbey to ask the people if they would accept her as their queen they replying in the affirmative, and she giving a slow half-curtsey of acknowledgement. It was a gesture on her part of obeisance and yet tremendous majesty – the only occasion she will ever be known to curtsey. Indeed all day I was choking with emotion and unable to speak or cheer. Am neither proud nor ashamed of this.

The weather was damnable. It rained all day. The moment the procession started it positively poured, and the troops were soaked. Yet the procession was magnificent. The colour and pageantry cannot be described. Uniforms superb and resplendent. The most popular figure Queen Salote of Tonga, a vast, brown, smiling bundle with a tall red knitting needle in her hat: knitting needle having begun as a plume of feathers. Despite the rain she refused to have the hood of her open carriage drawn, and the people were delighted. They roared applause. Extraordinary how the public will take someone to its bosom, especially someone not very exalted who is putting up a good show. All along the route they adored her. Beside her squatted a little man in black and a top hat – her husband. Noël Coward, when asked who he was, said, 'Her dinner'. Public also gave special applause to the Gurkhas and coloured troops, with that unequivocal sense of fair play. As for the royal carriages the most beautiful was the Queen Mother's, the Irish coach; the most splendid the Queen's. Her gold and glass coach designed for George III's coronation by Sir William Chambers, with vast gold tritons and painted Cipriani panels like something out of a fairy tale, Cinderella's, drawn by six bays with grooms in eighteenth-century livery; and inside the Queen wearing her crown and carrying her orb and sceptre, and the handsome Duke in a cocked hat by her side.

Thursday, 4th June

Mr Berger the pedicure man who was cutting my corn this morning remarked: 'If I may say so, you have a placid and artistic foot.' He said that to him feet had more character than hands or even faces. The feel of them told him the personality and attributes of their owner.

Friday, 19th June

On Monday A. and I motored to Somerset to stay with Elizabeth [Mrs Mervyn] Herbert* at Tetton Park near Taunton on a strange mission. Long pre-arranged with her, it was to tackle Mr William Esdaile of Cothelstone House near Taunton. He is Shelley's great-grandson through the poet's daughter Ianthe by Harriet West-brook. Ianthe was married by her aunt Eliza Westbrook to a Somerset squire, Mr Esdaile of Cothelstone. The present Esdaile owns a notebook of early poems in Shelley's handwriting and/or Harriet's, and probably other undiscovered papers besides. Two years ago, staying at Tetton, I was taken to Cothelstone and shown the precious notebook† by Mr Esdaile's sister who conducted me round the house, while Elizabeth walked the old boy round the garden. The sister pulled the book out of an old ottoman in the attic and I had opened it only at the first page when she snatched it from my hands and thrust it back into the ottoman because she heard her brother approaching. Mr Esdaile is an eccentric old fellow of over seventy who won't hear any reference to Shelley, either because he is ashamed of the poet for having been an atheist expelled from Oxford or because he married Harriet who came of a non-armigerous family. Neville Rogers and Edmund Blunden who are editing the complete works of Shelley for the Oxford Press are very anxious to have access to the notebook in order to publish the poems, some of which have never been printed, and were missed by Edward Dowden, Shelley's first biographer. As a member of the Keats-Shelley committee I offered to help.

So on Wednesday Elizabeth Herbert took me over to Cothel-stone, an astonishing house. Built about 1810 for the Esdailes as a neo-Greek villa it was added to in Victorian times. Is chock-a-block with good things and absolute trash. A landscape by Gains-borough, some portraits by Reynolds and one by Wilkie, very good, jostle against prints of puppies sheltering under umbrellas, Regency furniture and Edwardian pianolas draped with lace

---

* Elizabeth, daughter of Ambassador J.E. Willard (USA), m. 1921 the Hon. Mervyn Herbert.
† Now known as *The Esdaile MS Notebook*, with Introduction, Commentary and Notes by Neville Rogers, published 1966. The original notebook is held by the Carl Pforzheimer Museum, USA.

tablecloths and littered with photograph frames. Nothing has been shifted since the turn of the century. Much pampas grass. The whole is fascinating beyond words. There is somewhere a portrait of Ianthe which I saw on my previous visit. We were ushered into Mr Esdaile's study to wait for him. He is slight, thin-lipped, white-faced, rather aquiline and patrician, with a stoop, not unlike Shelley's. I daresay when young he resembled the poet in physique. Mrs Herbert explained that we had come early because I wished to talk to him about the notebook. 'I don't know where it is. I believe I have lost it,' was all he said and instantly changed the subject. After he had blamed the weather, the government, the Communists, we returned to the attack. 'I believe you have got it,' he said sharply to Elizabeth, and again changed the subject. Finally we returned to the subject and I asked him point-blank for permission to have it micro-filmed by the Bodleian. I quoted Blunden and Harold Nicolson who attach immense importance to it. 'I don't like Nicolson's voice on the wireless,' was the answer I got. But he did not positively refuse me. Then he took us both round the garden.

At 4.30 A. and a charming American staying at Tetton, Mrs Fenwick, joined us at a huge nursery tea of jam, Devonshire cream and cakes in the dining-room. They were all wonderfully flatter-ing and persuasive, played up to the old man and teased him. He was delighted. It was time to leave so Mrs Herbert most cunningly said she was taking the women upstairs. I was left alone with Mr E. who I don't suppose was a bit pleased. But I said to him, pleading, 'I know you won't refuse my request, will you?' And he consented to have the notebook photographed so long as it did not leave the house. I think this was quite a successful visit.

We then motored to Dunster Castle to see round the house, this also arranged for us by Elizabeth Herbert. A servant showed us into an end room where Colonel [G.W.F.] Luttrell was sitting watching the Test Match on television. He did not get up or shake hands but said quite politely, 'I must see the end of the match. Sit down where you can.' So we did, and when it was over he took us round the castle with much affability. Salvin altered the castle a great deal in the last century. From below the hill the outside looks very romantic and from the front is gracious enough. But it has been altered inside. There is little work of the Jacobean Arnolds left – perhaps the thin plaster ceiling of the hall and an uncouth plaster overmantel upstairs dated 1620. The dining-room has a fine undercut Charles II ceiling and panelling, and several good family portraits, one of a radiant young man of George I's reign whose Christian name was Narcissus. We saw the oak bed in which Charles II slept when Prince of Wales during the Civil War and a priest's hide behind it. In such a hide that monarch was tended by Father Hudleston who was to receive him into the Roman Church on his death-bed. The leather hangings, painted to resemble tapestries, are surely unique. The muniment boxes are all labelled in the handwriting of William Prynne[*] whose ears were – quite rightly – cut off for spoilsportry (i.e. his book *The Unloveliness of Love-lockes*). Imprisoned here in 1650 Prynne catalogued the family archives. Mr Luttrell spoke with unqualified pride of the castle, its possessions and his ancestry – yet all the time he was living as a tenant of some land company to which after six hundred years of Luttrell ownership he sold the whole Dunster estate, including the castle.

Monday, 22nd June

Hugh Euston[†] and I touring round Northamptonshire and Staffordshire came to the gates of Drakelowe after dinner. The lodge and a splendid pair of gate-piers remain. The piers are carved with great precision in drops and wreaths. So we drove through them up a long avenue of neatly planted limes. At the end of the avenue we came upon – not the house; it was demolished in 1934 we afterwards discovered – a gigantic power station. Returning to the lodge we made enquiries of the occupants. They came to the door and said the Gresley family had always been haunted by the bloody hand, which, the occupants maintained, was their crest. Years ago, they said, an elder son had long been missing. One day the reigning baronet walked into the house at Drakelowe to see his wife embracing a young man. In an access of jealousy he drew his sword and slew the young man. The young man was inevitably the missing son. Thereafter, the lodge-keeper's wife assured us, every elder son turned out an imbe*cile* (with prolonged emphasis on the

---

[*] William Prynne, 1600–69, Puritan pamphleteer, was branded for seditious libel.
[†] Hugh FitzRoy, Earl of Euston, b. 1919. On the staff of the National Trust.

last syllable). It was the case till this very day, she said. Hugh was tremendously impressed.

This night we stopped at Lichfield. We were obliged to share a room which Hugh evidently disliked as much as I did. He is a well-trained, quiet sleeping companion but very restless. He said next day that I groaned throughout the night and was very disturbing. I said, 'You must have had worse experiences in the army.' 'No,' he said.

Tuesday, 23rd June

After looking at Boscobel* we drive to Whiteladies Abbey, that romantic-sounding ruin in which Dame Joan Pendrill is buried. It is miles from anywhere. Through a wood we walk in dripping rain to a field in a clearing. There stand the Norman monastic remains, but every stone rebuilt by the Ministry of Works; the whole surrounded by a concrete post and wire fence to keep out the cows and grazing sheep. Why? Within a hideous wooden hutch an old man in uniform, bored stiff, knowing nothing about the history of the Abbey, skulks. He makes a charge of 3d. only; so after paying him a weekly salary the Ministry will never get their money back. All they have done is to deprive this hitherto picturesque place of romance, and keep the picturesque cows and sheep out.

By contrast we find at Tong Castle the Capability Brown ruin (Moorish Gothick) far more interesting, but about to be demolished altogether and the beautiful trees round it and along the glen, felled.

We motor up the drive of Onslow Hall, near Shrewsbury. The garden abandoned, the windows of the house shuttered, the place entirely neglected and decaying. It is a neo-Grecian building of admittedly little merit – I have made notes of it. But the sinister thing is the stable clock, still going and registering the right time. Not a cottage or living soul within miles.

Sir Richard Leighton† upon whom we called at Loton Park, his Jacobean house, half William and Mary, said to us, 'We lived at Wattlesborough Castle before we moved here.' 'Before you

---

* Boscobel House, Shropshire, where Charles II was sheltered and hidden in the oak tree by the Pendrill family after the Battle of Worcester, 1651.
† Sir Richard Leighton, 10th Bt., 1893–1957.

succeeded or before the war?' I suggested. No. He meant the Leighton family before they built Loton in King James I's reign.

Along a lane we stopped the car because a cock and hen partridge couple were leading a newly hatched family of baby birds in great distress between the two steep banks. The hen acted as I had often read but never seen. She trailed her wing to feign being wounded in order to distract attention from the chicks. The hedges radiant with eglantine and the road verges covered with the bluest of blue field geraniums.

Again we had to share a room in the Mytton and Mermaid at Atcham. Hugh complained that I emitted maniacal laughter.

Wednesday, 1st July

After a deal of intrigue A. and I met a photographer, sent by the Bodleian, at Taunton station early this morning and drove him to Cothelstone by appointment. At last we have succeeded in photographing the Shelley notebook, not without difficulty. Notebook amounts to about ninety-five open pages. It is true the poems are certainly in two handwritings; and perhaps three. On the first page is inscribed the name, Ianthe Esdaile. I don't know how many poems are in Harriet's hand but I believe several are in Shelley's. I am certain a large number of the poems have never yet been printed. It was thrilling to handle once again, at leisure, the closely packed octavo volume. This time Mr Esdaile told me he didn't want to sell the book. I advised him to claim a reproduction fee for any poems published. This I have firmly stressed in letters to Neville Rogers and the Clarendon Press. Mr Esdaile said to me: 'You must understand that until the last few years Shelley's name has never been mentioned in my family. He treated my great-grandmother abominably. He even had the effrontery, while living with another woman, to ask my great-grandmother to come and join them in their adultery.' He said the notebook was the only relic of Shelley he possessed, apart from his christening robe. I did not ask to see this because I was so worried about getting the photographs taken. Mr E. was in a great hurry to get off for his annual holiday – the old limousine purring at the front door – and would not leave until we had finished. It was a good thing I went. The photographer was a raw, callow youth, well-intentioned, ignorant, and with no manners. He asked us in the car how he ought to behave on arrival. 'Be your best self,' I said. I was appalled at the rough way he handled the manuscript.

Mr E. is a nice old man, old-fashioned, correct and very shy. In the dining-room under the Gainsborough landscape is a hideous harmonium with *Hymns Ancient and Modern* on a music stand. Elizabeth Herbert said the squire and his sister played and sang hymns together every Sunday evening.

I have received a charming letter from Mrs Alington* thanking me for my collins to her. After being taken by Hugh for a night at Treago Castle I wrote that it was an honour to have stayed with my revered head master whom, though I never knew him personally at Eton, I had always looked upon in his Olympian detachment with admiration and veneration. She is the sister-in-law of Lord Frederick Cavendish murdered in Phoenix Park in 1882. Some link.

Friday, 3rd July

It was sad walking round Ashburnham House [Sussex], and seeing it half-emptied of its lovely things, all of which were in place the last time I went there – only two or three years ago on a visit organized by the Georgian Group. Then Lady Catherine Ashburnham† took us round herself, a middle-aged, shy, diffident woman with a gentle smile, fair skin and rather prominent, strong white teeth. Early this year she died and now every single object is being sold by a distant cousin. Thus ends another immensely long association of an ancient family that took its name from its land. She was the last Ashburnham of Ashburnham.

Over the front door was placed her hatchment. I have never seen this done before and doubtless never shall again.

In the beautiful Jacobean church is a table of the Commandments dated 1676, framed at that time. The frame is gilded with small figures of putti and birds in white plaster emerging from foliage on the border.

Driving across Kent to dine with Vita [Sackville-West] at Sissinghurst A. and I stopped to pick wild honeysuckle and privet – the

---

* Hester, 15th child of 3rd Lord Lyttelton. Married 1904 Revd. Cyril Alington, Head Master of Eton, and Dean of Durham.
† Lady Catherine Ashburnham, 1890–1953, daughter of 5th and last Earl of Ashburnham, of Ashburnham, Sussex.

latter bloom very abundant this year and sweet-smelling. Vita was adorably shy, not awkwardly shy which she can be sometimes. Ben was there for dinner which helped. He told us of his visit to Ashburnham three years ago. Whereas he remembered every painting and where it hung in the house he hadn't the faintest recollection what Lady Catherine looked like. This amused Vita very much for she showed great interest in the lonely, retiring spinster heiress and longed for detailed description.

Wednesday, 22nd July

I am alone again. Alvilde has returned to France and Clarissa has gone to her father (a rare event) before rejoining her mother in France. Thank goodness, because in London I have a great deal to do without having to look after her. I get impatient with young girl frivolities, especially when her mother is away. To live with adolescents is quite impracticable and really should not be suffered.

Went to the House of Commons on Wednesday to listen to the Third Reading debate on the Historic Houses Bill. Whereas when reading *Hansard* I am impressed by the high standard of reasoning and its presentation, when listening to an actual debate across the floor I think the MPs, with their halting delivery, are silly fallible creatures like myself and not the reliable, stolid, super-intellectuals which *Hansard* makes them out to be and I want them to be. Of all the speakers only Dalton, a man I thoroughly dislike, had the manner and spoke with the assurance of a trained, disciplined parliamentarian. Yet I was struck by the gaiety, bonhomie and boyish jokes between the younger MPs. They were all twitting each other in debate and in whispers along the benches. Among the younger ones like William Vane and Nigel Nicolson I detected that pre-1914 Rupert Brooke and Julian Grenfell goody-goodiness – a whiff of it – which was doubtless so noble and saved Britain in 1914 and again in 1939. It is irrepressible, that core of patrician, rational, hyper-decent Englishness.

Saturday, 25th July

Yesterday was a golden day and so hot that I stopped in Oxford for a short half hour and bathed in Parsons Pleasure. It is always a mysterious little world to me. A masculine world of lush green scythed grass, enclosed by wattle fences from prying eyes, behind

which all women are prohibited. Within it the young men strip
completely naked. Not a fig leaf is permitted. Secret, shared rites of
manhood may be meditated but are not enacted, freed from the
shackles of womankind which no doubt envisages all sorts of arcane
communion. How disappointed they would be if they gained admittance. The lawn is dappled by light and shadow from the
shimmering willow trees. The Cherwell leisurely flows alongside.
On the opposite bank a meadow of hay and wild flowers forms an
impenetrable boundary on the low horizon to the bodies stretched
on the scythed grass. I have only seen Parsons Pleasure in idyllic
conditions when the summer sun is fully shining. A disagreeable
note is struck by the old men with paunches like balloons over
scrawny, shrivelled thighs supported by stick-like legs. These satyrs
feed on visions of the young men who either play an endless game
with a football or lie in abandoned attitudes on the grass plucking at
their anatomies or smoothing the golden or brackish flue of their
chests. I am always fascinated by their unabashed acceptance of
nakedness, yet their pride of body, and at the same time sly interest
in their neighbours' – those would-be casual, swift but penetrating
glances, measuring up the dimensions of another's figure, and then
the relaxed look of self-satisfaction or envy. It is extraordinary how
vain the normal young man is. I shall never revisit Parsons Pleasure.
It must be the preserve of the young. But where else can one bathe
in a gently flowing river, which I infinitely prefer to the sea? For on
a river one can measure the distance of one's swimming.

Monday, 3rd August

Hugh Euston and I set off for a week's tour in my Wolsey. We
stayed this first night with Gerry Wellington at Stratfield Saye.
Gerry had got out of his safes all the treasures for us to look at, like
bejewelled miniatures and the Garter George which Charles I gave
to Bishop Juxon on the scaffold. I am amused by the notices and
directions written in the ducal hand, scattered about the house and
signed Wellington. In the downstairs WC is one beginning, 'Pending the installation of a washer, please allow water to flow into the
pan before use.' In my bedroom were two: 'Please keep the blinds
drawn lest the sun fade the watercolours', and 'Coathangers not to
be removed from Room no. 43', as though there were more than
five bedrooms in commission. At dinner the dull librarian at-

tended. The two dukes (I anticipate Hugh's dukedom a bit) were discussing their relations and lineage while the librarian and I sat in silent subservience drinking it in. Talking of hatchments – and Gerry criticized Rupert Gunnis[*] for putting up someone else's for Lady Catherine Ashburnham – we asked humbly whether it was 'done' to have a religious text beneath one's arms on an escutcheon instead of one's own motto. 'People like us don't do it' was Gerry's retort. 'Who does do it?' we didn't dare ask.

Tuesday, 4th August

After luncheon the three of us went to look at Herriard Park. It belongs to Colonel Jervoise[†] of an ancient family. His forebears built it in Queen Anne's reign. Gerry thinks Talman was the architect, but it seems hardly worthy of the architect of Chatsworth. Herriard has no ceilings and little of distinction inside although a dear old place. The architect's model of the house is kept downstairs in a wooden box made for it at the time. House spoilt by being stuccoed over. Some nice pictures, particularly a Lely of Mrs Purefoy and two Jansen-y portraits, very fine.

I noticed how there is about Gerry the smell which common soldiers have. Not strong and not unpleasant, of dried oil. I am very fond of him.

Hugh and I looked at an old farmhouse near Sherborne, only interesting on account of its name – Font le Roi.

We stayed at Coker Court. Last time I was there I took Ted Lister,[‡] and dear old Mrs Walker-Heneage[§] threw her arms round my neck and embraced me with a cooing sound. Now Coker is lived in by her daughter-in-law, recently widowed young Mrs Walker-Heneage, an extremely attractive woman with a most seductive mouth. In fact I don't know when I was last so attracted by a woman. Before going to bed she told us of the ghost whose

---

[*] Rupert Gunnis, author of *The Dictionary of British Sculptors, 1660–1851*, published 1953.
[†] F.H.T. Jervoise, 1872–1959, Squire of Herriard Park, Hants.
[‡] E.G. Lister, 1873–1956, of Westwood Manor, Wilts., which he saved and reinstated.
[§] Dorothy Margaret Helyar, heiress of Coker Court, Som. Married 1904 Colonel G.D. Walker(-Heneage).

steps are distinctly heard in the early mornings. Having shut my door (of the willow-papered room) I got into bed. Five minutes later it deliberately opened. I jumped out to look in the passage but there was no one there. Rather disappointing.

Old Mrs Walker-Heneage couldn't bear touching people or things, and always wore gloves. Perhaps she mistook me for a ghost.

Wednesday, 5th August

After a discussion with young Mrs W.-H. and Bill Batten who is her solicitor, we looked at Leigh House and the Court House in Chard, where we lunched. This afternoon we called (I write 'called', but in truth we were trespassing in my old car up the long drive of Ugbrooke. To our dismay we had a puncture and were obliged to seek help from our host's chauffeur) on Lord and Lady Clifford of Chudleigh,[*] who felt obliged to give us tea. Within five minutes they produced for Hugh to see the original 'Secret Treaty of Dover' between Charles II and Louis XIV and a letter from Charles's sister Minette[†] to his ancestor Clifford of the Cabal. Hugh naturally was thrilled since his ancestor Arlington was one of the *A*s of the Cabal. The Cliffords have fine Lelys of Clifford, Monmouth and Catherine of Braganza. They do not live in Ugbrooke which is empty and decaying, dreary and ugly outside. Lord C. said that when Disraeli stayed there he observed while his carriage approached the front door, 'This house must be the worst specimen of a bad period', namely, the eighteenth century.

Thursday, 6th August

Lord Morley[‡] succeeded his brother at Saltram a year ago. He is 73, permanently drunk, has had to pay enormous death duties, has no children, yet has nobly spent over £10,000, his agent informed us, in decorating the state rooms from top to bottom. It is v. well done by Keebles [the decorators], and one of the best Adam interiors I

---

[*] 11th Lord Clifford of Chudleigh, 1887–1962.
[†] Princess Henrietta Stuart ('Minette'), Duchess of Orléans 1644–70, and sister of Charles II.
[‡] 5th Earl of Morley, 1878–1962, of Saltram Park, Devon.

have seen. Lord Morley was away but in the saloon was his butler, wearing his lordship's Brigade uniform, the earl's coronet and coronation robes at his elbow, sitting to a pretty American female artist.

Antony where we stayed the night is in splendid condition. The Carew Poles* live in princely style. I am delighted with this early eighteenth-century house, and with him. With her not so much.

Friday, 7th August

Alex Moulton† is looking for a pair of library steps on which he can stand at his bedroom window in order to shoot with his bow and arrow half a dozen arrows at a target in the garden every morning before breakfast. His black retriever is released to bring back the arrows.

Saturday, 8th August

This afternoon Alex took me in his boat, made of tin, up the river Avon. He attaches a noisy engine to the stern. Standing in the prow I watched the placid brown water ahead quiver from the vibration of the approaching engine like the retriever wrinkling its nose. Weather divine at last, no wind, and hot, baking sun. Banks of the river covered with clumps of purple loosestrife, tansies, epilobium, both mauve kinds, and deadly nightshade. We sailed through avenues of tall, bunchy willow trees from which the country boys hang a rope with a stick on the end. They swing on the rope, gathering momentum, then let go and plunge into the water. Scenes of idyllic youths bathing recalled that late Victorian artist, Sir Luke Fildes. Having passed the bathers Alex and I disembarked, took off our clothes and lay in a field of cut hay. Pricked by stubble and stung by nettles was exhilarating agony not to be long endured.

At Westwood [Manor] staying with Ted Lister. He has at last put in electric light, discreetly it is true, but a pity. It was strange and

---

* Sir John Carew Pole, 12th Bt., 1902–92, and his wife Cynthia Burns.
† Dr Alexander Moulton, b. 1920, of The Hall, Bradford-on-Avon, Wilts. Innovating engineer and inventor of the Moulton bicycle and motor-car suspension.

sad not to have Ted lighting one's chamber candle in its hurricane globe and not to stumble upstairs to bed in semi-darkness. The old man is to be 80 in November.

Wednesday, 19th August

This afternoon I followed a young woman with two small children into Queen Anne's Gate. There was a conflict of wills in evidence. One of the children was in a pram, the other being led. The led child behaved abominably, yelling and hitting the mother. She, a young working-class woman, was becoming desperate. She picked the child up fiercely and dumped it in the pram with the other. Promptly it kicked, yelled louder and threw things out of the pram on to the pavement. Exasperated the mother took it out, shook it and told it that if it didn't follow her properly and quietly, it could stay where it was – and doubtless be damned. By this time people were watching. I exuded sympathy for the mother and distaste for the child. Mother and pram went on. Child sat down on a doorstep, refused to budge and bellowed blue murder in anger and fear; an exhibition of utter loathsomeness. Mother paid no attention and went ahead, determined to give it a lesson – but in vain. People went up to the child, saying 'Poor little mite. It's a shame, etc.' I was so incensed that I found myself saying, 'Poor little mite, my foot. It's a damnable child. Serve it right if its mother knocked it on the head.' 'O, I say,' they remonstrated. However the outcome was that the poor mother was obliged to give way, routed by this odious offspring. Obliged to leave her pram and pram child, and retrace her steps for the truant. Consumed with fury and indignation in her turn, and stung by humiliation, she defiantly seized the child's arm and dragged it after her in open view of a gathering crowd of detractors, all but me who could easily have killed the child and embraced the poor young mother in pity.

This morning, working upstairs in Thurloe Square, I listened to the rag-and-bone man in his cart. His is one of the Cries of London not yet extinct. I heard him approach down Alexander Place. As he passed my window I looked out. He was young, spivvish, seated on a pile of scrap, holding the reins of an emaciated pony. No one paid any heed, or stopped him. No one felt inclined to do him a favour. At regular intervals he cried very fast and rhythmically what sounded to me like, 'Any, any, any knives, or!

Any, any, any knives – or!' The *or* was a kind of tenor's gulp on a higher note than the knives. I should have run after him to enquire what exactly he did say. Alas, the hurdy-gurdy-and-monkey man, along with the muffin man, a large tray on his head and a bell in his right hand, these of my youth are gone for good.

Banister Fletcher* has died, very old. He was on the SPAB committee when I joined. A thin, short, quizzical, humorous and modest little man, yet very distinguished. We stood together once under the Somerset House portico and he said that the classical vault, Chambers's I suppose, was the very best piece of English eighteenth-century architecture to survive. And then he licked his lips in relish. So too has Hilaire Belloc died. I used to meet him staying with Mary Herbert[†] at Pixton during the war. He was ailing and querulous. He seemed to exist only on wine, then very difficult to get. But Mary somehow provided it and he sipped it all day long, smacking his lips and complaining how indifferent it was. From time to time he warmed up, and talked, and talked, and talked. Was sardonic, but brilliant. Was very class-conscious, referring to himself as the epitome of the middle class, and Mary that of the upper. He wasn't wrong. He always wore the same dirty old cloak. One night there was a great noise. Mr Belloc going to the bathroom with a candle set himself ablaze. Mary put him out after filling the bath tub with water. Then she called me for help. There was a smell of burning next morning and the bathroom was full of ash from his rusty old cloak. In similar circumstances he died recently.

Thursday, 20th August

Eardley the dear creature came to breakfast. We motored in his car to Avebury and lunched with those awful Keillers[‡] (whom Eardley however loves) and Professor Hawkes[§] who brought with him an extremely genteel Miss Smith, archaeologist, gauche and shy. She

---

* Sir Banister Fletcher, d. 1953. Author of *A History of Architecture on the Comparative Method*.

† The Hon. Mary Vesey, b. 1889. Married 1910 the Hon. Aubrey Herbert, MP and traveller who declined the throne of Albania.

‡ Alexander Keiller of Avebury Manor, Wilts., amateur archaeologist.

§ C.F.C. Hawkes, b. 1905, Professor of European Archaeology.

hardly dared speak for fear of mispronouncing her *ows* and invariably did mispronounce them. I went from Swindon by train to Plymouth and stayed at the Grand Hotel. Before bed walked along the Ho! and round the exciting town.

Friday, 21st August

Had to pay £13 for new ball-bearings to my little Wolsey, once [Aunt] Deenie's car, and drove to Watermouth Castle in North Devon. Over Exmoor the road banks are of gorse and heather, inextricably interwoven. The gorse no higher than the heather and the two a daze of gold and purple. Beautiful day of blue sky, patches of sun and deep storm clouds. I thought how lucky I was to be alive. I have finished my Inigo Jones book and have nothing more to do to it. It will be out in October. Miss D.M. Stuart* has protected me from making a fool of myself, although I am not sure that her pedantry is always acceptable. 'Commence' for 'begin', 'Abigail' for 'maid'. I am well on the way with my next book – Rome. I have bought out of my inheritance money from Deenie and my book a drop-head Rolls coupé, which is frightfully distinguished (second-hand of course and immensely old, 1936). Absurd perhaps; snobbish possibly; aesthetic certainly. On Monday I go to France for six weeks; after this interval I long to be with A. again. I go to Lytes Cary this evening; and hope Giles [Eyre]† will be nice to me. He makes a v. good tenant of this ancient NT manor-house.

Sunday, 23rd August

Mama talked for hours into the night about her marriage problems with which I entirely sympathize, yet can't decide whether the whole thing is, or is not, for her best. She is not the least in love with her man. He is with her – which is so strange. As she says with awe, 'I am about to become a great-grandmother. Isn't it indecent?' Yes, it is rather. He is terribly correct, and it is his religion which induces him to press the matrimonial suit. She doesn't want to marry a bit. Yet does not want to lose him. So like a woman. He crosses himself before meals. She has become far

---

* Dorothy Margaret Stuart, d. 1963, poet and biographer.
† Giles Eyre, b. 1922, dealer in water-colours, and art reviewer.

better mentally as well as physically under his guardianship; for he takes her on long drives and this broadens her outlook. Ma has told me things that she has told no one else about the wooing. I rather wish she hadn't. And I made her promise she never would tell anyone else for fear of ridicule. Besides, the disloyalty. I must say I love the eternal child in her which makes men die for love of her at the age of 69. Well do I remember Papa and Deenie tormenting themselves about her health and happiness, and how was she to be kept alive; and here she is well enough to contemplate re-marriage while they are both ashes.

Monday, 24th August

This afternoon in the bus going back to Thurloe Square, having completed my shopping and final jobs, I found myself sitting next to a male tart. Rather handsome he was in a Modigliani-like way with a long, oval, pale face and almond eyes. He gave me one of those sidelong looks I know so well, expressionless and full of deep meaning; a second look was of the most languishing and seductive nature, yet one which if seen by a third person would not be noticed. That is so clever of this tribe; brought about by aeons of persecution, like the Israelites. They know how to elude detection. They have to, and the consequence of their subterfuge is a terrible dishonesty. We were not alone in the bus, yet I noticed how he touched my arm without appearing to, or in fact without actually doing so. I asked him where he lived and he said South Kensington. Then in mincing tones which made me feel a trifle sick, with a preliminary click of the tongue he asked, 'Have you done a little shopping?' I was strung with paper bags. After another languishing look as though satisfied that we had thereby clinched an engagement, nothing further was said. When at my stop I suddenly got off the bus without giving him a glance or fond goodbye I hoped he was not surprised or affronted. Tonight I fly to Nice.

La Meridienne, Roquebrune   *Tuesday, 25th August*

Landed at Nice airport at 3.40 a.m. and was driven in a taxi to Monte Carlo. Just before 5 dawn broke. It was a flush of liver red on the sea towards Italy. I left my luggage at the Hôtel de Paris and walked in the early morning light the five or six miles to

Roquebrune. As I left the casino *place* it was still almost dark, lamps alight and a man leisurely sweeping up horse dung into a pan. Lights appeared at windows overhead and shutters banged open. When I could glimpse it between the houses the sea became mauve. The first smell here, even detected on the asphalt of the Nice aerodrome, is a resinous one, of pine and cistus. I climbed the hill to the village. A tinkle from the church bell. I walked into the house and up to A.'s room where she lay asleep under her mosquito net. I threw off my clothes and jumped in beside her.

Monday, 31st August

Last night we dined with the Mosleys[*] at the Hôtel de Paris. The only other guest was Bob Boothby.[†] Before we accepted there was hesitance. How tenuous are human principles. I argued that if they were Stalinists I should not go, but I had never felt as opposed to Fascists, much as I detested Hitler whom alas the Mosleys liked and honoured. Besides was not Diana Diana, the Diana I had known and loved since childhood? Love comes first. I sat between Diana and Tom. I think she is the most flawlessly beautiful woman I have ever seen: clear, creamy complexion, straight nose, deep blue eyes and grey-gold hair dressed in a Grecian bun swept rather to one side of her nape. Her figure so slim. Is spare the word? She is just as beautiful as she was at 17 and more so than when first married in her early twenties, or late teens was it? Tom Mosley is fatter, rather greyer. He is well-mannered and attentive. His good manners almost make me shy. His interests seem chiefly political still and when he gets talking he is on the verge of delivering a platform speech or rather a benevolent dictator's harangue. I was reminded of 1931 when I canvassed for him and the New Party at Stoke-on-Trent and attended so many of his meetings when chairs were flung at him and furniture was smashed. Since those days his views seem balanced and eminently sane. He talks of England as though it were a foreign country and the English as 'they'. Diana is the first woman I really was in love with – although she never knew.

---

[*] Sir Oswald Mosley, 6th Bt., 1896–1980, and his wife, the Hon. Diana Mitford.

[†] Robert (Bob), Lord Boothby, 1900–86, politician and television commentator.

A. and I are extremely happy together and it is as though we were having another honeymoon. I am well and interest myself in getting brown; not a very exalted ideal perhaps, but harmless. I swim every day at Monte Carlo, intending to develop my chest muscles.

Undated

A young cousin of A. and Clarissa called James Armstrong who is staying in Mentone walked up to dine. He is a lieutenant in the Navy and considered a straightforward, no-nonsense, tough extrovert, though clever. Eminently personable too. A perfect sailor I should say. Strong sense of duty, loyal, ambitious to shine in his career. When he rose to go, having delighted us with tales of his exploits and evident success in that career to which God had directed him, I said I would accompany him to the chapel at the top of the hill overlooking Mentone. On the way he told me his favourite books were *South Wind* and Connolly's *Unquiet Grave*. I found this unexpected. When we reached the chapel he sat down on the wall with his knees beneath his chin. There was no moon and the stars and lamps of Mentone and Ventimiglia gave no light. So I could not see his face. He told me that far from being what he probably appeared to his relations he pondered deeply about the fundamental things of life and death, had few friends and was fearfully lonely. As I turned to go home he rose, shrugged his shoulders and said, 'Well!' In walking back I ruminated.

When the Mosleys lunched with us on the terrace I was more than ever struck by his moderate views. He is no longer extreme; whether to hoodwink or through bitter resolve who can tell. He said that only amateur politicians in England harboured bitterness against each other; the professional ones, among whom he included himself, did not. As examples he gave Bob Boothby and that old fiend Beaverbrook whom he had for a generation opposed on all matters of political principle. Yet they always remained the closest friends. Bridget [Parsons]* who stayed with us afterwards said that no considerations of guest for hosts would have made her meet the Mosleys here. She was sure that Diana would as willingly shovel

---

* Lady Bridget Parsons, 1907–72, sister of Michael Rosse.

us all into a gas oven as smile on us. I can't imagine it. Peter
Quennell* on the other hand said he would willingly meet them
because they are now rendered utterly innocuous.

Sunday, 20th September

Bridget left us yesterday after a ten-day visit. She was a perfect
guest and entered into all our fagging, waiting and washing up. I
love her but she is lazy, selfish and insincere.

Three days ago we drove up the Nervi valley from Bordighera,
to Dolceaqua, a village with an old bridge like a rainbow and
streets like caverns underground, lit at intervals by arches in the
sides, or tall, narrow courts like ventilator shafts. The *pavé* uneven,
undrained and caked with dirty straw and excrement. The drive
behind the sea coast to San Remo is more unspoiled and beautiful
than any Italian country I have yet seen. The mountainsides
clothed with forests of olives and Spanish chestnuts. Villages like
Apricale and Ceriana, medieval conglomerations on peaks, are
unaltered as they were in Augustus Hare's time. The blackberries
are larger but less tasting than the English ones. The wild figs
refreshing to walkers. Recently Peter [Quennell], Bridget and I
walked from the golf course at Mont Agel down to Roquebrune,
having started from La Turbie. The walk took us three hours.
They both agreed the view from the *col* overlooking Italy as lovely
as any on the Mediterranean to be seen. Both are my match for
walking and endurance.

Yesterday morning at breakfast came a sudden, violent thunder-
storm, the sort that destroyed Shelley. Very black sky over Mont
Agel while the sun was shining on us and upon the sea towards
Italy. Ominous silence while we put under cover the garden
cushions. Then a wind which twisted the cypresses almost into
knots. Heavy drops. And a torrent. Poor Foo, A.'s beloved white
Pekinese, ran and hid under the table at the first thunderclap. The
storm lasted one hour. When it subsided I watched the layers of
cloud around us and overhead dashing about in a whirlwind.
Gradually the inky splodge over Corsica dissolved as the sea grew
greyer and flecked with silver streaks. Within another half hour I
was sitting out on the lower terrace and reading in the sunshine

---

* Sir Peter Quennell, 1905–93, poet and man of letters.

which seemed stronger than ever. Delicious, fresh, earthy smells, rare here. The tall cypresses on either side of me crackled in the sun's rays as the moisture dried within them; and drops of rain formed on the twigs like brilliant cut diamonds, and fell. Within no time spiders' webs were stretching from tree to tree. Walterine calls them *les voiles de la Vierge*. The water was literally sucked out of the ground in gusts of heavy steam.

When there is a full moon in these parts night is almost like day, and buds of flowers unfold. For instance, the blue water hyacinths, which last but twenty-four hours, come into bloom during the full moon I have noticed. The peasants sow their seeds here only during the waxing moon.

There is an old woman in the village reputed to be a witch. If she dislikes you, you may find your pillow stuffed with rats' tails. On Fridays she has the power of overhearing and understanding, no matter in what language, whatever is said at any distance. Her husband breeds rabbits but no one in the village will buy them. Many villagers, including Louise who does our washing, cross their fingers when they pass her.

Lately I have had nightmare after nightmare. Three nights ago I had four of which I remember three. (1.) The corpse of my 'first' wife, murdered, was in the *grenier*. I begged Alvilde to have it moved before it was discovered. I saw the bare legs of it protruding from a blue skirt. But A. wouldn't, saying she must wait until they moved the drawing-room carpet from the *grenier* in the winter. (2.) Lord Zetland* was making a speech in the House of Commons (not Lords). He was on all fours on a table and he delivered his peroration, laughing, 'The path to the grave is smooth and easy.' (3.) I had a bed sitting-room in the House of Lords. It was empty when I went to the bath. On my return the Chamber was packed with peers. I had nothing on but my pants. Gibbons, the wine waiter at Brooks's, produced a trolley on wheels. Pushing it in front of me I hid myself while moving out of sight. The fourth dream I forget. But last night I was in a church, ensconced within a niche. The church was about to be blown up and I counted the seconds for the fuse to go off.

---

* 2nd Marquess of Zetland, KG, 1876–1961, Chairman of the National Trust, 1935–45.

I believe the nightmares may be caused by the mosquito net. Perhaps it is wine; perhaps it is going to bed too soon after dinner; perhaps it is a bad conscience.

1954

―――――――――――――――――――――――――――――――

And here we are, A. and I, back at Roquebrune. I haven't written a word in my diary since I was here last summer. We arrived ten days ago and shall presumably stay until April. In London my time is so occupied working for the National Trust that I have little left for anything else. In November my *Age of Inigo Jones* was published. Up to date it has had excellent reviews, far better than my previous books, which is not surprising, and for the first time in my life I have experienced a modicum of achievement. A modicum, I repeat. The *Times Lit. Supp.* frankly laudatory, also *Spectator*, *Tablet* and *Time and Tide*. Harold Nicolson in the *Observer* gave it a review which anyone might covet. No carping notices yet. On Xmas day which we spent with the Moores at Parkside I was able to compare my state of content with the previous Xmas there, when that very morning I received the terrible letter from Eddie Marsh saying the *ms.* was so frankly bad it was a waste of his energies to read it.

Now I have begun sketching out a new book; *Roman Mornings* it is to be called. I asked Rupert [Hart-Davis]* if he would consider publishing it and he said yes – would consider. It is a new experiment. I want to write about architecture in a readable manner, that will be informative and literary. Shall I succeed? After which I have in mind a book on Lord Burlington and the Whig architect peers. In fact I wish to venture on biography. I am inspired with confidence by the good reviews of I. J. But I must not indulge in self-satisfaction. O no.

Strange that Duff Cooper is now dead. I did not find him appealing. Yet A. loved him. He was very much a woman's man. He loved women and was indeed an arch-pouncer, which was one reason why I didn't care for him. He put my hackles up in the way they rise when I see big lecherous dogs making themselves so

---

* Sir Rupert Hart-Davis, b. 1907. Publisher, editor, writer, and J.L.-M.'s oldest surviving schoolfriend.

offensive to Foo. Lecherous Duff was like many physically small
men. I am assured he was a poet underneath.

Tuesday, 19th January

There was a total eclipse of the moon last night at 3.15 here, 2.15
in England. I read about it in *The Times*. I set the kitchen alarm
clock but woke without it before 3. I saw the full moon already
turned into a crescent on its back, yet the outer circle of the whole
was visible, the rim seeming illuminated. Oddly there were small
specks on the rim's surface which looked lit too as though they
were mountain tops catching the last rays of the sun. But this I
think is not possible. I had no binoculars. As the crescent slowly
disappeared the full moon assumed the quality of alabaster, then of
opal. Although the eclipse was 'total' it didn't look to me absolutely
so. Perhaps it was only quite total in England. Then the moon
turned into a large grey pearl. Then it became smoky as it might
be were one looking at it on a fairly clear night in Manchester.
After that I left it and returned to bed, having been watching it off
and on for an hour. In the meantime the night was deathly still
except for some cock-crows. The sea was hardly audible as though
the tide had been arrested and the waves had stopped. Men and
creatures are subdued, albeit unconsciously, by such phenomena.

On Monday Moira Shearer[*] lunched with us. She is with the
Dolin Ballet company at Monte Carlo. We saw her on Monday
night in the *Spectre de la Rose*. She is very sweet and intelligent;
looks younger than she is. Has snow-white skin and coral-red hair.
Very thin with too delicate arms and legs. Faint Rhodesian accent.
Old Henry May[†] was asked to meet her. He delighted in her.

Sunday, 7th February

In horrid Monte Carlo yesterday I watched the starlings gather
before sunset. Each evening they behave in the same fashion. It is
a kind of drill before settling down for the night. They congregate
as though from nowhere and in a dense cloud wheel round the

---

[*] Moira Shearer, b. 1926, ballerina and writer. Married 1950 Ludovic Kennedy.

[†] Henry May, cultivated Henry Jamesian American living in European capitals. Then in Mentone hotel.

town and over the sea, at great height, at great speed. The remarkable thing is their formations which vary from a packed ellipse, sometimes horizontal, sometimes vertical, to an echelon, then a diamond. Is one bird the leader? How do they manage to fly together like guardsmen in perfect spacing at this speed? Finally they swoop upon a particular indiarubber tree in front of the Casino where for twenty minutes they keep up a tremendous clamour before shutting off for sleep.

The starlings are about the only birds on the coast. At the moment the snow on the mountains has driven down to our village a few robins and long-tailed tits.

Nancy [Mitford]* gets quite cross with Alvilde for complaining about the pigeon-shooting from the Casino. Fat Italians, Alvilde says in her best *donna inglese* manner, sit in armchairs potting at tame pigeons, pigeons let out of bags in which they have been kept several days in total darkness and without food. In the sudden sunshine the starved creatures are blinded and bewildered. They are ruthlessly shot into the sea. 'It is no worse than slaughtering hand-fed pheasants in England,' says Nancy, Anglophobe. This is an old argument. I consider all sport revolting on analysis. Cruelty to the pigeons does not come into the picture. It is the moral depravity of the killers which I find distasteful.†

How is it that one dislikes a person with whom one shares a secret depravity? The more closely the depravity is shared the more one dislikes the person; and when others speak ill of him or her the more one feels inclined to agree with them.

Tuesday, 9th February

Last week Willie Maugham gave me Dylan Thomas's *Collected Poems* to read on condition that I told him what I truly thought of them. Yesterday we lunched with him and I returned them. 'Well, Jim?' he began. So I said that for modern verse there was a certain amount of music in them; that there was a great vigour and power of expression; that undoubtedly the poet had something intense to say; that the syntax was deplorable and there was little intellectual

---

* The Hon. Nancy Mitford, 1904–72. Eldest Mitford sister, novelist and biographer. Married 1933 the Hon. Peter Rodd.
† No. Today it is the cruelty I deplore.

content. They made no sense. I believe that if they had made sense
(and this sounds very Irish) then I should not have liked them very
much. Willie said they meant nothing to him. He had been
brought up on Shelley and Tennyson who did make sense; these
were a kind of post-Impressionist painting. He believed there was
something to them, but what, he did not and never would know.

Thursday, 11th February

Nancy says that music to her is delicious manure. At a concert this
evening at Mentone I realized that to me it is like drink or a drug.
It accentuates the mood of the moment. If one is writing, or in
love, it inspires one to write or love better. This afternoon I had
been annoyed by two letters from England. When we went to the
concert I had forgotten about them. But throughout the concert I
thought of nothing else and was inspired with the most devastating
retorts, which now an hour later have fled from me.

At luncheon with us today Willie said after a silence, 'I have just
come to a decision. All women ought to be kept in harems.' I said,
'I suppose Alvilde's presence has brought you to this conclusion.'
He then watched A. put two lumps of sugar in my coffee for me,
and said, 'When my wife was really cross with me she used to say,
"I forget whether you like sugar in your coffee." '

London   *Monday, 15th February – Sunday, 21st February*

Much against our wills we were back in London for the week. A.
had feared that either she was going to have a baby or she had
cancer. She went to St Mary's Hospital, Paddington, and was
curetted. There was nothing amiss. A very great relief either way.
I too was suffering from distressing sciatica. Was x-rayed at St
Thomas's Hospital and told I had arthritis of the spine. Went to a
Harley Street orthopaedic surgeon who said it was a displaced disc.
He tried to put it right by wringing me like a wet rag. It declined
to be put right. There is in our village, Roquebrune, a sorcerer, or
rabatteur, who cures all the village folk of rheumatism, sciatica, and
more, with a herb which, tied to the heel of the sufferer, produces
a blister. When pricked the blister discharges all the poison the
herb has drawn down.

I met the sempstress on a walk who told me that a grey cat – it
must be grey – applied to the affected area cured sciatica. Cats of

other colour were no good at all and must be avoided. The breath they exhaled was lethal to children. So too was the scent of freesias, which nevertheless made an excellent wine. I must remember grey cat's breath when exasperated beyond words by little ones.

This week which I very much hated for the anxiety about A. and the pain in my back and because Thurloe Square was let and I had to stay in Eardley's flat, was spent hobbling around in the rain. However I enjoyed the evenings. The Sutherlands dined with E. one night. E. believes Graham is extremely noble and self-sacrificing in coming from abroad to give evidence against John Rothenstein in the Tate Gallery case.[*] Another evening spent with Edward Le Bas[†] in his studio (very nice man who thinks too much about boys and drinks too much); E. benefits from Edward's tuition at the easel. Another evening with Harold [Nicolson] and Alan Pryce-Jones.[‡] Alan in one of his worldly moods. He said there were three women he might marry: 1. Bridget Parsons (little hope). 2. A very rich Rothschild unknown to me. 3. Elizabeth Cavendish[§] (does she know of this?). In a disingenuous manner he then said, 'But how could I, a person of little position in the world and with an income of a mere £3,000 a year, ask one of these women to share the squalid life I could offer them?' Another evening dining with Rosamond and Joshua Rowley.[¶] Ros said she once had a maid who gave birth to an illegitimate baby which the lover murdered. It all happened in R.'s house.

Italy   *March*

The dome of Impéria was built by Gaetano Cantoni, 1745–1838, whoever he was, and the street next it is called after him. For a late church it is a remarkably interesting piece of architecture, and intricate too, a symphony of circles and domes.

---

[*] Case in which the art critic Douglas Cooper insulted John Rothenstein, director of the Tate Gallery, at a reception: fisticuffs were the result.
[†] Edward Le Bas, 1904–66, artist and collector of modern paintings.
[‡] Alan Pryce-Jones, b. 1908. Man of letters and reviewer, and editor of *Times Literary Supplement*, 1948–59.
[§] Lady Elizabeth Cavendish, b. 1926.
[¶] Sir Joshua Rowley, 7th Bt., b. 1920. On National Trust staff and Lord Lieutenant of Suffolk, 1978.

San Satiro at Milan more sophisticated than I remembered it. Even A. who dislikes Italian Renaissance church architecture thought so. The fantasy about it is almost rococo, viz. the round windows set in a halo in the crossing arms; same arrangement appears in Santa Maria delle Grazie I think, and in the exquisite chapel at San Eustorgio. There is a jewel-like quality in these Milanese works of Bramante and his school which is essentially fifteenth-century, quite unlike B.'s Roman buildings. They recall Michelozzo who in fact built the Portinari chapel. When B. got down to Rome he became a different architect altogether, more avant-garde, more strictly classical. How and why did this happen? Rome more sophisticated – and the court of the Popes. Then at Pavia there is something almost baroque in B.'s duomo, in the strange pointed piers of the crossing, like the prows of ships about to collide. Bold inventiveness.

Another Bramante bit of unorthodoxy is the single column in the centre of the windows of the delle Grazie apse; links up with the unorthodox single column in each bay of the della Pace cloisters at Rome.

Back to rococo again. I have said in *Roman Mornings* that rococo was not an architectural style. No more it was when one considers Bramante's rococo-isms, and indeed Michelangelo's of the sixteenth century which the pundits now call Mannerism – really the same aberration only two hundred years earlier. Again, what more heterodox than the hideous Casa dei Zuccari (1590) in Rome with its portal and window made of monster faces, the one swallowing the visitor, the other the daylight – gobbling up both with their awful jaws.

At Turin where we also were this month I looked carefully at Guarini's work. S. Lorenzo, 1687, is in convexes, making the entablatures jut forward into a number of points, which is ugly. It is a riot of deformed lines. The ribs of the cupolas stand out like girders, purely structural, not even camouflaged, which is too much. The décor is polychrome. Guarini wanted to do one better here than Borromini at S. Carlino, Rome. In the Sudario chapel spire he tried to emulate the spire of Borromini's S. Ivo. But it is heavy and involved. Horrid really. But fascinating. The inside cupola ribs criss-cross like a junction of tram lines. The Carignano palace however is singularly beautiful. So are the two staircases. Both are rotundities and not angularities.

The Santuario of Madonna de Vico came upon us all of a sudden as we drove past. An astonishing thing to discover unexpectedly. The great oval dome, 110 major axis by 80ft.

20 Thurloe Square, SW7   *Monday, 5th April*

Before leaving by the Blue Train for London tonight Graham [Sutherland] allowed A. and me to have a look at the portrait he is doing of Eddy Sackville-West.* We thought it extremely like, sensitive yet un-caricatural. Really an astonishing work. Its present stage is head and shoulders, rather a finished sketch, for there was another huge canvas only in outline which is to be the finished thing. Graham works by a curious system. He paints part of the figure, head, torso, legs separately and then copies these parts faithfully on to the big final canvas, sewing the various limbs together so to speak.

Thursday, 22nd April

Jamesey Pope-Hennessy[†] dined alone with me last night. He had come from a meeting with Christopher Hassall,[‡] to whom Eddie Marsh left everything. No doubt Eddie loved Hassall dearly. Both Hassall and wife treated Eddie with greatest kindness. Jamesey asked him outright if Eddie had ever loved anyone physically. And H. replied that the furthest he ever went, as far as he knew, was to take his, H.'s foot, and polish it with his handkerchief while holding it against his bosom. Oddly enough Harold Nicolson told me only last week that before the first war Eddie was said to delight in taking off the hunting boots of his young men friends. Hassall suggested that since during his puberty Eddie's voice didn't break properly he may never have developed properly in other respects.

Hassall has inherited all the Rupert Brooke correspondence which he generously proposes to sell to King's College for £100, having been offered £5,000 by an American university. There is

---

* Edward Sackville-West, 5th Lord Sackville, 1901–65. Man of letters, reviewer and musicologist.
† James Pope-Hennessy, b. 1916, writer. Murdered in 1974.
‡ Christopher Hassall, 1912–63, poet, biographer and playwright.

one letter to Eddie Marsh, written after Rupert Brooke's death by
a New Zealand sergeant. The sergeant reminds Eddie how he first
met Brooke in the Brompton Oratory. He was looking at a statue
of St Cecilia when a strange voice accosted him. He turned round
and saw the most beautiful face in the world. Rupert Brooke, he
went on, struck up a warm friendship with him and used to call
him 'my St Cecilia' – which is slightly off somehow. A surviving
friend of Brooke's told Hassall that no photograph could ever do
justice to his good looks and that his complexion was flawless.

Today I went to Nurstead Court near Gravesend and close to
Owletts. It belongs to major Edmeades* who is a nephew of Lady
Baker† of Owletts. Nurstead interesting only for its semi-remain-
ing aisled hall of great round columns in timber instead of stone.
Condition deplorable. The major's old mother lives with him. The
place terribly down at heel, messy, smelly, in fact squalid beyond
the bounds of Alan P.-J.'s imagination. I went on the roof. It is
perished, tiles off, lead rotten, water pouring through in wet
weather. No servants. Poor major! How are the gentry fallen.
Edmeades cannot afford to mend the roof. He has to find thou-
sands of pounds to pay off death duties. Then he showed me some
of his trim labourers' cottages, all with television. A good landowner. He works every day as long as the light lasts, like a farm
hand, but without holidays; for he never goes away.

I went to see dear Lady Baker at Owletts. It was in 1937 I first
went there when Sir Herbert was alive. I have great admiration for
this family, for they are charitable, devoted, dutiful, fruitful and
successful. Sir Herbert was a superlative human being, a remarkable artist and architect. I love the ethos of Owletts, this nice old
Charles II house with its well-designed-and-made furniture of Sir
Herbert's. All the children now married and the house full of
grandchildren. The garden ablaze with daffodils, cherry blossom
and crown imperial lilies.

Wednesday, 21st July

Gerry Wellington asked us to luncheon today. A. is away but I
accepted. I wanted to see the part of Apsley House he lives in. At

---

* Major R.W. Edmeades, b. 1914.
† Florence Edmeades, widow of Sir Herbert Baker, architect, who died in
1946.

the NT meeting this morning Gerry whispered that luncheon was at 1.30 and the Prime Minister and Lady Churchill were coming. We were to be only eight in all. I took a bus and walked into the courtyard of Apsley House just as the PM's motor drove in waving the flag of the Warden of the Cinque Ports. So I made a dash for G.'s small side door before the Churchills should enter. The other guests already assembled. I knew only the American Ambassador[*] and Mrs by sight and Muriel Warde[†] by more than sight. I sat next to Muriel and the Ambassador's daughter. Muriel was between me and Sir Winston.

Sir W. looks like a small, fat and frail doll, or baby, with a white and pink face, most unnatural in an adult, and no lines at all. There is a celluloid quality about the skin which is alarming. He shuffles. His back view is funny. He was wearing too short a black jacket exposing a shiny striped seat. The front part of him is different in that it is smartly dressed. An expanse of white, semi-starched shirt and cuffs with links, the habitual white winged collar and spotted bow-tie. The shirt bulges out as he slumps in his seat. He has sparse wispy white hair, and is a very spruce old gentleman – in the front. I suppose he does look old; or rather unreal. It is hard to detect a human being behind the mask. Everyone deferred and played up and when he did vouchsafe a word, laughed rather too hilariously. When he left Gerry said he was in fine form, and splendid humour, which simply means that when he is not, he must be terrifying. The Ambassadress and Muriel kept up a running badinage which he was either relishing or deliberately paying no attention to, I couldn't make out which. General conversation did not get far and yet we were all so determined not to miss a word Sir W. might utter that no one listened to his neighbour. However, all he said that I recollect was that once at the age of 25 he danced a *pas seul* (he explained he never could dance with a partner, but by himself danced beautifully). At the end of this performance he thought he had a heart attack and the next day a lump appeared over his heart and he felt very ill. So he went to see a famous heart specialist in France who told him he must never drink effervescent liquids or smoke again. If he strictly obeyed these directions he might pull

---

[*] Mr and Mrs Winthrop W. Aldrich, US ambassador to London, 1954–7, and his wife.
[†] Muriel Warde (Mrs), daughter of Arthur Wilson of Tranby Croft, Yorks.

through. Twenty years later he again visited the specialist, who congratulated him on his remarkable recovery and survival. 'How wise you were', he said, 'to obey my injunctions.' 'So I had the satisfaction', said Sir Winston, 'of telling him that every single day since my last interview I had both drunk effervescents and smoked. Doctors still know very little.'

Before luncheon I overheard him asking Muriel who I was. Then as we went into the dining-room he said, 'Does Oldham mean anything to you?' I knew he referred to his first election when my grandfather and Papa supported him and had him to stay. He told me he remembered it all vividly and asked if Crompton Hall was still standing and if we lived there now. I said it was pulled down last year. Then he asked about the Milne mill and I said we still had it and Dick [my brother] managed it.

Conversation between Gerry and Churchill struck me as Trollopean. 'Now, Prime Minister, will you have one of my cigars?' 'No thank you, Duke. I've got one of my own.'

There is no peasantry left in England, yet very occasionally I see a flash of something which denotes it, rather a memory of it. While motoring through a narrow lane near King's Lynn in Norfolk this month I passed a middle-aged countryman leaning against a bicycle talking to a woman. He wore no hat but a chaplet of hop leaves on his head, absolutely unconcerned as though he might be Bacchus himself.

1956–1957

20 *Thurloe Square, SW7*   *Friday, 30th November 1956*

At dinner Ivy [Compton-Burnett] in that precise, clipped manner
of speaking with never a pause for premeditation: 'Yes, I am going
away to avoid the purely purgatorial aspect of Christmas.' And in
talking of the Suez crisis: 'I consider Conservative stupidity worse
than Socialist roguery and malice. At least roguery and malice do
not endure; whereas stupidity expands and accumulates like the
universe into infinity.'

La Meridienne, Roquebrune   *Sunday, 7th September 1957*

Rhoda Birley* having been with us several days went on to stay
with the Churchills who have been lent Lord Beaverbrook's villa
at Cap d'Ail. Lady Churchill had tea with us last Tuesday to fetch
Rhoda. We were asked to lunch at Cap d'Ail today.

   We arrived at midday in order to bathe from their private rock
first. I changed in Anthony Montague Browne's† pavilion in the
garden where he is quartered. Then we had drinks on the terrace.
At 1 o'clock Sir Winston's figure appeared at the door leading to
the terrace. Much smaller, less broad, and slighter; immaculately
dressed and clean like a doll. Face not so celluloid as the last time
I met him at Apsley House, but very fresh looking, pink and white
and quite expressionless. He was wearing an ordinary blue suit and
that familiar semi-starched piquéd shirt with collar of wide wings
and spotted bow-tie. He stumbled down the steps and shuffled
across the terrace. On his head a large cowboy hat of white felt.
His manners noticeably courteous in an old-fashioned way I don't
remember before, doffing his hat and nodding welcome. When we
left he held his hat in hand to shake hands with A. and thanked us
for having come.

   He is very much older and rather pitiable; so deaf that I doubt
he heard Alvilde at luncheon for she sat on one side of him and

---

* Rhoda Pike, widow of Sir Oswald Birley, portrait painter.
† Anthony Montague Browne, b. 1923, diplomatist. Private secretary to Sir
Winston Churchill, 1952–5 and 1956–66.

Rhoda the other. I was exactly opposite him. I heard him question
A. about her father whom he knew well: what regiment had he
been in during the Boer War and in what battle of the 1914 War
had he lost a leg. She didn't know but answered gallantly and tried
to start occasional conversation. Willie Maugham and Alan Searle
were the other guests. Willie said he was older than Winston; but
he is far brighter and talked like mad. I don't think Sir W. registers
much that is going on. When the women left the table the men
stayed on for about three-quarters of an hour. He drank brandy
and smoked two cigars which he sucked until an inch and a half
were left, and very precisely laid on the ledge of a silver cigar-stand
which Wendy Reeves[*] has given him and he is proud of. Then he
warmed up a bit and talked of obituary notices in *The Times*. I told
him that the regular writers of obituaries were sent their contribu-
tions after an interval of ten years or so to add paragraphs, if the
subject was still alive, for which they were paid a supplementary
fee. This seemed to amuse him. He told Willie that had he won
the 1945 election he would have been obliged to give India
self-government under the pledge made by the pre-war Conservative government and this would have much gone against the grain
with him. He said he was all for leaving India to stew in her own
juice, but added with a twinkle, 'I am now merely a retired, and
tired, old reactionary.'

I don't think he had the slightest idea who I was – not that there
was any reason why he should. I talked to him a little after
luncheon about Randolph[†] and Johnnie[‡] whom he criticized for
being a bad husband to his second wife. Boring for him doubtless
and awkward for me. He seemed in another world already and
occasionally sighed. But he ate well, second helpings of everything. He wears a crested signet ring on the finger next the small
one of his right hand, which is strange. Said he was very indignant
that Ruskin Spear, who had submitted a gross caricature of him to
the Royal Academy without Sir Winston having either sat or even

---

[*] Her common-law husband was Sir Winston Churchill's literary agent.

[†] Randolph Spencer-Churchill, 1911–68, MP, journalist and biographer. Sir
Winston's son.

[‡] John G. Spencer-Churchill, 1909–92, painter and composer. Son of Major
J. Churchill and nephew of Sir Winston.

been approached, came up to be introduced at the last Academy dinner. We asked, 'What did you say?' 'I said, "I don't want to meet him. Take him away." I could not have been more discourteous.'

When I got back this evening Mlle Marie, the Curé's cousin who lives with him and his mother aged 92, showed me some old panelled doors she presumes we might like to buy. After we looked at these she told me about Bar-bar-a, the tame hen which the ancient mother kept in the house for twelve years. Bar-bar-a used to roost at the end of the mother's bed while she dressed in the morning, and at nights slept in the bed. '*Mais, monsieur, je vous assure, elle n'avait jamais sali les draps. Quand elle voulait faire ses besoins, elle chantait d'une voix spécialle, etc.*' Truly remarkable. I said how wonderful and sweet the dear bird must have been. But Mlle Marie, who is renowned for her love of animals, said to my surprise, '*Non. Pas du tout. Elle était terrible.*' She suffered from B. prodigiously. When M. le Curé came home of an evening B. would walk all the way up him as he lay stretched with his feet on a stool. First she would peck the bottom button of his cassock, then the second, then the third and so on all the way up, finally roosting under his chin. '*Mais elle était terrible.*' She sang several tunes and when M. le Curé sang French songs she would accompany him, nodding her head approvingly. When he sang in Italian or English she made the most hideous discordant din, nodding her head the other way disapprovingly. Every anniversary of her death, Mlle Marie is made by the mother to put flowers round the photograph frame, in which is a likeness of Bar-bar-a and on top of which is a spray of her tail feathers.

Saturday, 13th September

I was writing in my pavilion this morning, when at 12.45 I was distracted by a strange sound of tearing. Looked out of the window and saw a cloud of smoke coming up the garden. Rushed out and met Alvilde also gazing. Today is the third day of violent mistral and there are fires everywhere. Apparently this one was started by a train at the bottom of the hill only a quarter of an hour previously. I have never seen flames spread with such speed. Our lowest terrace was ablaze. We got hosepipes which Javier, Clarissa's nice Mexican friend, and C. played gallantly but ineffectually on the flames. Then the Algerian boy now working on the new room – one of the builders – jumped over the fence with a *pioche* and hacked at the undergrowth. Soon the whole village was in the garden for the tocsin bell was droning from the church to call the men back from work. By a miracle the wind changed and the fire took a right-angle turn for 50 yards and proceeded to blaze a trail up the *vallon* beside us. Had we been out today our trees might have caught and the whole place would have gone. As it was, for a moment we thought all was up. Alvilde even packed her jewellery and took down the Bonnard painting and Cézanne drawing which she moved to the gate – for anyone to steal. She was beaten rapidly backwards by a huge flame. This I did not see for I was below trying to save the olive tree with a hollow inside which was red-hot like an oven. Claire our new little maid was almost in hysterics. This fire made a clean gash up the *vallon* beyond us into the mountains. The whole of Mont Agel is in flames and the cinders are falling as though from Vesuvius.

Went in the evening to the Churchills for drinks and were considered very heroic which of course we had not been. Sir Winston sitting slumped in an armchair in the middle of the room, to whom we talked in turns. A. told him how much she was impressed by Nevil Shute's book *On the Beach*, which he too had read. He said he was sending it to Khrushchev. She asked would he not also send it to Eisenhower? Sir W.'s retort: 'It would be a waste of money. He is so muddle-headed now.' The 'now' is significant. He said to Montague Browne: 'I think the earth will soon be destroyed by a cobalt bomb. And if I were the Almighty I would not recreate it in case they destroyed him too the next time.'

Relations with close neighbours are always hazardous. And when the neighbours are decent people relations are not necessarily made easier, for one hates to offend. Now the Curé and Mlle Marie are good, kindly, considerate and beloved by all. It is unfortunate that our telephone wires get inextricably entangled with Mlle Marie's jasmine, which seems to flower the whole year round. And she has the habit of watering it every evening between the hours of 5 and 7 o'clock which is when Alvilde indulges her habit of telephoning or receiving telephone calls. This means that during her hours of busiest communication with the outside world reception is rendered practically inaudible by a concatenation of excruciating crackles and often total cut-offs. Because of our happy relations, which we would be loath to jeopardize, we can do nothing to ameliorate matters. In fact we do not like to say anything.

1964

Alderley Grange, Wotton-under-Edge   *Tuesday, 29th February*

Rory Cameron[*] went to Mount Athos last autumn with Henry McIlhenny.[†] Told us he spent a fortnight there which made me admire his toughness until he disclosed that every night but two they went to sleep on Henry's luxurious yacht moored alongside. However, the morning after the first night spent in a monastery he was astonished to overhear, while shaving at his cell window, the sound of what he fancied was a woman's voice speaking with a man's. Nothing female of any kind, human or animal, is of course allowed on the Holy Mountain. On leaning out of the window, so he alleged, he saw a young monk talking to an older monk and putting on this voice. 'They were clearly lovers,' said Rory, and on spotting him appeared embarrassed. I am not inclined to believe this. It is the sort of anti-monasticism dig I have heard before. At least I don't want to believe it.

Wednesday, 21st March

Hugh Euston's old bedmaker came to see him the other day. She said that in the street in which she lived she was the only Conservative. Of her neighbours she remarked to Hugh: 'Poor things, they try to be but can't; and since they can't, how can they?'

Sunday, 11th April

I am not often moved emotionally by paintings. By poetry and music, yes, continually. As for oriental art I don't understand it and in my total ignorance am usually bored by the mannered formalism. But today I went early to see the Siamese Exhibition at the V & A, called of course the Thailand Exhibition (Does one now refer to Thailand cats and twins?). The sculptured heads of Buddhas,

---

[*] Roderick (Rory) Cameron, 1914–85, American travel writer, resident on Cap Ferrat, French Riviera.
[†] Henry McIlhenny, d. 1986, collector and philanthropist. President of the Philadelphia Museum of Art.

mostly of the earliest style, the Dvaravati, sixth to eleventh century
AD, did move me – profoundly. I have never seen faces of such
accomplished other-worldliness, faces of such selfless meditation,
contemplation, mysticism. The beauty of holiness is in them, more
startlingly so than in any sculpture of western Christianity I have
so far seen. Were the Siamese in these centuries mystics who
arrived at the ultimate divine reality which St John of the Cross
hints at, and which only saints in our Church are said to attain? I
know nothing of their train of life, their state of civilization, and
little of their religion. Perhaps their apparent mysticism was merely
perfunctory, or assumed, but I can hardly believe it.

And now I wonder so much what it is to be religious? It was
thirty years ago last month that I became a Papist. Within the last
two to three years I have given up the pretence of believing. I am
utterly without faith, and am irritated by rather than sympathetic
toward Catholicism. I don't think I ever really believed, even
thirty years ago. I merely wanted to believe, and looked upon the
Church as a necessary rock in a disintegrating world of material-
ism. Now that the world has disintegrated I can no longer maintain
the fiction. Besides, so many of my best friends, by whom I mean
most *good* friends, who are dead, Kathleen Kennet,* Vita, and even
my mother, were without a scrap of faith. Rosamond [Lehmann]
goes burbling on about the *occult*, which I find more irritating
than the recognized sects because there is no dogma, no ethic,
nothing in the way of discipline to be found in it to guide its
followers. It is surely sillier to believe in spiritualism than in the
Immaculate Conception. Yet I so dearly love Ros that I am glad
she gets something, whatever it is, out of her strange, nebulous
beliefs.†

May

The last week of May Eardley, Dadie Rylands‡ and I went on a
walking tour in Cornwall, along the south coast. We spent only
four days walking because of the absolutely odious weather. We

---

* Kathleen Bruce, 1878–1947, widow of Captain Falcon Scott and wife of
Edward Young, 1st Lord Kennet of the Dene.
† This irreligious phase of J.L.-M.'s life did not last long.
‡ George Rylands, b. 1902, Shakespeare scholar and Fellow of King's Col-
lege, Cambridge.

started at Looe, arriving the first night at Fowey, the second at Mevagissey, the third at Nare Head, the last at St Mawes. We followed the coastline as far as we could. This was difficult because the paths ended in nothing and we found ourselves plodding through gorse and bracken, or over ploughed fields, and up and down cliffs. For months we had looked forward to this expedition. The first day it pelted, the second was sweltering, the third there was a dense sea mist, the fourth it deluged. We carried haversacks on our backs, and this spoilt the enjoyment of the walk for me. Eardley and I were dismayed to discover that Dadie looked upon the expedition as some sort of penance; we imagined it was to be pleasure. Had we two been on our own we would never have set out on the deluging days. As it was Dadie drove us forth with scorn and scorpions.

Sunday, 28th June

At Bredwardine after the commemorative service to Kilvert this afternoon A. and I walked away from the churchyard with William Plomer.* He said, 'You heard the clergyman ask for our prayers for Kilvert's last niece, Thersie's daughter, still alive, but ailing, and aged 84. She didn't deserve them.' I asked why. He said: 'I went to see her some years ago and she greeted me with the words, "Mr Plomer, I have been very naughty. You will be angry with me." "Never," I answered, little knowing. Then she continued, "I have burnt all Kilvert's manuscripts, now that you have extracted the best bits and published them." ' Plomer said he was furious and could easily have killed the old woman. He said he thought he had omitted only repetitious passages, and a very few indiscretions, these latter, I gather, relating to little girls. So perhaps the old woman's bonfire was not too disastrous after all.

In relation to his cousin Richard Rumbold's diary William [Plomer] said that much of it was repetitive, and some of it indiscreet; that the greater part was introspective, going over and over again the same old self-questionings, and it was these passages which he omitted in the published book because they were boring.

---

* William Plomer, 1903–73, writer, poet and editor of the Kilvert Diaries.

A. and I then went to Moccas court, having telephoned the McBeans* this morning. He said his wife would certainly not see us, and then she who had been listening in on her extension spoke to me and said she would. What we found was indescribable. The filth and squalor worse than ever. At the front door an old motor car without tyres on the wheels used as dog kennel for a scruffy old spaniel. In the hall dog-bowls half full of rotting food, half-empty tins and rags. The staircase hall a pile of stinking dog blankets. The large Savonnerie carpet that belonged to Nelson ruined by stains. The drawing-room was covered, every chair, stool and the sofa with blankets no less stinking. Windows tight shut, and radiators full on. Heat and airlessness insufferable; the smell appalling. Dogs everywhere with running sores, one with piles, unable to do its business and stinking so that I thought I should be sick. She will not let them go for walks further than the door-step because she fears poison from the agricultural sprays. The two McBeans looked like creatures that had emerged from under a stone. His bald head covered with sores, his cheeks wan. She like an old witch. They have not left the house for seven years; all their shopping things are sent from London by post, including the bread. Of course they are mad. Or rather she is and he toes the line. She was a great beauty and now she is ageing and can't bear to be seen. Won't go out and won't entertain friends.

In Much Marcle church this weekend I was struck by the resemblance of the recumbent figures of Sir John Kyrle's tomb to those of the Sandys tombs in Wickhamford church. Clearly, I said to myself, they are by the same hand. Looking through Mrs Esdaile's[†] book on my return home I notice that she has spotted the same resemblance, but has not discovered the sculptor.

Sunday, 5th July

The Peter Scarletts[‡] staying here [Alderley Grange] over the week-end both speak warmly of the present Pope [Paul VI], and will

---

* Alec and Eileen McBean were tenants of Moccas Court, Herefordshire, seat of the Cornewall family.
† Katharine A. Esdaile, author of *English Church Monuments* (1946).
‡ Sir Peter Scarlett, m. 1934 Elizabeth Birchall and was Minister to the Holy See, 1960–5.

not hear a word of criticism. He thinks it is as well he is lacking in Pope John's glamour. If Pope John could have nominated his successor Peter is certain he would have chosen Montini. Paul VI shares all the ideals of his predecessor. Whereas the late Pope was an inspiration, this one is an intellectual of much brilliance who will carry through the other's policy. Archbishop Heenan they dislike. Say he plays to the gallery, and sets out to please too obviously.

How injurious a diary can be if it is not strictly truthful. It is not easy to be truthful; nothing is less easily expressed than the truth, and one should not always blame chroniclers for untruths, which often they may not have intended.

Tuesday, 7th July

John Kenworthy-Browne* and I looked at two new buildings in Oxford today. St Catherine's College is still unfinished. So too is the Institute of Technology & Something-or-other. St Catherine's is pretty ghastly. Of a brash, ugly yellow brick laid with wide, sunk pointing. The Hall is of the same material inside as out, rough, grim and cold. The undergraduates' bed-sitting rooms have their outer walls entirely of glass. A flimsy net curtain covers each wall, but not so as to prevent one seeing everything happening within. For instance we saw the scout making the beds. He saw us and came down and asked if we would like to look inside since we seemed interested. We did so. If the undergraduate does not wish to be seen in bed he may draw his thick curtains which means dressing in the morning by artificial light. He cannot have any privacy during the day at all unless he draws the curtains which on summer days he presumably does not consider doing. Shoddiness, shoddiness is the hallmark of all the work in this beastly building. The Institute of Technology on the other hand we found rather beautiful; indeed the first rather beautiful contemporary building I have seen in England. It is horizontal, also of yellow brick, but of sympathetic texture. On one side it is approached by a wide, almost baroque staircase. The inside is not as good and on a sunny midsummer day the library had the electric light on. In this large

---

* John Kenworthy-Browne, b. 1931. On staff of National Trust and expert on neo-classical sculpture.

library there is not one single book which I would accept as a gift. *Chacun son goût.*

What reasons, other than quality and a harmonious posing of horizontal masses and a lack of extraneous projections like tanks on the skyline, I have for approving this building I cannot say.

Thursday, July 9th

Osbert Lancaster* is a great gossip. After lunching with the Beits he and I left together and got a bus at Sloane Square. I had sat between Lady Harewood† and Lady Alexandra Metcalfe,‡ and told him I found the first heavy and the second delightful. He said Lady H. had left Lord H. for someone else and the Queen had forbidden a divorce; that Lady A. was a bore (on the contrary she is highly intelligent and informative) and that after three minutes' conversation with her he knew how a fly felt on being flitted.

When I arrived at this luncheon party – I go to such parties once in two years now, if that – with Diana Cooper, whom I met on the pavement, and saw some ten sophisticated guests grouped in the Beits' large and opulent flat, I wondered if I would not faint. Then I thought I must make a dash for the door and bolt. I might have done so if A. had not been there. Agoraphobia seizes me on such occasions. Terror grips me and a sense of inadequacy as well as intense dislike of everyone. I ended by enjoying myself, but is anything worth the pain of arrival?

---

* Sir Osbert Lancaster, 1908–86, Cartoonist, painter, theatrical designer, writer. Married 1933 Karen Harris who d. 1964.
† Marion Stein, m. 1949 George Lascelles, 7th Earl of Harewood.
‡ Lady Alexandra Curzon, m. 1925 Major E.D. (Fruity) Metcalfe.

1968–1969

This summer I received a letter from the Cardinal Secretary of State couched in the most courteous and flattering terms, addressed to L'Illustrissimo Professore, etc., telling me that the Pope had set up a small Commission of six persons to investigate the authenticity of St Peter's Chair, kept inside Bernini's great bronze cathedra at the far west end of St Peter's. I answered that I was greatly honoured to be invited, while pointing out that I had few qualifications to assess this most precious relic. I thereupon received a slightly tart reply that His Holiness had made the selection himself, and it became me to accept without further ado. Of course he did so because of my book on St Peter's, which I know he made the Italians translate against their will, and which he gives to important visitors at audiences. So I could do nothing but agree to serve. I was naturally pleased, and excited, although a little apprehensive because my Italian is so shockingly bad.

They never gave me proper notice of the first meeting in September. And because Alvilde had bought tickets for a very expensive cruise to Turkey in September, I felt unable to go. However, I was sent the very full minutes of this meeting at which questions of when and how to move the Chair from the cathedra, how to treat it, and who to get to do so, were considered. I was then summoned to the second meeting, at which the Chair was to be revealed to view, on Tuesday, 26th November.

I went to the office of the Ingenere della Fabbrica at 5.30. This is in the enormous Sacristy building. You pass through the arch at which two Swiss Guards stand holding halberds, then are stopped by papal police at the barrier the other side of the arch. Extreme politeness is shown. The Engineer, Vacchini, whom I met two years previously when seeking permission for special photographs to be taken for my book, is a brisk, efficient, neat, very co-ordinated man, with a well-trimmed moustache, rather like a British captain of a line regiment. I came to have the greatest regard and respect for him. My five colleagues are Monsignore Michele Maccarrone, the President, a small, dark, bright man, and very good chairman. He is I think a historian. Monsignore Balboni, portly, an archaeologist who has written an incomprehensible book, more footnotes than text, about the Chair; Padre Ferrua, SJ, a little, delicate, oldish Jesuit who is in charge of the catacombs and had much to do with the excavations under the Basilica for Pope Pius. Like so many intellectual Jesuits he has that abstracted, maddeningly unruffled, slightly contemptuous air. Professor Romanelli, little beady eyes; a German, Ernst Schramm, Professor of Carolingian art, and the Englishman, J.L.-M., professor of nothing. Schramm is the only one who speaks English, and badly. He understands only what he wants to understand. Maccarrone speaks fairly good French. The others no French. Communication is not entirely satisfactory. At first I was shy, then went bald-headed, speaking in any language that provided me with the phrase I needed.

At six, by which time the doors of the Basilica are shut, we proceeded by way of the Scala Braschi into the south aisle of the Basilica. It was very impressive. Most of the lights in the church were out, but dozens of servants with torches were searching in confessionals, behind pillars, in nooks, crannies, and under the red baize curtains of benches for possible hiders. Vacchini explained to me that visitors habitually conceal themselves in the Basilica and spend the night there, either from access of zeal to be alone beside the Apostle's grave, or to leave firebombs.

The front of the cathedra is entirely concealed by sheets and behind it are strong arc lights blazing. As we pass we drop to our knees and reverently pray for a few seconds to the Apostle, turning our faces to the Confessio. We step over those two porphyry steps from the old Basilica, which thrill me, towards Pope Urban VIII's tomb. On it we leave our hats, coats and notebooks, or briefcases. Then we climb up steep ladders behind the sheets. The scaffolding is carefully prepared. In fact every precaution has been taken by the Ingenere. Every eventuality has been foreseen. Clambering up the two ladders, the old men groan, and move extremely slowly. I realize that I am still lithe and active, for these ladders have no terror for me, and my movements are still brisk. I am appalled to find that the four Fathers of the Church who uphold the bronze cathedra are hollow behind. I expected them to have hollow insides, but not to lack back sides, so to speak. For the two front Fathers of the Western Church are merely hemispherical. As I reach the top I pat the head of St John Chrysostom. It has a square hole in the skull.

The plank floor on which we stand is about twice the height from the pavement that the Alderley Grange roof is from the drive. It is on the level of the base of the throne. There are cameras, two or three cameramen and three workmen already up there. The arc lights focused on the bronze throne make it look rather tatty. The dark rear part of the throne is scratched. The right-hand putto's papal key is either crooked or loose, and looks as if it were coming off. The gold rays so striking from below have lost their sharpness. They are planks soused in gold semolina pudding. The edge of the bronze cushion on the other hand is delicately edged with gold dolphins, tiny, which cannot be seen from below. The crease of the bronze cushion is awfully good. So are the bronze reliefs on the side of the throne which I have never noticed before. The faces of the two angels leaning against the cushion are strong but not sensitive seen close to.

Two workmen in grey overalls immediately jump on to the throne seat. Vacchini is rather embarrassed that the two keys which Bernini had made with which to lock the cathedra in the seventeenth century can nowhere be found. He mutters as though shocked that such carelessness after a mere three centuries can be laid at the Treasury's door. With a hammer and chisel one workman takes the pins from the hinges, breaks the clasps and wrenches off the lid. I see that underneath the lid there is an intricate lock mechanism. I recall the lovely description of the Chair being installed in 1666 to the singing of *Te Deum*, swinging of censers, and the two keys being handed to Bernini's brother. Where on earth had he put them? A stool is fetched to enable the short-legged Monsignores and Professors to peer over the edge into the cavity below. Within a red velvet lined chamber stands the sacred Chair, covered with a drapery through which an outline of the pedimented top beneath is quite distinct. The drapery (called the *copertura*) is of cut velvet, gold, green and scarlet of Pope Sixtus IV's reign (1471–84). In the centre of the velvet an embroidered representation of St Peter seated on the very Chair, most carefully and accurately delineated. Monsignore Maccarrone announces that the della Rovere (i.e. Pope Sixtus) arms are also represented. The *copertura* is indeed the most beautiful object imaginable with the silks perfectly preserved. It is however covered with dust, which blows around and gets into our eyes and noses.

Then a workman jumps inside the cathedra. Everyone is so excited and anxious to get the Chair out that I am fearful lest an injury be done to it. Another workman starts removing the glass panels (there are 3 of them) behind the gilded bronze grille underneath the cathedra, between the legs. Occasionally he pops his head above the seat. His head is pouring with sweat. He has difficulty removing the glass because the old screws and bolts are stiff to undo. The Ingenere produces a tin of oil with which to loosen them. One of the Monsignori asks if it is the oil can Bernini used. We all snigger. The glass panels as they come out, covered with dust, are green. It must have been through these glass panels and the grille that important visitors in the eighteenth century were on special occasions allowed a glimpse of the Chair, because a glimpse through the back of the cathedra or shell would, I now see, not be possible. Next the workmen, with the help of the Ingenere, who is splendid, immaculate in his black velvet coat, yet authoritative, wrestle with the grille itself. The grille is finally wrenched off and carefully stacked at one side next the glass.

Vacchini and one workman crawl inside. They start tilting the Chair in order to bring it out between the feet of the cathedra. The hole made in the seat where the locks were picked is too small for it to pass through. I advise that they remove the *copertura* which otherwise may get torn. With little difficulty they drag the Chair out, and take off the *copertura* with the utmost care, fold it once only, and put it on a large square board, specially constructed. Encrusted with dust it is laid aside. The Chair is then lifted on to another board, recently made with little sockets to prevent the legs slipping. The dimensions were taken from a *modello* made by Bernini of the Chair, kept in the Sacristy. They were not quite exact and one socket has to be altered by a carpenter with the greatest expedition. The Chair revealed is exactly as shown in two indifferent likenesses taken when it was last exposed to view. Whereas in England after centuries it would have been attacked, even destroyed by worm, deathwatch beetle, or fungus, here owing to the Mediterranean climate it has hardly changed at all. Therefore I see little reason why it should have changed appreciably since it used to be shoved around the basilica before 1666, or even since it was put together many centuries ago.

An iron cage with a ring on the top is placed over the Chair and its base, clamped down, and attached to a hook and rope over a wheel. The whole contraption is slid to the edge of the platform over the nave. At this stage I go down the ladder to watch the Chair descend gently on to a trolley with wooden wheels on the pavement.

I should have said that at every stage photographs are taken of the Chair's passage from the cathedra to the pavement. The organization has been almost perfect. Much excitement throughout. Incessant chatter. The others come down the ladder. Monsignore Balboni looks down, feels giddy, and murmers *Mamma mia!* We all follow the trolley down the south transept, making only a perfunctory bow to St Peter's tomb because we all are so excited. The trolley is pulled silently and smoothly towards the Sacristy. Here we six members of the Commission are photographed beside the Chair. The Italians push themselves forward. I in my Anglo-Saxon fashion remain in the background, conscious however that being taller than the others my head will be seen above theirs.

The Chair is taken to a small room off the Sacristy, of which the walls are hung with white cloth. The Chair is picked up by the rings attached to the sides and placed, board and all, on a revolving low table, or platform.

Next day we are made to attend a funny little ceremony during which workmen take out the old lock of the door of the Chair's bedroom, put in a new one and three keys are handed to Vacchini, his secretary, and the President of the Commission. This precaution seems most odd. Throughout the previous twenty-four hours the Chair was presumably not so adequately protected by the old lock. Who on earth would enter and steal it now?

The two days following the extraction are spent in meetings, discussing what to do next. Very revealing how Italians behave during committees. They all talk and gesticulate at once. No one listens to anyone else, but everyone delights in his own ideas and expressions. They talk at breathless speed. I give up, and sit mute.

The morning of the 28th we spend in the little room reserved for the relic. Mercifully Romanelli and Ferrua are not present, so it is possible to study the chair at close quarters. Professor Schramm is rather a nice old boy who makes heavy Teutonic jokes. He keeps pointing out to the others how the legs of the Chair are worn by devout Anglo-Saxons having picked little bits off. He refers to my ancestors' damage, and won't believe that his did the same thing. He is also extremely careless, as I have noticed experts tend to be with works of art. He is always tapping the Chair with the end of his fountain pen, and in fact he knocked off a piece of decayed arm. When I pointed this out to him he was rather cross. But Maccarrone is quite severe with him.

What amazes me about this chair is how roughly, rudely put together it is. When they fitted the Carolingian chair inside an earlier carcass, they used great nails with heads an inch in diameter, which they hammered through the ivory carvings, right in the middle of a figure, or delicate carved head. The ivory plaques between the legs were cut ruthlessly to fit, and three actually nailed upside down.

Two experts from the scientific institute which is going to take radio carbon tests were busily picking samples of dust from the Chair and putting them into test tubes. Innumerable photographs are to be taken and sent to each member of the Commission.

[The conclusion reached by the Papal Commission's scientific examinations and deliberations was that the wooden carcass of the Chair and the splendid Carolingian ivories adorning it dated from the '80s of the ninth century AD. The Emperor Charles the Bald (823–87), whose ivory likeness is carved in the centre of the chair-back, was probably enthroned in it by Pope John VIII.

J.L.M. 1993]

Alderley Grange 28th May 1969

Old Tom assured A. today that the Gloucestershire saying is infallible: Two moons in May – No sun, no hay.

She asked: did that apply if there were new moons on, say, 30th April and 28th May? He couldn't be sure.

Today I noticed that a patch of common stinging nettles in a sheltered corner of Winner Hill in full sunshine gave out a strong sour-sweet, rather musty smell, not disagreeable. There were no flowers on the nettles.

Chuff and Fop [whippets] disturbed a hen pheasant and two of the tiniest hatched chicks. The hen flew away agitated. The chicks remained in the grass stock still, trying to camouflage themselves I suppose. Even when a day old they have this cunning instinct. Unless they are petrified with fear, which is presumably not so much an instinct as a reaction.

Sunday, 8th June

Lionel Esher[*] staying here with Christian last weekend recounted a piece of horrifying news told him by his brother-in-law, Evelyn Shuckburgh, our retiring ambassador in Rome. I was telling Lionel how last November I visited the Protestant Cemetery and made recommendations to the Embassy how Keats's grave might be treated. I asked Lionel if the two dead pines overhanging the graves had been felled yet. 'Ye-es,' he demurred. Then he said the Italian workmen, instead of felling, dragged the trees out by the roots. In doing so they dislodged the graves of Keats and Severn, drawing out and smashing the coffins. He begged me not to tell anyone on the Keats-Shelley committee. They would be upset, he said. I asked how badly the coffins were smashed. He said, very badly.

I went with A. last week to Sir Harry Luke's[†] memorial service in the Knights of Malta church, Clerkenwell. Sir H. Luke meant little to me. I met him once and thought him portentous. Did not take to him, and did not dislike him. I went for [his son] Michael's sake. Yet when that much overworked psalm 23 was sung I was nearly in tears. Why am I emotionally moved by these sorts of things? I feel ashamed. Even those in the congregation who may have loved him did not cry; or did not seem to. Nor, I suppose, did I seem to. At least I hope not. I except his grandchildren who were in floods of tears, which was very right and proper. And very sweet too.

---

[*] Lionel Brett, 4th Viscount Esher, b. 1913. Architect and poet: and Christian Pike, his artist wife.
[†] Sir Harry Luke, 1884–1969, colonial administrator and Governor of Malta.

1971

On my way yesterday to the Mutual Households Association meeting I took a large envelope of photographs for John Corn-forth at the *Country Life* office. At the porter's desk inside the front door I asked as usual, 'Will you be kind enough to deliver this to Mr C.?' Reply, 'I don't deliver letters any more these days.' I, rather nettled, 'What do you do then?' 'I sit here.' 'What fun!' I say caustically. 'It isn't,' he says. End of dialogue. So I climb two steep storeys to the office while the old bugger sits below gazing into space, and presumably earning £20 per week.

I am so conscious of the passage of time, or rather the little time left in which to do so much that I fuss and fret, and waste it rather than save it. For instance this morning I thought to myself 'What a bore having to review this book, Dorothy Stroud's *George Dance*, which will occupy three days, and how can I reduce the three to two?' so that I was not attending to the first five pages of my reading. Then woke up to the fact, and had to begin again from page 1.

Lunching with Raymond Mortimer* in Canonbury Place was just like being in the country. The pink dining-room window gives on to a long narrow garden with a huge London plane tree on a lawn. Outside roses scrambling and foxgloves, grass and leaves all fresh and green. Yet to get there one must walk through decayed streets, piled with offal, through demolished alleys, scruf-finess and horror. Dadie [Rylands] and Fanny Partridge† present. Dadie and Fanny talked so much and both together that Raymond and I hardly got a word in. Raymond quite silent, and I for once was anxious to talk, having quite a lot to say or ask. But couldn't. Dadie is good for R. because he teases him, particularly about his grand friends. 'Of course it's all right for Ray, because he gets the Embassy car to motor him wherever he wants, whereas Fanny and

---

* Raymond Mortimer, 1895–1980, literary and art critic.
† Frances Marshall, b. 1900, diarist and literary reviewer. Married 1933 Major Reginald Partridge who died 1963.

I will have to take the bus. We know our station,' etc. They were planning a tour in Italy together in September. Then these two left, and I stayed behind, in order to lie flat on the floor because of my bad back, and talk quietly to R. He says that Nancy [Mitford] is dying he is certain. She told him when in London that her Indian manipulator divulged, 'Your doctors think you are suffering from cancer.' What did Nancy say, I asked R? 'She said she didn't want to know any more.' That I think explains everything. She does suspect. How could she not? No one of her intelligence could fail to suspect cancer. I too when it comes to my turn shall not relish being told.

Dadie said that Roger Senhouse's* heir is a great-nephew, very nice, extrovert, sport-loving and stupid. As Roger's oldest friend, Dadie, when Roger was dying, saw the young man and warned him that he would be inheriting things of greater value than he might realize, viz.: modern pictures, ancient books and, moreover, letters from Bloomsbury friends. Notwithstanding his advice, the young man has sent to the incinerator hundreds of letters to Roger from Lytton Strachey, Virginia Woolf, Keynes and other Bloomsberries.

Friday, 2nd July

If it were not for the fact that *The Times* never publishes a letter from me on a subject other than historic buildings I would write one about the Harewood Titian. All this fuss and criticism of the Government for not buying it for the National Gallery for $2\frac{1}{2}$, or is it $1\frac{1}{2}$ million £s? I cannot see that it matters pictures of this importance – the Radnor Velasquez is another – and by foreign artists leaving this country. It is not as though they are going to be destroyed, or lost to the world. Whereas important works of architecture which are unique to this country are being destroyed every day. One must get one's values right. To my mind it is far more important to prevent, say, the Vandykes leaving the Inigo Jones room at Wilton, or some quite minor painting being removed from a beautiful overmantel for which it was commissioned, than Italian and Spanish masterpieces leaving England to be preserved and admired in another country. I would admittedly

---

* Roger Pocklington Senhouse, 1899–1971, publisher and bibliophile.

prefer that they did not go to America where they inevitably end up in museums and are never likely to move around in private hands again.

Saturday, 3rd July

Before dining with Jack Rathbone[*] I called at Rosamond's, and lying flat on the floor talked to her for an hour. She told me a strange story. I had sent her a week previously a cutting from some paper with a very small illustration of an eighteenth-century picture of Jordans house in Somerset, for sale at a London dealers. I remembered her having told me that Jordans once belonged to the Speke family, and her old mother-in-law, Lady Milford,[†] was a Speke. Ros said that she forwarded it to Lady Milford who to her surprise became tremendously excited. Being 92, deaf, almost blind, utterly miserable, and living in a world of darkness nothing had interested her for many months. She even wrote Ros a letter by return of post, saying how she had pored over this indifferent photograph with a magnifying glass, trying to detect the mulberry tree she played under as a child, that she was determined to buy the picture and was sending her daughter to London from Wales to buy it. While Ros was reading the letter, she received a telephone message from Wales that Lady Milford had had a stroke, and was in a coma. She died the morning of the day (30th) I was last with Ros. Ros thinks the excitement and pleasure of the Jordans picture killed her, and what a wonderful way out.

Sunday, 4th July

I hate Bernadette Devlin[‡] as much as I hate the Revd Ian Paisley, if anything worse. Now that she is to have an illegitimate baby and may be disowned by her beastly, pious Irish constituents, I find that I am pleased, and hope that they will chuck her out. Yet on principle I am all for sex freedom. In other words I, like the rest of the hypocritical world, am ready to seize any stick with which to belabour somebody whom I dislike. That is why buggers are so vulnerable. The moment they get into a fix their enemies will

---

[*] John Francis Warre (Jack) Rathbone, secretary of the National Trust.
[†] Ethel Georgina Speke, m. 1901 1st Lord Milford.
[‡] Bernadette Devlin, MP 1969–74. Founder of Irish Republican Socialist Party.

round on them because they are buggers, not because of the fix
they have got into, which may be something quite venial.

Tuesday, 6th July

Attended the Bath Preservation Trust Committee for the first time –
not without embarrassment, for in the past I have been v. critical
of this Trust and even resigned my membership. Now I join as
the result of constant, persistent pressure from Christopher Chancellor,* and A. says it is my duty to join. When welcomed by the
Chairman, Chancellor, I thanked them for their forbearance and
said what nice people they must all be. Unless I am strongly
interested by a particular item I find it hard to concentrate on the
subject discussed at the committee meeting. I am riveted by
entirely irrelevant matters, and matters is the word, viz.: the
freckles adorning the chest, arms and hands of my handsome but
plump female neighbour; the side whiskers of the youngish man
opposite which are already grizzled grey; the Chairman's icy
politeness and deft parrying of bores; the Deputy Chairman's
prosiness and smelly pipe, the Secretary's coyness, and indeed the
extreme niceness of one and all, met here to attempt the uphill task
of preserving Bath which they passionately love against the depre-
dations of philistine officials who don't care one damn how they
spoil the finest city in England. The singleness of purpose of
British people is splendid. The outside world is hostile.

Last night A. and I had a tele dinner, i.e. off a tray while
watching *Panorama* which was about Pakistani refugees, five millions pouring into India during heavy monsoon rain. Commentator describing the heaps of human beings, lying starving amidst
urine and excrement. A. and I silently eating, not caviare, and
drinking, not champagne, but eating the remains of curried
chicken and strawberry mousse left over from the weekend, and
drinking white wine. We felt sick, not from guilt, but disgust. If
this does not convince viewers that there are too many unwanted
people in the world, nothing else will.

---

* Sir Christopher Chancellor, 1904–89, chairman of Reuters and Bowaters.

Thursday, 8th July

I admire people who have no sex life, or at least appear to have none, which is why I approve of circumspection, or hypocrisy if you prefer. For sex should be solely an individual's concern, and speculation by others about it makes for interest. What I mean is that I admire people who are so original as not to derive pleasure from the same old, over-played game, with its lack of variation, its dreary, repetitive gambits, its inconclusiveness, its vanities and always *post coitum animale triste est.* I refer to lust not love of course.

Pam [Jackson]* dining here on Tuesday said that Nancy's sudden illness and operation for cancer two and a half years ago coincided with Palewski's† marriage, or rather immediately followed it. She and Diana are certain that a lot of her trouble is psychosomatic, that tiresome word. Her dreadful pain is worse when the Colonel fails to keep an appointment. She lies in bed waiting and waiting for him to telephone or visit. Pam hates him, and considers him the root cause of her illness. I find this hard to credit. For how can a woman so intelligent as Nancy nourish so hopeless a passion for a man for nearly thirty years when it has been hopeless from the start?

Friday, 9th July

Went to an orthopaedic surgeon in Gloucester, recommended by the nice one who twisted me about last week in London. Whereas the London one was impeccably professional, the Gloucester one was not, and moreover charged me 6 guineas instead of the other's 4. The Gloucester man was nearly everything that a doctor should not be. He was grubby, loud, vulgar, with a stentorian laugh, trying to ingratiate himself by using four-letter words, then said things like, 'Put your tootsies on that stool.' I could hardly bear it. Why must people try to be what they are not, or why do they not try to be what they ought to be? I'm sure most patients want their doctors to be first of all scrupulously clean, then quiet, respectful, authoritative and withdrawn.

---

* The Hon. Pamela, 1907–94. Called Woman by her intimates. Second of the Mitford sisters. Married 1936 Professor Derek Jackson.
† Colonel Gaston Palewski, 1901–84. Chef de Cabinet to General de Gaulle, and French ambassador to Rome.

Monday, 12th July

Dog days. After the wettest, beastliest June on record we are enjoying a July which brings back halcyon memories of those childhood summers which were a perpetual sunshine, of lazing on lawns under the shade of large spreading lime trees. For the past ten days we have had every meal from breakfast till dinner on the terrace. The garden is fragrant with roses which clamber over every wall and intoxicate the senses. People who come here give A. unstinted praise and say this is the most beautiful small garden they have ever seen. I believe it must be the fullest of roses ever seen. It is the greatest tribute to her, for she has created something which, if ephemeral, is a work of art. It is more than I have yet done, for I have yet to create a work of art.

Nothing gives me more happiness than sitting in the library with the holland blinds drawn down and the bright sunlight filtering through, while the outside world is sizzling and I am cool as a cucumber within.

The dogs are too silly. In this heat they pant and stalk unwillingly at my heel when I take them out. Yet so conservative are they that in spite of it they follow me round the house in the afternoon with exasperating looks of expectation and reproach, oblivious I suppose of the fact that they don't enjoy walks in the heat. I suppose they have no memories, and their conservatism prevents them reasoning. Rather like me in my old age.

Mrs Mason away this weekend from Friday till Tuesday, and we hoped to be alone having had guests every weekend this summer. But A.'s Australian god-daughter Léonie Matheson and Rod* wrote that they wished to see us, so A. invited them down. Only stayed one night and a more civilized, charming couple could not be invented, with the most perfect manners. I like Australians.

Wednesday, 14th July

Walking from Brooks's John [Kenworthy-Browne] took me through a tunnel passageway beneath a house between Spencer Ho. and the old Salisbury house, which I never knew existed. I had not been through it before. We were looking for Samuel

---

* Judge Roderick, b. 1928, and Léonie (née Downer) Matheson, living in Adelaide, South Australia.

Rogers's house which I well remember and think must have been destroyed in the war. When we reached Hyde Park Corner a park attendant was waiting to let us through the gate which he was about to shut with a bunch of keys in his hand. He was friendly. We asked 'Is there much point in locking the gates of the Green Park when one can slip under the rail all the way along Constitution Hill?' He laughed. 'We have to do it,' he said.

I went to tea, or rather Dubonnet, which I did not the least want on a hot afternoon, with Gwladys Chaplin.* She is having her operation next Thursday, the cancerous lump removed from her jaw, and thought it was the week after. The lump is far more prominent than the last time I saw her which cannot be more than a month ago. Poor old thing, she is very courageous. She said, 'It isn't much fun being ninety, and I want to go. I rather look forward to the operation, and don't think I shall get through it.' Then in the next breath spoke of the parties she would be able to give because of the nice new cook she has just got. She was very pleased that her portrait had arrived at Alderley. It came just as I was leaving at luncheon on Monday. 'He's a famous artist, Ellis Roberts,' she said, 'and you would get a lot of money for it if you sold it.' I said we would never sell it and A. would leave it to Clarissa on her death. Indeed it is charming, very Romneyish, painted in 1905. She couldn't remember the sitting at all, but that her husband liked it, or why she was clasping a dove for she hated birds.

On Tuesday as arranged I lunched with Bridget [Parsons]. On arrival the French maid said to me half-way up the staircase, 'I am afraid you will find her ladyship rather depressed today,' and gave me a knowing look. There was no one in the drawing-room. Then I heard a growl and a pair of shoes shot through the door on to the floor, narrowly missing my head. In came Bridget, stumping and complaining. To my surprise she was wearing a very tight pair of black satin hot pants, and a shirt so *decolletée* that her bosom was all but totally visible. When she sat I could see her navel. She was pulling behind her a pair of trousers which she then put on. We had a delicious luncheon of cold trout and raspberries. Conversation consisted of exaggerated praise of the maid very loudly so that she outside should hear every word (I suppose poor B. realizes

---

* The Hon. Gwladys Wilson, m. 1905 2nd Viscount Chaplin and d. 1971.

that this woman is more important to her than anyone else in the world), followed by complaints of the disloyalty of her friends, one after another. When she said she could not dissociate A. from them I said, 'But Bridget, you are so apt to jump on people that they are rather frightened of coming to see you.' 'What rot!' she exclaimed. We called a cab and with difficulty she hoisted herself in. The Curzon cinema was practically empty, mercifully, for B. fell fast asleep, and snored. After an hour she woke up, said it was a rotten film, which it was, and suggested leaving. I accompanied her back to the flat and left.

Thursday, 15th July

Waiting in the Ritz for Joan Drogheda* to lunch I saw Geoffrey Gilmour† also waiting. I asked him if he thought our rich, spoilt women friends expected to be met at their houses and conducted out to luncheon. He said, 'Certainly not. One must treat them tough. That's what they expect, and like.' I watched the clientele milling through the hall. Less chic than in the war days when I lunched there constantly. Joan at last appeared. At once, before I actually recognized her, I knew this was the right thing. She still has the most beautiful trim little figure. She walks like a goddess, and was dressed in a beautifully made lime-green dress with brass buttons, simple, no nonsense. How frail, superb and elegant she is.

I told her about my yesterday's experience with Bridget. She said it never pays to make duty visits out of kindness. Last week she received a letter from K. Clark who has had a serious operation, asking her to visit him at Saltwood. So Joan got her friend Lady Poole‡ to motor her from London. K. having said he had to rest immediately after luncheon Joan asked if he would like her to arrive at midday. This was accepted. Lady Poole dropped her at 12.15. K. met her at the door. 'Oh, you are here already. I haven't shaved yet. Oh dear! I suppose I shall have to show you round the garden. How awkward.' Although the Clarks have an able-bodied butler K. insisted on bringing the clean plates from and taking the

---

* Joan Moore's husband had become 11th Earl of Drogheda in 1957.
† Geoffrey Gilmour, 1907–81. Collector of *objects d'art* and resident in rue de Bac, Paris.
‡ Daphne Heber-Percy (née Bowles), m. 1952–65 to 1st Lord Poole.

dirty ones into the kitchen, thus interrupting the conversation. As Joan says, people who think that by indulging their servants this way they are ingratiating themselves into their esteem make a mistake. After luncheon Lady Poole failed to return on time, whereupon K. slunk off. 'And what earthly good did this expedition do to K., or me?' Joan asked. I said, 'In spite of everything K. is the greatest man we know.' Joan agreed.

Sunday, 18th July

Mr Barker our builder of whom we are very fond has sent his own son David, and adopted son, little Billy, a black foundling, to Rosehill boys' preparatory school in this village. He says that whereas David is doing moderately well, little Billy is doing brilliantly at both work and games, far excelling the other. And Billy has had a terrible childhood in that having been parked out with the Barkers as a baby he was reclaimed at the age of 5 by his mother, an utterly hopeless white girl – the black father unknown. The child and the Barkers were miserable, really broken-hearted, and Barker had a collapse in consequence. After a year, the mother having abandoned little Billy again, the Barkers managed to retrieve him. As Barker said, such experiences were enough to make a delinquent out of little Billy. On the contrary he is an exemplary child so far. His success surely proves that there is less in heredity than is generally supposed; or perhaps one could say, more in upbringing than is supposed.

Last night I woke at 3 with terrible cramp in the right leg. However much I moved about, even getting up and struggling round the room, it persisted. When I told A. this morning she reminded me how Eddy [Sackville] always maintained that after 50 a man must expect to have something wrong with him at least once a week, if not more often.

At the Royal Society of Literature annual prize-giving on Wednesday there was the usual tea break. In the crowd I found myself talking to Bobbie Speaight[*] and Joan Haslip.[†] Affectionately I took hold of what I supposed was Joan's arm and began stroking it while looking at Bobbie. On turning round towards Joan I saw with

---

[*] Robert Speaight, 1904–76, actor and literary scholar.
[†] Joan Haslip, 1912–94, biographer. Resident in Florence, Italy.

horror that I was fondling her right breast. I dropped it like a hot coal and felt extremely embarrassed. I said nothing. She seemed unconcerned. She has very good manners.

Lord Butler (R.A.B) our president gave the address on autobiographical writing. Quite good, yet as he modestly warned us, amateurish. He kept referring to Charlotte Brontë's *Villette* when he meant *Jane Eyre*. He also pronounced autobiographers as autobiogrophers – surely odd, though possibly right.

I have often noticed how women who achieve success never cease rubbing it in to one. They have no idea of modesty. In fact they are damned pleased with themselves. Nancy never stops intimating what a great writer she is – which of course she is not. Yesterday Joan Evans* lunched here. She is undoubtedly *very* clever, and highly respected as antiquarian, scholar and art historian. Yet all her stories redound to her credit. 'I was the first British woman to become a member of the French Wine Tasting Society', or 'As the only woman to become President of the Society of Antiquaries', or 'I floored him [never *her*] when I pointed out that I had carried off the Brackenbury Prize in 1909.' Vita Sackville-West on the contrary was an exception. She never boasted, never spoke of her writing or prowess, and was humility itself. I remember Kay Kennet once telling me in all solemnity that Peter Scott was the best living artist because he made more money out of those ghastly watercolours of ducks flying across marshes; and also because he was her son and no one else was.

Wednesday, 21st July

A. is just like my Mama about her birds. When they fly into the house and make dreadful messes, which are indelible, on the new lamp shades she is pleased. The right birds can do no wrong; the wrong birds can do no right. That is to say right birds are blackbirds, thrushes, tits, swallows, wrens etc., most birds in fact. Wrong birds are starlings, sparrows, crows, hawks. When they come to her bird trays in the winter and eat the food she chases them away in a rage; and is surprised that they are so foolish as not to understand that they are the wrong birds. These glorious days

---

* Dame Joan Evans, d. 1977. First woman president of Society of Antiquaries, and writer on art.

when we have most of our meals on the terrace the young
blackbirds almost eat out of our hands. They are quite fearless and
pick up the bread we throw them. They manage to pick up piece
after piece in their beaks without dropping or swallowing the
previous pieces, before flying off to the nest in the vine on the east
wall of the house. A. and Nancy in Versailles have an interminable
correspondence about the respective merits and demerits of their
birds. Nancy works herself into paroxysms of anxiety over the
possible fate of her blackbirds. From Nancy this is surprising for I
would not say she was very nature-minded.

Thursday, 22nd July

My dates are all wrong – never mind. On Tuesday afternoon I
thought I would visit Chavenage near here. It is now open one
afternoon a week. A pretty Elizabethan manor with nothing whatever inside. Had to join a party which was shown round by the
butler, a nice man, who has been with the family since the 1920s.
He read every word from a large sheet of paper attached to a
board, and his ignorance after all these years was very remarkable.
There were two framed colour photographs of the Wyatville
drawings for Windsor Castle recently found in the attics. At the
door into the garden the butler dismissed us and passed us on to
Major Lowsley-Williams [the owner]* who showed us the chapel
(over-restored in the last century and badly pointed). The Major a
happy, plump, friendly man. While our party of twelve slowly
dissolved, one member, an Anglicized German, and I were left
behind feigning an interest in the carved altar front which the
Major was extolling. It was obviously made up from a James I
bedback or overmantel. The German got down on his knees to
examine it, and said: 'There is only one man who could give an
opinion on this, and he is James Lees-Milne. Now in his book
Tudor Renaissance he is not necessarily . . .' I foolishly put my hand
on his shoulder and said laughing, 'You had better be careful what
you say, because I am he.' The poor man had a shock. The Major
kept repeating, 'It is the most extraordinary coincidence I have
ever known.' It was not that, but it was fairly extraordinary. The

---

* Major Philip Savile Lowsley-Williams, d. 1986.

German said he had once met me with Hiram Winterbotham,[*] and that he was the author of a book on baroque architecture for which I wrote a Preface more than ten years ago.

Telephoned Bloggs Baldwin.[†] Told him that his cousin Monica[‡] and I now addressed each other by our Christian names, much to our mutual embarrassment. Bloggs said, 'You can't very well blush on bumph.' I asked outright, 'Is it a fact that Elspeth really hates going anywhere, and refuses on principle?' He said No, it was her low blood pressure which tired her. In fact, he said, only last week, 'Elspeth looked at me (I never look at her) and said "We are losing all our friends. And it is your fault." ' 'What then?', I asked. 'We have now decided to accept every invitation that comes our way.' 'Then you can both come to dinner with us on Saturday.' 'Alas, I am afraid we can't.' I said that perhaps it would be a mistake for Monica and me to meet after these years of correspondence, like Ellen Terry and Bernard Shaw. He said it wouldn't be a mistake. 'Take my word.'

At the Chinese Ceramics exhibition at the V & A, I was too mean to buy a catalogue, and do not know the difference between or the dates of Sung and Tang. No exhibit was labelled, only the number given. So my interest was not intellectual, solely visual and aesthetic. Anyway I learnt why Chinese porcelain is superior to its Western imitation. It is flawless and pure. I thought, of course the slow evolution of traditional motifs is what makes the greatest art. Like the Greek Doric all over again.

On my way out of the exhibition passing through the Latest Acquisitions room my eye was caught by two framed coloured drawings by Wyatville of the Windsor Castle rooms, approved and signed by George IV. These were not the identical ones I had seen yesterday in copy, but from the same set. The Queen bought the greater number. Lowsley-Williams said he had no idea at all how they came into his attics.

---

[*] Hiram Winterbotham, b. 1908, Gloucestershire intellectual, traveller and eccentric.
[†] A.W. Baldwin ('Bloggs'), 1904–76, 3rd Earl Baldwin of Bewdley, biographer, and his wife Elspeth Tomes.
[‡] Monica Baldwin, d. 1976. Cousin of Stanley Baldwin and one-time nun. Authoress of *I Leap over the Wall*.

Friday, 23rd July

My happiest mornings are those when I wake up to the realization that I have no plans at all for the day, not even a meeting with the Diocesan Architect at the church, not even a visit to the tailor in Bath – nothing.

At Lyegrove yesterday Diana [Westmorland]* described how she lunched at Firle. She sat on George Gage's right,† June on his left. Neither could hear a word George Gage said, he mumbled so. 'Finally by sitting on his lap and eating out of the same plate I managed to catch one word from every other sentence,' she said.

In writing the last paragraph the telephone rang. A village neighbour asking us to have a drink this evening.

Saturday, 24th July

A., who continually says that were I not so stand-offish she would have our neighbours to drinks more often, complains that I accepted last night's invitation without consulting her. How would I like it if she had accepted without consulting me? Anyway it was next door, and only lasted half an hour. I can never refuse over the telephone. That is my weakness.

On my walks I don't look around or above enough. My eyes are fixed on the ground, or rather are looking within myself. I am too introspective. I don't consider the natural world around me as I should. Yet I am tremendously susceptible to my surroundings, and could for that reason never be happy living in ugly country. I think this also goes for Raymond [Mortimer] and Desmond‡ who love Long Crichel, yet – unlike me – never go for walks, never set foot outside their garden. A. asks me why they bother to live so far from London when they would be just as happy in Surbiton, and since the country means nothing whatever to them. The fact is, it does. Something of the Dorset landscape sinks in. Just the same

---

* Diana Lister, d. 1983. Daughter of last Lord Ribblesdale. Married her third husband, the 14th Earl of Westmorland, in 1923.
† Rainald (George), 6th Viscount Gage, 1895–1982, of Firle Place, Sussex.
‡ Desmond Shawe-Taylor, b. 1907, literary and musical critic for *New Statesman* and *The Sunday Times*. Lives at Long Crichel House, Dorset.

with me here. My walks are of course made by the dogs, without whom I would be even less responsive to nature.

The fly mentality is incomprehensible. At this time of year they congregate in the rooms, and circle round and round some central object, a chandelier or hanging lamp, without apparently alighting, just round and round aimlessly, contentedly. What is it all about?

Monday, 26th July

I suppose the reason why I have never been invited to join the Historic Buildings Council is my sullenness and despair. It is the only committee I have ever wanted to be on, and I used to feel deeply over the slight, like Lewis Namier* who was not given a fellowship at All Souls – because, Raymond tells me, he was the most egregious bore of all time, not I think my worst failing, which is possibly sheer dullness. I was one of the first people in the early movement to save country houses. In an indirect way I instigated the foundation of the HBC through Esher when I was secretary of the Trust's Historic Buildings Committee. I believed I could not be left out, and dire was my disappointment when I was left out and some with a tithe of my experience were put on. Oliver Esher and Jack Rathbone several times approached the chairman (that odious Alan Lascelles) on my behalf, with no results.

Telephone rang whilst I typing this. Elspeth Huxley to thank for luncheon yesterday and to say how attentive Raymond was to her. I said he was one of the nicest of men, that I used to be frightened of him but wasn't any longer. That in any case he would enjoy talking to her because she was on his intellectual beam. 'Oh, but', she said, 'I am not a highbrow, just a country bumpkin with intellectual leanings, whereas you . . .' 'I', I said, 'have never considered myself a highbrow even with intellectual leanings. I am a simple, rather stupid man . . .' The conversation continued on these self-deprecatory lines.

Tuesday, 27th July

The most charming letter from Raymond this morning. I think no doubt he enjoyed himself. Full of praise of A.'s garden and her

---

* Sir Lewis Namier, 1888–1960, historian.

cooking. He ate nothing however, and looked frailer and smaller than formerly. Fanny Partridge was robust in comparison, although her face is ravaged.

Wednesday, 28th July

I regard the *Geranium pratense* as a sort of miracle. Walking back from Wotton across the fields under a grey leaden sky my melancholy was dissolved by the clusters of five little petals as blue as the Mediterranean. They mock the dark and dismal north and make me long to fly off to the sunny south.

Thursday, 29th July

Yes, autumn. A faint mist on the lawn this morning which on close inspection turns out to be a light dew. While dressing I habitually listen, first to the news summary, then to the gramophone records. Mozart symphony practically reducing me to tears. All the pathos of all the youth of the whole world since creation in it. No composer moves me more. Meanwhile Fop on the furry rug by the fireplace, shivering with anticipation, with a slight smile, alert expression, ears cocked, is totally oblivious of the music and what it is meaning to me. If instead of the Mozart a mechanical tree-saw were screaming in the room he would not alter his expression or cease longing for me to let him join Chuff downstairs, and gallop out of the front door with lunatic barks and yells.

Friday, 30th July

Last night after dinner I called A.'s attention to the swarm of insects under the ilex tree on the drive. They were swirling round and round each other in a tight ball, at a hundred miles an hour, and what is more, never colliding. It was a dead calm evening. No breath of wind, so it was not as though they were caught in a current of air, a pocket. There was clearly a purpose. Were they catching other lesser insects, cannibals in the insect hierarchy? Was it a dance of sex, or death? We must ask Anthony [Chaplin]* when we stay with him in August. Another question is why the human is the only creature to laugh.

---

* Anthony, 3rd Viscount Chaplin, 1906–82. Zoologist and pianist.

Going for a walk I rang the Gascoignes'* bell. Midi not back
from London yet. Bamber and Christina[†] were sunbathing in the
garden and made me talk for five minutes. I noticed that the
figures of both were the same. Both slim, slender, with small hips,
Bamber's waist as narrow as mine was five years ago – eheu! She
has no bust. They are very alike in other respects – points of view.
Before dinner they came and sat with us on our lawn. Pity we had
not known they were to be alone or we would have asked them
to dine, without their parents, and possibly have *talked*; for Bamber
is a highly intelligent boy although I have not yet got beyond
expressions of jocular esteem, skimming the very surface of things,
and not down to earth. This is often the case with children of old
friends. Seldom conversation. He said his father never read a book –
which does not surprise – and so was quickly bored. Had been
tyrannical until his children were self-supporting and independent
of him when he became utterly uncritical and indifferent to their
views and habits. In fact most fathers are the same. So long as they
are paying for their children they expect them to conform to their
ways. Money is the root cause of power claims. And when both
parties have money there is no longer call for exercise of rights.

Off to Ireland today. I hate going away, when the time comes.

Wednesday, 4th August

And I hated being away – as I knew. The flight from Bristol was
horrid. A mingy little plane like a moth which danced about the
clouds. The ventilation was not working. Only hot air came out.
There were dozens of children screaming their heads off. At one
moment I thought I was either going to have a heart attack, or go
mad. We bumped as I do not remember doing since the early days
of air liners. It was worse than the sea because although the sea
rock is rhythmical and can be come to terms with, the air rock is
intermittent and could come to anything. Is unpredictable and
therefore frightening. It is fear in my case. I am scared stiff. Good
Mona Baring and brittle Joan Haslip waiting for us at Belfast with

---

* Derick and Midi Gascoigne, living at the Mount House, Alderley. She
died in 1990.
[†] Bamber Gascoigne, b. 1935, author and broadcaster, and his wife Christina,
photographer.

McIlhenny's car. The drive to County Donegal two and a half hours.

Derek [Hill]'s* house is set in a relentlessly green salad bowl. One feels like a slug at the bottom trying ineffectually to climb out of it. I told him that the place was like a dream or a scenario in Alain-Fournier's *Le Grand Meaulnes*.† And truly the house is as pretty as can be, a sort of real rectory, with rector. It is the landscape of Ireland that is dead in spite of the green and luxuri-ousness of the vegetation. No birds sing. The inhabitants stand for hours with their mouths open. Withal they are horrid, cruel, stupid people, whose only outstanding quality is a long memory; and this is to our disadvantage.

Peter Montgomery‡ was staying. I have not seen him since the war and the incident of the Piccadilly Hotel bombardment described in the last chapter of *Another Self*. No longer golden-haired, he is grey-haired, but unlike me has all his hair. A distinguished face, albeit grey too for like all Irishmen he drinks much. Derek, whose drink he consumed liberally, pointed this out to no avail. Peter is a good, easy, nervous, ineffectual man, but positively musical. All his spare energies flow into orchestras and symphonies.

The boiler having burst just before our arrival, and it being Ireland's Bank Holiday weekend, there was no hot water in the house from Friday till Wednesday. It did not much matter. We had occasional baths in the cottage, 100 yards away, through the rain. I had mine after dinner the first night, and in my dressing-gown lay on the floor talking to Derek and Peter before going to bed. I found them deep in discussion of the alleged refinements of sexual practices current among the old English aristocracy and the *gratins* of the New World. Some so nauseating, others so comical that the mind boggles. I don't see that sex can be much joy either while one is vomiting into others' mouths or convulsed with laughter. These sorts of things are not done in Ireland for the inhabitants are prudish. If they have not many virtues then they have circumspection.

---

* Derek Hill, b. 1916, painter. Lives at St Columb's, Letterkenny, Co. Donegal.
† Published 1913. Novel about a child's dream world.
‡ Peter Montgomery, 1909–88, squire of Blessingbourne, Co. Tyrone. Con-ductor of Northern Ireland Symphony Orchestra, 1933–8.

Glenveagh Castle, County Donegal, is a miniature Ludwig of Bavaria castle, but oh so tame if you compare it with Neuschwanstein. The architecture is not bold enough to please me. It is 1870 or 1880 and there are not enough towers and battlements. The outside is parsimonious. The inside has been made very attractive by Henry McIlhenny, and is filled with Landseers. He has 8 gardeners, 8 indoor servants, 20,000 acres and 28 miles of fencing to maintain. He is a friendly, absurd, cosmopolitan-society, American, millionaire queen. But shrewd, philanthropical, and a genuine connoisseur of the arts, with good taste. And he laughs at Derek's oversensitivity. Derek cries with vexation over Henry's overbearing proximity, he the comparatively poor man at the gate. But he ought not to mind, or try to compete, for he has the great advantage of being no millionaire, yet being comfortably off, and a good artist beside. He has all the advantages, come to think of it, yet is driven to frenzies of resentment at Henry being there at all. Mutual friend-snatching a recurrent cause of strife.

Coming home, by which I mean on the first stages by way of Belfast, we stopped at Derry for luncheon, having motored through Bogside: first, the Catholic area of dilapidated, slummy streets, scarred and battered; then the Protestant quarter, every street and alley ablaze with bunting, Union Jacks and Long Live the Queen. Even the street curbs are painted red, white and blue. Most provocative. The wretched soldiers are posted on the top of an arch, within sandbagged watch-towers. The same thing in the Falls area of Belfast. It makes one sick. There is no end to it seemingly. Prots and Caths in Ireland sharing one single emotion to the exclusion of all others – hatred. The Prots' professed loyalty to the Queen means nothing beyond an expression of loathing of Catholicism and the South.

Friday, 6th August

My birthday. I woke oblivious of it, concerned only with a pain in my left eye. While I was shaving A. came in and kissed me. She did not believe I had forgotten, and I believe it is the first time I ever have, because now a birthday means little to me. I wish I could ignore it totally. I am 63. I used to despise, yes, despise people who had reached that age because physically they were repugnant to me. They still are. A. overwhelmed me with presents –

a suitcase with initials, an ink-wash by Charles Tomlinson* of dragonflies, the very one I admired the other night when he brought a selection to show us and Raymond and Fanny were staying, two ties and a brown pullover. A. loves giving as much as receiving.

Thank goodness our visit to the Chaplins next weekend is put off because poor old Gwladys is failing. After the operation for cancer of the jaw a fortnight ago she seemed fine, now the wound is suppurating and she is what the nurses call 'poorly'.

Saturday, 7th August

A. says, having watched the astronaut walking in space and appearing to be floating horizontally without any apparent sensation of speed, although the space-ship to which he was attached by a thin cord, not even taut, was travelling at 20,000 miles an hour: 'I catch a sudden glimmer of understanding of what the universe means; but it disappears instantly.' Indeed to witness such things on the television screen makes one begin to understand how, if speed of such velocity has no meaning, then doubtless time has the same lack of meaning in outer space, as we are told. The mind tries to grasp these wonders, but it can't.

Horrible things happen to the body. Weakness of valves, etc. Greater care must be taken to be clean. I hate admitting to wearing plates; and because on Tuesday next I have to surrender my bottom plate to Mr Plowman the dentist for adjustment, and shall not have it returned till the following day, I am reluctant to go to the theatre and dine with Freda Berkeley on Tuesday evening. A. thinks this absurd, saying that it is not as though I had no front teeth; and it is only some back teeth which are missing.

This morning A. doing flowers in the church for Sunday met a young couple at the door and talked to them. He told her he was writing a book about Brian Houghton Hodgson who lived in our house for thirty years till his death in 1894. She suggested that they came and saw the house. This they did, and were thrilled. But when I suggested that they might care to go round on their own,

---

* Professor Charles Tomlinson, b. 1927. Poet and Professor of English, Bristol University. Married 1948 Brenda Raybould.

and take notes, they declined. Which makes me question whether he is serious or merely curious.

Dining with the Gascoignes a solicitor called Dickie. As we were leaving Dickie asked me if I remembered Isabel Kellet. I said I didn't. He said she had been a niece of the old Empeys, and had many a tale about Mama and how good she was to the Empeys and how funny. Then I remembered the niece. As for Mollie and Emily Empey they can never be forgotten. They lived in a cottage of ours in Wickhamford, and bicycled every Sunday to church. Mollie had a beard and looked like an old Irish priest, and Emily wore pince-nez and was very blind. They would hop and hop before venturing slowly to throw themselves on to their saddles, then wobble perilously until they got going. Very worrying to watch. Once going they never dared look to side or backwards but kept their eyes glued to the front wheel. As children we were obliged to have tea with them once every holidays, which bored us considerably. And whenever we called or left a message we were given a ginger biscuit. Although we loved them when we were young children, we soon grew out of them, and I fear became horribly offhand and cruel. I am sorry now that it is too late to make amends and to tell them what darlings I know them to have been. Emily had been Mama's governess.

Tuesday, 10th August

Dickie is Midi's solicitor. The first time she visited his office she stepped briskly into the room, rather pleased with herself, and said: 'Mr Dickie, you will be glad to hear that *I* know exactly what I want.' 'Then all I have to do is to tell you why you can't have it,' was his reply. She took to him at once.

With Eardley to Berkeley Castle yesterday. Ten years ago when I went as a visitor I thought it was ghastly. That opinion was confirmed yesterday. The rooms are badly arranged, the contents indifferent and badly looked after. The Stubbs picture badly in need of repair. Horrible shapeless rooms; and bare stone walls are a poor background for gilt furniture. The best furniture, with sofa, chairs and mirrors *en suite*, splendid in themselves, has been badly regilded with oil, not water gilding. The late Earl fudged up the place by introducing Gothic doorways, galleries and even windows brought from France. Much of the outside is badly restored.

Bad, bad, bad nearly all the way round. The only good thing is the
terraced garden. This is beautiful. The situation is not impressive.
Yet the outside is better than the inside. Seen from across the
meadow at twilight the Castle does look like a crouching tawny
lion, about to spring.

Had a horrid nightmare last night. Some schoolmaster or don
was correcting my Latin prose. He was devastating me with
sarcasm about my illiteracy. I was feeling miserable and humiliated.
At the back of my mind I was thinking, 'This beastly man does not
realize that I am capable of better writing than this. If he only
knew, and would take the trouble to find out my potentialities. I
know I can write, I know I can. Damn him!' In fact I was
retrojecting myself to my Oxford days when I had nothing to
show for myself, when my education was thoroughly neglected,
and I resented this neglect, and yet fostered secret and intensely
passionate ambitions to write.

Thursday, 12th August

Mrs Golda Meir, the Israeli Prime Minister, interviewed on *Panorama* on Monday came across as a transparently sincere woman,
astute, tortured, but honest. Impossible not to like her, and admire
her. In the course of the hour she said she did not want to be
remembered, didn't want any place or prize to be named after her.
She had never kept a diary. Which remark made me ask myself
why on earth I did. No doubt I explained why in 1942. Then no
doubt the reason, even if I was not honest enough to give it, was,
partly at least, a contemptible, vain desire for a vestige of immortality, idiotic though such a craving was. Now it is different. I am
going to keep this diary only for six months, just to see if I can
make a book out of it, out of everyday events, thoughts, nothing
much, nothing at all perhaps. But one must be candid. That is the
first absolute necessity. Unfortunately one cannot always publish
candour.

In a crowded bus from Paddington to Oxford Circus I found
myself standing above a young, rather beautiful negress, who was
sitting in a single seat and wearing a white blouse. It was stuffy in
the bus. I was admiring what I could see of her bosom from my
bird's-eye view. I caught a strange, sickly sweet, rather vanilla-like
smell, which persisted after the bus emptied and I got a seat behind

the young negress. Then I moved away, and the smell ceased. So it is all rot to say that negroes do not have a different smell to white people. They do; and doubtless we have a smell which they don't much care for.

Some days, usually mornings, I am so conscious of my own hideousness, my absurdity, my dour presence that I dread encountering people I know, and having to speak to and be recognized by them. I move in a capsule of self-consciousness. At other times I merely feel so brittle, so incommunicable that contact with another is unthinkable. To make the effort of communicating is out of the question. I feel so fragile, so dazed, so doped that I belong to no world and float in my own. I am not happy during these moods, but just mentally, psychically ill. My confidence is not so much subdued as non-existent. I feel inferior, unable to cope. Tormented too with *Angst*.

Friday, 13th August

No, the chief purpose of keeping a diary is to keep one's hand in. It keeps the fingers flexed, and the mind. Even so, I pay not the slightest regard to style, syntax or grammar. I forge ahead without any consideration of good prose. I wonder if Harold [Nicolson]* whose diaries are impeccably written took trouble, or ever rewrote. I believe not. He was a disciplined, trained and professional writer, who simply could not go wrong, even when improvising. I remember him typing his diary at the end of the day, and early in the mornings. He did not use all his fingers, and his typing was not fast, but he never wavered, never hesitated, and went straight through like cutting butter. So it seemed to me listening to the click, click in the next room in King's Bench Walk. That was in 1934–5, when I was a paying guest.

I know no agony greater than having a manuscript turned down. It has happened to me several times, and the pain, humiliation and disappointment are always devastating. This past winter I suffered from acute depression because my novel was rejected by literary agent David Higham, and publishers Hamish Hamilton and Jock Murray. Yesterday I began to read through it once again after a

---

* Hon. Sir Harold Nicolson, 1886–1968, diplomatist, writer, MP. Married 1913 the Hon. Vita Sackville-West (d. 1962).

break of nine months at least, probably longer. I have nearly finished reading the first part which I know is the best, or least bad section. I think it is worse than I had supposed. It reads in a stilted, old-fashioned way, and I am old-fashioned. I have a dreadful belief that old writers today, unless tremendously distinguished, are simply not wanted. Look at the way Leslie Hartley* is now treated by reviewers, as an old, fuddy-duddy reactionary without an original idea to convey.

Yesterday walking with the dogs along the lane by the Post Office tower at Ashcroft the verges of the lane were filled with oats. The fields on either side were still growing barley, I think. Were these oats spilt from wains that had been passing along the lane at harvest time last year? At any rate in these pools of oats were jet-black slugs, with smooth heads and corrugated bodies. I looked at them closely. They never moved and did not seem to be eating. They repel me, yet I am grateful for any living creature's existence that is not a human's.

Saturday, 14th August

Joan Drogheda, brought to dinner by Diana Westmorland and Julian Fane,[†] talked about Jamesey [Pope Hennessy], whom after a long interval she recently asked to luncheon. He was charming, but she says never again does she intend to be involved with Jamesey. He is a bad friend. After discussing his unorthodox loves she said, 'Mine have always been orthodox.' 'Never sadistic or masochistic?' I asked. 'No,' she said, 'unless my bad failing is falling out of love when another falls in love with me. Nevertheless although I don't want him I don't want anyone else to have him. I must keep him around, being irritated.' 'That,' I said, 'strikes me as dog-in-the-manger, with a touch of sadism.' 'You don't think so?' she said, wide-eyed.

Yesterday was A.'s birthday. Today is Dick's.[‡] As we get older I think with dread of the awful possibility that she may die before me. Pray God it may not be. Yet I wonder what she would do without me to revolve round. I dread to think, because she has not

---

* L.P. Hartley, 1895–1972, novelist. Author of *The Go-Between*.
† The Hon. Julian Fane. b. 1927, novelist. Younger son of Diana Westmorland.
‡ Richard Crompton Lees-Milne, 1910–84. J.L.-M.'s brother.

many intimate friends. Nor indeed do I have many left. I think I could make new friends more easily than she somehow. Today she has motored to West Wycombe to stay with Clarissa, and all day I have worried about the roads.

Sunday, 15th August

Dogs are lucky in having no memory. This morning while it was thundering Chuff was terrified. He clambered on to my knee while I was writing. He shook with terror, and kept swallowing and licking his lips, a thing dogs only do in extremity. I comforted him, kissed his ears and assured him there was no cause for alarm. He would not eat his dinner. Then the weather cleared, the thunder ceased. He saw me prepared to go out to lunch with Eny Strutt,* and at once gambolled around and barked with excitement when he realized that I was taking him. The hideous terror of five minutes ago was totally forgotten. Joan said yesterday that nothing would induce her to subscribe to the refugee Pakistanis, whereas instead she had sent a contribution to the Battersea Dogs' Home. Quite right.

Marianne,† Eny's Dutch friend whose surname I forget, was staying. I said she really ought to write her memoirs. She resolutely refused; the things she knew must be left unrecorded. She played an important rôle in the Dutch Resistance movement. I said, 'You knew Queen Wilhelmina very well, didn't you?' 'I was Secretary to her Cabinet for many years.' Queen Wilhelmina was brought up in a cotton-wool world. Her three brothers had died before her father. She was the only child of a second marriage, and succeeded to the throne when still a child. Her father King Willem III had wanted to marry Olda Willes's mother who was a great beauty and an aunt of Eny. His son the Prince of Orange had wanted to marry someone ostensibly suitable, and Parliament endorsed the marriage, but King Willem resolutely refused to allow it, because he knew that the real father of the girl was a very close relation of his,

---

* Baroness Irene de Brienen (Eny). Married second husband, Admiral Arthur Strutt, and died in 1974.
† Marianne Tezgers, active member of wartime underground in Holland and confidante of Queen Wilhelmina.

and already the Dutch royal family had intermarried, '*trop de cousinage*'. Eny said that as a child she went with her sister and cousins to the royal palace, when the Queen was still a girl. The ceremony was strict. The children assembled in the hall. A door would open and a chamberlain in sky-blue breeches banged a staff on the floor and announced '*Sa Majesté!*' The children were not allowed to play with the Queen as they would with each other. One little boy pulled the Queen's hair, and was never allowed inside the palace for the rest of his long life. During the war the Queen in exile in England started to invite every Dutchman or woman who had escaped. She had them to tea with the utmost informality. When she returned to Holland she began to live in the same informality and simplicity and her ministers had to remonstrate with her. She had been brought up by her German mother to suspect all her ministers, and in consequence treated them with hostility. Marianne said very quietly that she knew the Queen as well as anyone else. And when we were saying goodbye she said, 'Having worked with Queen Wilhelmina I am not afraid of Eny.' Queen W. was intensely proud of Juliana, and referred to her always as '*My* daughter,' giving the *My* great emphasis.

On the sofa after luncheon Eny began showing me a photograph album of the twenties – titled women in cloche hats, and men in flannel trousers and homburgs, all looking alike and exclusive. Suddenly I could bear it no longer and was impelled to jump up and go. One should never do that with the old, but I just could not stand another minute of it.

Monday, 16th August

As there was no Holy Communion at Alderley this Sunday I decided to go to Hillesley at 9.30, the first time I have ever attended a service there. It was what is called Family Communion which I don't like, with sermon and four hymns. But I was much impressed with the wonderful state of this church brought back from a near ruin solely by the efforts of the Rector Norman Sparks who himself repaired the roof, ravaged by beetle, and painted the walls and did improvements generally, with his own hands. For days and weeks he was up scaffolding. He rallied the young of the village to co-operate. Yet I did not notice a single young person in the congregation this morning.

Wearing my spectacles (the sun shining through the south windows) I noticed what I have so often before noticed, the reflection,
much magnified in some part of the lens, of my eyelashes. They
appeared like a forest, each lash, seen distinct, tall, upright, or bent
in so clear a vision that would never be revealed to me if I looked
at them in a mirror. I don't quite understand how this comes
about. And actually my eyelashes are diminutive.

The elm disease in this county is worse than ever known. It is
an epidemic. Everywhere one sees the trees dying, or dead. Within
a month of being attacked they die, beginning at the top. The
cause is a beetle. The effect strangulation of the tree's life-blood.
But the cause of the virulence of the beetle is the loss through
pesticides of some other insect or bird which formerly ate this
beetle. Some say it is a wasp which used to eat it and has now been
eliminated. In any case the loss of these noble trees is terrible,
especially in the Vale which is wooded with them.

Tuesday, 17th August

I enjoyed reading in the *Observer* the three astronauts' [of Apollo
15] accounts of their moon experience. Although they could have
been more graphic they are the first accounts of a descriptive kind.
Hitherto accounts have been as muzzy as the photographs. These
men have been almost poetic. I derived some impression of the
steep mountains, 12,000 feet, enclosing the deep valley where they
landed, and the golden colour of these mountains against a pitch-
black sky. Then the astronaut who was left circling the moon
wrote that going round the far side meant entering total darkness;
that on his re-emergence the moon hills on the horizon were first
touched with dawn light, then on his coming round to the earth
side – the relief of it – suffused with a burst of blue light. None of
these men spoke of being lonely, or frightened. They even felt
homesick for the moon on leaving. How strange, unearthly, sub-
lunar, marvellous. No noise; deadly quiet; rock minerals glinting
like silver. As they drove their jeep in the valley one of them
quoted a verse from the Psalms, 'I will lift up mine eyes unto the
hills: from whence cometh my help.' The experience, he added,
confirmed his faith in God. I wonder how voices sound on the
moon.

Wednesday, 18th August

How one cannot face up to realities, and how one is full of cant! Walking through the Newark woods I thought, every second of the day some creature's death agony is ringing in my ears. And do I heed it? No. I hear a musical accompaniment to my happy stroll under these idyllic trees, or a lullaby in the bird's notes as I complacently offer my face to the sun. What in fact I am hearing is some little bird being torn to shreds by a hawk, a squirrel being skinned alive by a crow.

I enjoy teasing the dogs. In the woods I let them run ahead, then step aside into the bracken and lie down as though dead. Instead of going on they soon come back. They always find me. Chuff approaches and, satisfied, sniffs around without a comment. Fop gives me one cursory lick and waits. Rather bored; and not amused.

Derek Hill asked one of the inhabitants of Tory Island, twenty miles off County Donegal, what they did in the summer. 'In the summer,' he answered, 'we fish and fuck. And in the winter we don't fish.'

Thursday, 19th August

Motoring John Cornforth to Kemble station this evening I was turning right off the Kemble lane into the station yard. John uttered a sharp yell of terror. And I saw a van coming towards me at great speed over the hump ahead. I put on my brakes. It put on its, and with a terrible screeching drove into the bank. Looking out of the back window I thought it was bound to topple over. It didn't. I stopped. A young man got out of the van. I walked to meet him. I think we both felt guilty. He had been going a tremendous pace. I was talking and should have been more alert. I presumed he was going to curse me. Not so. He asked if I had had a scratch. I said No, we missed each other by a cat's whisker. I was much shaken. So was he. 'O what luck!' we both said. And we laughed idiotically. 'Let it be a lesson to us both,' we said piously in duet. We were overcome with relief, and emotion. We moved towards each other, smiling, and with mutual apologies and con-gratulations. I am sure if John had not been there I should have fallen upon his neck. What an introduction to a lifelong friendship it might have been.

We were out all day. First we went to Westonbirt, all round house and garden for my article on the place in *Country Life*. Lunched off hot chicken eaten with our fingers at Bourton-on-the-Water, in a small hotel garden. Bourton is a beastly village, crammed with trippers, and not even pretty. When we got home met at the gate a charming young man who asked A. and me if we lived at the Grange. He was the grandchild of a former Miss A'Deane who owned this house. We gave him a drink and I took him to the church to see the A'Deane mural tablets. He was thrilled.

Friday, 20th August

John Cornforth* thinks that David Vicary who lives in Kilvert's Rectory outside Chippenham is the best exponent of the post-John Fowler style of decoration. His understanding of colour schemes is 'the tops', J.C. says. Certainly when I was last at the Rectory, a rare little George II house, I thought it enchanting inside, nearly all the contents fascinating and desirable, and the fabrics pretty. But, oh my! the muddle and chaos. You could not move for the clutter, far worse than ours here. This is doubtless the prevailing fashion and can be compared with the way in which the expensive (not the indigent) young dress, messily, everything thrown together in an uncoordinated, happy-go-lucky manner, the outcome of which may be successful, or not. It seems a toss-up how it will turn out; fortuitous.

I took John Cornforth to call on Don Nicholas† at Temple Guiting, in order to return some Stuart books he had lent me. Notwithstanding his tremendous knowledge of the Stuarts D.N. is self-deprecating and tries to make you think he knows nothing and that you have much to teach him. This is bad for me and makes me bumptious.

Saturday, 21st August

I walked through Newark woods to leave a letter on the new tenant of the house. A girl on a pony passed me. She had a sweet old-fashioned face, almost demure. Turning her head she said,

---

* John Cornforth, on staff of *Country Life*: architectural historian.
† Donald Nicholas, author of *The Portraits of Bonnie Prince Charlie*, 1974.

'Good afternoon,' and, I think, blushed. Her eyes shone like diamonds. She and the pony seemed one. The pony's face had more expression than hers. Hers was purposeful, yet melting. I longed to say, 'You are a poem. I could love you. I want to hug you and whisper the nicest messages into that pink ear of yours.' Instead while she was passing me I no doubt was looking severe and professorial; and she said to herself, 'Poor old man, he has never known what the word love means. He has had no romance in his life. He is dry-as-dust, half dead.'

Sunday, 22nd August

Nigel Birch, now Lord Rhyl,[*] was staying with Sally Westminster.[†] After dinner we talked of Tom Mitford,[‡] dead these twenty-six years and more. Nigel said he was no good as a barrister, for reasons he could not make out, but good as Judge Advocate. Said he doubtless would have given up his indiscriminate sex life, have married and borne many children, become a model husband – and, I added, probably a disciplinarian father. Talked of his beauty, and Randolph's, which lasted until the latter was 21 when it vanished. He repeated that Randolph was the most beautiful creature one could imagine. This is true. He had magnificent eyebrows, and deep-set eyes, like Lady Randolph Churchill's to judge from her photographs. Nigel said he and Tom were Randolph's best friends, his only friends in fact; and R. died as much from excessive eating as drinking.

Monday, 23rd August

Extraordinary that Ksheshinskaya should still be alive. Last week her birthday was announced, aged 99. She was the mistress of the late Tsar Nicholas II before he married, in the last century. A ballet dancer, she married a Grand Duke. Sachie recommended her memoirs which I read last year. She was temperamental, and rather maddening. But what a link.

---

[*] Nigel Birch, 1906–81. MP and economist. Created Lord Rhyl 1970.
[†] Sally, 1911–91, widow of Gerald Grosvenor, 4th Duke of Westminster.
[‡] The Hon. Thomas D. Mitford, 1909–45, son of 2nd Lord Redesdale. Killed on active service in Burma.

Desmond Shawe-Taylor is staying with us for the Three Choirs Festival, as vital, as delightful, as fussed, as ebullient as ever, though older. Slightly round-shouldered, and deaf. Since he is determined to grasp the meaning of every word uttered by others he repeatedly holds up conversation. Dadie Rylands told Eardley that of all the critics and reviewers in the world of literature, of art, of music put together, Desmond is the best and cleverest.

Beverley Nichols[*] told Desmond that the director, having staged a rehearsal of Melba's final goodbye speech at Covent Garden to culminate her last performance of *Bohème* (which reduced the audience to tears), said to Melba, 'You must add some pathos, and give praise to the stage hands. For instance, mention the door-keeper.' 'What? That silly old fool!' she said. In the speech she referred to 'that dear Mr So-and-So who for forty years has faithfully handed me into my carriage, to him I say Farewell with all my heart.' It brought the house down.

The buffet-car attendant on the London–Salisbury train trots down the corridor, announcing, 'Teas, Horlicks, coffees, Oxos, Bovrils,' which when he gets to the last carriage amounts to 'T-h-i-cs-ox-obsils.'

Tuesday, 24th August

Went for a walk with Desmond through the fields and Foxholes Woods. He is the sweetest fellow, very entertaining, funny and extraordinarily quick. A really brilliant man. Very affectionate too. But his fussiness is a disease. At times he can't enjoy himself for worry whether his shoes will get dry before departure, whether he will leave them behind in the boothole, whether we would forward them if he did so, and how to get himself to his brother's house at Andoversford. With his great, quick intelligence he must be driven almost mad by his own fussiness. He has to have a simple statement of fact – the sun rises at 5.30 a.m. today – explained and argued over before he will accept it. But when one can steer his mind away from these domestic worries he is immensely stimulating.

One sad thing about advancing years is that old friends become, with few exceptions, more trying to live with, some too trying to

---

[*] Beverley Nichols, 1898–1983, author, composer and playwright.

be with for more than a day. *Ergo*, one should love but not live with them.

In a rage with the Midland Bank this morning over the telephone because my bank statement, prepared by computer, does not explain whence come payments into my account. The bank was unable to tell me who or what sent me a cheque last October for £42. So I said in these circumstances bank statements no longer served a useful purpose and they might just as well cease sending me mine. If I had actually been in the bank I would probably not have lost my temper; whereas confronted over the telephone with a faceless voice, which is hostile and dogmatic, I quickly do lose it.

Jeremy Hutchinson* at luncheon at Lyegrove today asked, 'Have we done the slightest, tiniest bit of good minding so desperately about the worsening of the world physically, morally and all? Has our minding contributed one iota to lessening this appalling declension?' I said No. It has merely made us miserable. The others, all but Jeremy, thought it had (the others being the three women, Diana Westmorland, June and Alvilde).

Friday, 27th August

For two days I have been in bed with a temperature, another 'go' of influenza; the last at the time Jim Mossman† died in Feb. I think. Feeling very ill.

One false illusion of my life has been that sweet reason will win through, and that in no circumstance need man resort to force. On the contrary, events since the war have taught me at last what years before wiser men than I discovered, namely that force is essential to uphold right. Right must be might, even if might is not right. Violence has reached such a pitch that only violence can restrain it. The thugs of this world cannot be checked by light sentences and comfortable cells, but by being executed, got rid of by the quickest, least offensive means, a prick in the arm and a gentle slipping away to God decides where.

---

* Jeremy Hutchinson, QC, b. 1915, created Lord Hutchinson in 1978, and June (née Capel), his wife, daughter of Diana, Lady Westmorland.
† Jim Mossman, television commentator, d. 1971.

Saturday, 28th August

Whenever I am so ill that I am reduced to bed I imagine it is a etribution for some sin, and I rack my brains to discover what sin.

Gwladys Chaplin, having reached the brink a week ago so that Anthony telephoned us to expect the end at any time – the doctors gave her days only – is better again, and walked round Chelsea Square on the arm of her New Zealand nurse whom she adores, and who apparently adores her. The nurse says things like 'Come on, old lazy-bones', which no one would have dared say to Gwladys in her grand days. Anthony has gone back to Devon, chastened no doubt. A. and I could not help smiling for we know that devoted though he be, and dutiful as he has become, he really thinks it time she died. It is a terrible thing how one can want the death of those one loves deeply if one is heir to what they possess. One tries to drive the thought from one's mind, is desperately ashamed, hates oneself, feels worse than a murderer, knows one loves the person and wishes him (or her) nothing but good, would go to the stake to save him (or her) pain – and yet, so strong is the human instinct for self-betterment, one cannot stop oneself anticipating the benefits from the loved one's will. I confess to having harboured these sentiments when my dear Aunt Dorothy was so ill. Even when my dear Mama was so ill. Now I can hardly contemplate these sentiments without deep shame. A novel could be written around this theme.

Rachel Savory[*] meeting A. in the churchyard. A. told her that while the school holidays were on, and only one service a week was held in the church, attended by five people at most, it seemed absurd to arrange enormous bowls of flowers; that she was only going to do the two altar vases during her stint. Rachel said piously that she, A., could do what she thought proper whereas she, Rachel, was certainly going to continue the full decoration. 'I don't do the flowers for the congregation, or the school, but for Him,' pointing to the skies. A. was so taken aback that she said nothing. I said, 'You should have replied, "In that case, Rachel, there is no need to do the flowers at all. For He can see them more easily growing in our gardens, without having to look through the church roof, especially now that the south aisle windows are temporarily boarded up." '

---

[*] John and Rachel Savory, friends living in Alderley.

Sunday, 29th August

I believe that one ought to pay the utmost respect to old people who have been clever, successful or distinguished. At least, I was brought up to do it. It is not now generally accepted. Indeed why should one pay the same measure of respect to the ex-distinguished person of today as to the distinguished person of yesterday, who may now be foolish, drooling, useless, ugly and an encumbrance, for the last is no longer the same person as the first? You do not treat the callow child the same way as you will treat him when he becomes distinguished years ahead. You treat him as he deserves at the time, roughly perhaps, crossly, chastisingly if he demands it. Therefore you should treat the old, gaga person with disdain, disregard. That is the rational corollary. Thank God I was brought up the way I was, is all I can say.

Monday, 30th August

When Midi told me with smiling eyes that Bamber's new book on the Moghul Empire had already reached her, and that his novel has been accepted, my immediate reaction was envy. I contained it, and said jubilantly how splendid the news was – it is – and how glad I was, and now am. That I should be even slightly envious of this charming, successful young man is preposterous and reprehensible. How can any good be expected of humans who are subject to such degrading instincts as these?

Tuesday, 31st August

In the evening picked mulberries, or rather picked those which had fallen from the old tree on the back lawn. In no time I filled a kitchen bowl. Very satisfactory it is too, garnering one's own produce. Such lovely, lush deep-dyed fruit with crinkly, corrugated surfaces. I thought, as I picked, of old Brian Hodgson who used to sit under this tree a hundred years ago, and probably was made by his wife some August evening to do what I was then doing.

Friday, 3rd September

The Countess of Albany wrote in a letter: '*les personnes qu'on a le plus aimées, si elles revenaient après deux ou trois ans, elles causeraient plus d'embarras que de plaisir. Cette idée est désagréable. Il y a bien des vérités qui déplaisent.*' Her letters are chock-a-block with verities. I think she was a more remarkable woman than she has ever been given credit for – wiser than Madame de Staël her friend, than Alfieri her impulsive, undependable lover, than vain Bonstetten, her lifelong adorer; but of course common sense, the one virtue on which she prided herself, does not make a woman romantic, and she was derided for being unromantic and materialistic by her contemporaries. The remark which I have quoted may have been a reference to her meeting with silly old Bonstetten after an interval of nearly thirty years.

Saturday, 4th September

I thought I should read one of Alfieri's tragedies. So in the train read *Saul*, considered one of the best, and one which so moved the French artist Fabre* that he painted a colossal picture on the theme and dedicated his life to ministering first to Alfieri and after his death to the Countess of Albany. I read an 1850 translation, a rather literal and pedestrian translation in English. Nevertheless in discounting the lost poetry of the original, which I must accept and which is of course lacking in translation, what I read bored me heartily. How could someone with the panache, the passion and the enthusiasm of Alfieri – for he was not a boring professional man of letters, but an amateur of flesh and blood, a kind of prototype of Byron – turn out a drama with little action about some Old Testament figure? I suppose one could say that his Saul has some of the qualities of Shakespeare's Lear, and Shakespeare's *Lear* in an Italian translation might be pretty dull. But the theme of *Saul* is ponderous, portentous. Above all *dull*. But then I find Greek drama boring. It all seems unnatural, un-human, static; and the situations which are meant to strike the reader with horror, the accumulation of destiny's appalling retributions, seem to me contrived, unreal and lacking in emotional truth. I mean I cannot believe in them. I become impatient with the characters for being such asses as to get into these absurd predicaments, and being such fools as not to find the easy way out.

---

* François-Xavier Fabre, 1766–1837, created Baron by Charles X. Historical and portrait painter.

Last night dined with Charles and Brenda Tomlinson. Perplexed why I did not enjoy their company more than I did. I like them both. I admire them both. He is an intellectual and by repute an excellent poet. She is a sensitive and very clever girl. Their ideas are right; they are literary. Yet their literalcy – if there be such a word – rather stifled me. Nerves on both sides I daresay. In a future context we shall feel cosier because, all said and done, our sympathies are compatible.

Sunday, 5th September

The Fall is such a good alternative to the Autumn. We are having some lovely days after much rain and cold in August. The dead quiet of the autumn is a characteristic. Such solemn, tranquil, golden days presaging unmerited savagery to come, blustering horrors with the equinoctial gales. It is the absence of wind, an absence seldom experienced in the spring, which is so welcome. In fact the spring in England is one prolonged disappointment; the autumn seldom is.

A. called me out on to the drive yesterday morning to watch the behaviour of the swallows, or house martins. They were flying in swarms against the front of the house, not settling on the walls as they sometimes do before leaving us, but rushing at the house and ricocheting off at an angle, some few dashing into the two nests they made earlier in the summer at the corner where the three-centre bay juts out, their favourite, and constant, nesting place. I suppose they were after insects: certainly not lime from the walls. They find the lime on the south wall which is not ashlar, but rubble, and is loose and flakey, with much thick, untidy pointing for them to nibble. Half an hour later I went out and the swallows were high up in the sky again as they normally are during fair weather, which the barometer indicates at the moment.

Today I watched the butterflies on the mauve buddleia opposite the octagonal game larder by the back path. I thought there were not going to be any this year. But I have never seen so many. Each spear head was bending under the weight of five or six. There were tortoiseshells, peacocks, cabbage whites – not so many – and one white admiral I think. But it is so long since I have seen one I cannot be sure. Yet I am fairly sure it was not a red admiral. This is a very encouraging sign.

Midi spoke to Bamber about my novel, and told me to ring him up because he had advice to offer. I did so last night and was just slightly, only slightly, nettled. I expected him to say he would give me an introduction to his friend at Cape's who had taken his novel. Instead he said he could not bother the friend who was so very busy without first reading my novel himself to see if it was good enough to pass on. I did not say, 'The hell you won't', but did say that I would not bother him, and had already decided, since his mother had spoken to him, to submit it to Norah Smallwood[*] of Chatto's. I thought Bamber slightly patronizing. But it is silly to be proud, and I did not show it. In fact I worked myself up to be indignant after I had put the receiver down. This sometimes happens with me, and it is not until later that I realize I have been miffed. Now today I have written to Norah Smallwood. I daresay I am making a mistake and that I ought to rewrite Part 3 before submitting to anyone. However there it is. Or rather, 'Here it isn't', as old Lady Vernon[†] used to say. Now the worst of being old is that one does not like the young treating one without a certain – what is the word? – 'consideration', or rather treating one as disposable rubbish. This is an absurd admission, I presume. And Eardley says 'consideration' is the last thing he wishes to be treated to by young or old; and I should not wish it either, should just shut up, and be thankful if anyone deigns to speak to me at all.

Monday, 6th September

When I went to see Gwladys Chaplin last week she was fully dressed wearing her diamond brooch, sitting regally in an armchair in the upstairs drawing-room. I thought her a little more frail than the previous time before her last operation for cancer of the jaw. I asked her how the Holfords of Westonbirt became so very rich, having been ordinary Gloucestershire squires, to be able to build that huge house and Dorchester House in Park Lane. Gwladys's reply was: 'Oh, but people were rich in those days.'

Last night we went to see Eny [Strutt] sitting or rather lying in her summer house, the sun full on her face. Her eyes were hollowed out as though by an instrument. She looked so feeble

---

[*] Publisher. Chairman of Chatto & Windus, d. 1984.
[†] Doris, widow of Sir George Vernon, 2nd Bt., of Hanbury Hall.

that a puff of wind might blow her away. Wearing too a padded collar. She is kept together by stays and collars, and yet she told us how dreadful it was for some friend she knew whose marrow had disintegrated in her bones, the very thing that has happened to hers. Her voice has become strangely quavery which is a bad sign. By the time we left she was very animated, and told us many secrets, not to be repeated, evidently enjoying herself. She called me back to beg me not to repeat them. The truth is I have already forgotten what these secrets were, they did not interest me enough to remember, so I may forget if they do recur to my mind that they were secrets and repeat them.

Last night the harvest moon rose from behind the hill in the east through the branches of the magnolia tree. We watched the process from the upstairs landing window. There was one faint light in a cottage window. The moon quickly cleared the hill and tree. It was full and not silver but like a golden guinea. The moon's mountains were perfectly clear even with the naked eye, or rather through my naked spectacles. Standing in the drive I wondered what it would look like through my strong magnifying glass. I could not focus the glass, but instead a blur of every colour of the rainbow appeared, violet, green and yellow. The front of the house with the moon behind it became a pearly grey rectangle with no features.

Tuesday, 7th September

After breakfast at 8.45 I was at the kitchen window talking to Mrs Mason when she said, 'There's the Duchess of Westminster!' and Sally's smiling face was looking at us. She had come with her gardener to pick up our crab apples on the lawn, the tree behind the catalpa and in front of the garden house, which is covered with the Kiftsgate rose. They rushed at the crabs with a basket. The gardener said these are Siberian crabs, the best possible for something or other. I have often eaten them in September, or rather chewed them and spat them out having chewed them. They have a delicious but sharp taste.

At Westonbirt this afternoon I met the *Country Life* photographer, who could not read John Cornforth's directions, but I was able to tell him which photographs he wanted taken. J.C. had also written, '3 more garden photographs to be chosen by A.L.-M.' Since A.L.-M. had refused to accompany me J.L.-M. chose them, views showing as much of the garden architecture as possible. The dogs found a rabbit and I had a splendid view of the chase. They were catching up on the rabbit when it disappeared into the churchyard, into a grave presumably. The head gardener spoke to me about the mistake women make in feeding the tits in winter with fat. In consequence the tits no longer eat the aphis eggs in the winter, which explains why aphides are now so prevalent in gardens. He said the burning of stubble was the wickedest thing done these days because the field mice and all living creatures were destroyed.

On my return this afternoon a letter from Norah Smallwood saying yes, send the novel. A. advises that I do send it, with an explanation that I am not satisfied with the ending. She who began rereading the last chapter, can't finish it. She finds the story so disagreeable and is shocked that I could have thought of such a theme. I knew she was shocked last year when she first read it which explains why I have been rather cagey about referring to it again.

Wednesday, 8th September

All day suffering from terrible *Angst*, a gnawing in my vitals and a dread that something ghastly is about to happen; a total inability to enjoy the day, which is an exceedingly beautiful one – the last week has been divine. What is the cause? Maybe it is the fact that today I have packed and posted my typescript to Norah Smallwood. I think my terror is of making a fool of myself. Am I doing so by persistently hawking this bloody novel around? Turned down already by my agent and two publishers. I vow, I vow that if it is turned down by this one I shall dismiss the thing from my mind for ever. Am I too insecure to write about incest, homosexuality, bestiality, necrophilia, coprophilia and the divers nasty little habits that flesh is heir to? I don't know.

Alvilde frightens me with her driving. She is a good driver, but she goes very fast and her movements are sudden. Why do old people suffer more from fear than young people? It ought to be the other way round because when one has had the better part of one's life one ought to be indifferent to the remainder, ought to be prepared to go; and when one is young one is ignorant of consequences.

Tomorrow we set forth to Scotland and shall be away for nearly three weeks.

Saturday, 25th September

A. had such terrible toothache towards the term of our Scotch tour that when we reached Blair Atholl I put her on a train to Edinburgh where she got a seat and flew direct to London. The next day Mr Plowman took out a wisdom tooth. Why does this particular tooth always cause trouble? In consequence I motored alone to stay with the Drummonds* at Megginch Castle for two nights. I cannot give a detailed resumé of our tour, which took us to Skye and Lewis and Harris. First we stayed with the Fulfords† at Barbon in Westmorland; next one night with the Glenarthurs‡ at Mauchline, Ayrshire. Matthew, whom I had not seen for thirty years and who besides being a cousin was once an intimate friend as well as my brother-in-law, greeted us drunk, and remained drunk throughout the visit which lasted till after breakfast the following morning. A. didn't like him much. I cannot dislike him for underneath he is still the same rather feckless, sweet, bumbleish person I was fond of when a boy. Margaret his charming wife is very handsome indeed. Then hotels in Connel, Mallaig, Skye, Culloden, hideous and expensive. We stayed also with Elizabeth Sutherland§ at Uppart and she took us to Dunrobin. I enjoyed it all and found the western Highlands, where not spoilt, and much of them are as yet unspoilt, to be more sublime, more subtle in colouring, more awe-inspiring in wild weather than any mountainous region in Europe that I have seen.

The proprietor of a newspaper shop in Stornoway said, 'This country is not what I fought in the War for.' I said No, it is worse than it was before the War began. He said, 'Why, I was never allowed as a lad to read a line on a Sunday.' I said, 'That was a bit

---

* Humphrey (né ap Evans) and Cherry Drummond, 16th Baroness Strange in her own right, of Megginch Castle, Perthshire, m. 1952.
† Sir Roger Fulford, 1902–83, biographer and editor, and his wife Sibell (Adeane).
‡ Matthew Arthur, 3rd Lord Glenarthur, 1909–76, and Margaret Howie, his wife (d. 1993).
§ Elizabeth, 24th Countess of Sutherland, b. 1921. Scottish landowner.

severe.' He said, 'It may have been, but not to read on a Sunday was better than taking drugs on a Sunday.' A bit of a *non sequitur* I thought. I said, 'You don't have to take drugs any day of the week.' He went on, 'Even today when I glance at the newspapers on a Sunday – mind you, I only glance – my conscience pricks me.' 'And yet you sell them,' I deprecated. He was a nice man, but this aspect of the Scotch does not appeal to me. When we were sitting in our stuffy, middle-class hotel at Culloden an old mother and middle-aged son were at the next table in the dining-room – dinner at 7 sharp, and tea served at 9 o'clock. They never uttered or addressed one word to each other. After dinner they sat in the lounge in deadly silence. There were two foreign girls present who could bear it no longer. One politely asked the son if his mother would object to their turning on a gramophone record, Menuhin playing Bach. The son looked appalled, and glanced nervously at his mother for her opinion. She frowned and murmured that she supposed she must consent. She sat throughout frowning, the record playing so softly one could hardly hear it. The Presbyterian side of these people would prevent me living in Scotland.

On the staircase of this hotel is an *art nouveau* settee. Along the top in beaten brass are the words, 'Welcome comes with Smiles.'

Lunched with Lord Lovat* at Beauly. An extremely handsome man, tall with snow-white hair, in kilt and sporran. Neither A. nor I could extract any response from him. This gallant, ex-Commando, extrovert figure, the father of God knows how many children, is singularly vain. A. caught him passing a mirror and giving himself a sidelong glance of approval, just as dear Angus [Menzies]† does. His jolly daughter Fiona took us over Beaufort House and showed us the portraits and Bonnie Prince Charlie's hair – the Highlands are stuffed with his hair, enough to provide wigs for a dozen bald men. Like so many people of this sort she professed to know nothing about her ancestors and to care less. The aristocracy is either like this or like Mr Hornyold-Strickland‡ of Sizergh who bores one stiff with the long, illustrious lineage of the Stricklands.

---

* Simon Fraser, 15th Lord Lovat, b. 1911. Large landowner who served in the Commandos in 1939–45.

† Angus Menzies, 1910–73, A.L.-M.'s first cousin.

‡ Henry Hornyold-Strickland, 1890–1975, of Sizergh Castle, Cumberland.

When I got to Edinburgh alone on the 22nd, I tried in vain five
or six hotels. Exasperated I found a horrid, commercial hotel to
take me. Then I had to find somewhere to park the car. Round
and round I went, nearly mad with frustration and rage. Driving
into Princes Street from a side street with no traffic lights, a
policeman on point duty whom I had not observed, signalled me
to stop and reverse. This was more than I could endure. I shouted,
swore foully and looked doubtless red in the face and furious and
foolish. The policeman came up to me. I said, 'I have been circling
round this damned town for an hour and am fed to the teeth.' The
policeman with a charming, open smile, said, 'I know how you
feel, but I am here to control the traffic, so you must obey me.'
Very gently. I was able to apologize, and thank him for being so
forbearing. He smiled again and waved me on. I felt ashamed of
myself. My confidence in the decency of others was restored. Not,
however, for long.

Sunday, 26th September

I had a ghastly experience. Depressed by my miserable little
bedroom, and having telephoned to A. in London, I decided since
it was not yet dark (6.15) to venture outside the city in search of
the site of the Battle of Prestonpans. Found it and then dined early
at a road-house. Motoring back, already within the outskirts of the
city, I was stopped for rather a long time at some traffic lights. A
man in a dusty blue raincoat, sallow-faced, about 35, not a hippy,
not apparently labour-class, called out, 'Are you going to the City
Centre?' Yes, I said, Jump in. He did. Immediately I regretted it
because he stank of whisky. We were within less than ten minutes
from Princes Street. He kept repeating that he wanted a drink, and
asked me to stop so that we could drink together. I said I would
not have a drink, but that if he wanted one, that was his affair, only
I suggested that he had had enough drinks already. This made him
very cross, and disagreeable. He questioned me, Who was I, where
did I come from? I was reticent, but said that I came from England
which must have been apparent from my accent, or lack of one.
When we got to Princes Street I tried to stop and get rid of him.
But he would not get out, and there being still much traffic, the
cars behind me became impatient and blew their horns. So I was
obliged to drive on. To reach my hotel I had to make a one-way

circuit. In one of those residential streets behind Princes Street I drew up along the pavement, The man asked me for money. I said I was damned if I would give him any, and said 'Get out immediately!' He wouldn't. For a second or two I sat and thought what do I do now? The street was fairly empty. Suddenly he seized a coat of A.'s from the back seat and threw it over my head, while he rifled the pocket on my left side. Took two or three pounds. Luckily the rest of the money I had cashed that afternoon was in another pocket the far side from him. I managed to grab hold of the door handle by feeling for it, ducked, and got out on to the pavement. Through the open door I launched a blow at him, but could not hit him hard enough because of the awkward distance from where I was standing. He then slipped into my driver's seat and began starting up the engine. I managed to blow the horn violently, to no avail. Then there was a tussle for the key. He struck me on the nose with the edge of the book I had been reading over dinner. My nose poured with blood. In the tussle he broke off the keys in the ignition lock. In a rage he then got out and started pummelling me on the pavement. A young man and girl friend approached. I beseeched them to help me, and tried breathlessly to explain what had happened. 'I was giving this bloody man a lift. He has attacked me. Is trying to steal my car,' etc. 'On the contrary,' the man shouted, 'he has assaulted me.' The couple whom I begged to fetch a policeman walked off. Another man in bowler hat and swinging a furled umbrella merely said, 'Compose your differences, my good men', and declined to interfere. It was only when a larger group of youths approached that the man ran off, with imprecations, saying 'I have got your keys. I have taken your number. You'll hear more of this.' Bewildered, shocked and miserable I got back into the car. What was I to do, with no ignition key? By some miracle the stump, though broken, remained in the ignition, although the boot and door keys had gone. I started up and drove off I knew not where. Eventually I found a lock-up garage, because the car was full of my and A.'s luggage. I walked back to the hotel. A sweet young waitress gave me plaster for my nose which bled like a pig's. I took two Mogadons before I could get to sleep. Next morning I was so upset that I drove straight home within the day. I managed the 300-mile drive along the motorway perfectly.

This affair has upset me more than I thought possible. The nose bash did not particularly hurt. It was only inconvenient, and is now unsightly. For two days I have felt ghastly.

Monday, 27th September

I think it is as much the realization, because this incident has happened to *me*, that the majority of the human race are savages and that we in this country have reverted to jungle society, as the personal indignity, which has upset me.

I have read Kay Hallé's* book about Randolph Churchill. What comes out vividly from the accounts of him by some thirty friends is that he was a resounding personality, positive and not, like the rest of us, negative. All admitted his brutish manners, his offensive tactics. His great qualities were honesty and courage. How I do admire courage. Had Randolph had my adventure in Edinburgh he would have acquitted himself with gusto. He would have pursued the man, bashed him, brought him to justice; not slunk off as I did, feeling myself lucky to be rid of the skunk.

Randolph just was not my type; nor was I his. Latterly whenever I saw him in Brooks's I avoided him. I had nothing to say to him, and hated his loud-mouthed, drunken manner. I vividly remember the first time I ever saw him. It was at Eton. I had been there, I suppose, two years. 'Up to' Sheepshanks, at the beginning of a new 'half' Sheepshanks called upon me to stand and construe some Latin verse. I hesitated; I bungled; I stopped. Suddenly from the rear of the classroom, amongst the new boys, who customarily remained dumb with awe for their first six months, a dwarfish figure with the face of an angel stood on its seat and said, 'I know, Sir, it goes like this', and started to spout the English translation with the utmost confidence and fluency. Whether the translation was correct or not I don't remember. The whole division was appalled by the audacity, the cheek. Mr Sheepshanks snubbed the individual. This was my first introduction to Randolph. Thereafter I used to see him with Tom, and staying with the Redesdales, the *enfant terrible* always. Unsympathetic to me.

The other thing the contributors remarked on about Randolph was his aristocratic side. He was an aristocrat, in that he did not

---

* Kay Hallé, d. 1992, American chronicler of Winston Churchilliana.

care a damn for anybody; was possessed of unbounded confidence, which amounted to insolence. I have noticed that aristocrats are either like Lord Salisbury,[*] gentle, attentive to their inferiors, courteous, while aware of their superior social status in the world; or provocative and combative and rude like Randolph, Edward Stanley,[†] Nigel Birch and others. Incidentally Nigel Birch told me the other day that Randolph's trouble, i.e. his failure in life, was largely the fault of his mother. Lady Churchill, far from being indifferent to him, positively disliked him from childhood onwards, and showed it. Randolph resented this treatment, disliked his mother in return, and bore her a grudge which induced his appalling effrontery to life thereafter. The usual Freudian explanation of ill behaviour for which the erring one likes to excuse himself by trotting out.

Tuesday, 28th September

Returning from Ozleworth down the Ozleworth–Wortley lane the sky over Winner Hill was a Poussin blue with purple storm clouds, the hill magnified into a mountain by the humidity, the windless atmosphere calm. You could have heard a pin drop on the lush grass in the combe. A classical scene. I would not have been surprised to see a half-naked peasant girl suckling her babe and a youth leaning on a shepherd's crook watching her as in Giorgione's *Tempestà*. But no, I was in the Cotswolds not in the Marche between Rome and Naples.

Having gone round Dunrobin Castle the other day with Elizabeth Sutherland, A. and I were leaving by the side door. At that moment the boys, for it is a public school run by Elizabeth on Gordonstoun lines, were returning from the playing fields and indeed bathing in the sea, for it was a gloriously sunny afternoon. Two brushed past us, naked to the waist, their bronzed, smooth, hairless torsos glistening with the bloom of youth. They must have been 18 in the plenitude of strength and beauty. As we got into the car one of the women said, 'What hefty looking creatures. They seem older than boys.' 'Yes, don't they,' said the other in a disinterested voice. 'Now we had better go home for tea.'

---

[*] Robert Gascoyne-Cecil, 5th Marquess of Salisbury, 1893–1972. Statesman.
[†] Edward, 6th Lord Stanley of Alderley, 1907–71.

Another letter this morning from Monica [Baldwin] in which she says I write fascinating letters. They aren't of course, and she is given to exaggeration. But it is curious how one's letters are good or indifferent according to the recipient. It is the recipient who is responsible for them as much as the writer. When I have to address my nearest and not necessarily dearest who may bore me, I can't write a good letter for nuts. Nor if I am writing to someone much my superior in intellect and wit like Raymond [Mortimer] of whom I am in awe can I do better than a pretentious private school master. Because I try too hard. But with Monica or Eardley with whom I feel at ease, of the same mental calibre, I can sometimes do all right. It should follow then that to write a good book one ought to have in mind one person for whom one is writing the book. This is a good point which I shall try and follow. The person must therefore be someone of one's own intellectual standing. One must not address someone above or below it. One must in fact not aspire to be what one is not, as I am always saying. The flaw in the dictum is that one will never move out of the rut into which one's limitations have stuck one.

Friday, 1st October

The last two days in London. Any break in the rhythm of life upsets the trains of thought; and makes the mind a blank. One should not go away from home more than once a year, and then for a brief visit only. I have always maintained that the best novelists were not travellers, but stick-in-the-muds like Jane Austen, the Brontës, even Proust, who left home seldom and never to go far afield. Willie Maugham would have been a greater, a more cosmic novelist if – and this may sound an anacoluthon – he had not been so restless, so constantly in the air or on the wave, so cosmopolitan, so deficient in territorial roots.

Monday, 4th October

Bruce Chatwin* and Keith Steadman† lunched with us yesterday. Bruce came in like a whirlwind, talking affectedly about himself. He has no modesty; he shows off. A. complains of this and says

---

* Bruce Chatwin, 1940–89, travel writer and novelist.
† Keith Steadman, horticulturist and Gloucestershire neighbour.

how different his manners are to those of James Ancaster.* But I say James Ancaster is of our generation, is a gent of the old school. Bruce is an attractive young man of different generation, Birmingham, ambitious, bubbling with enthusiasms, still very young, feeling his way, not self-assured, and on the aggressive. I like him. It is a pity he is already losing his looks. We talked hilariously and seriously of the young's revolt against the establishment. Bruce having listened to my views – surprising that he can listen – declared that I was basically an anarchist too. I am not quite sure of that.

He and I went for a short walk with the dogs through the Foxholes Woods. Then he was enchanting, and all his preliminary social, bombastic manner left him. He talked enthusiastically, that is what I like about him, sensibly, unaffectedly. I am certain that in another ten years he will have ceased to be bumptious. He said he felt happy only in the wilderness, the natural wildernesses of the world. Feels constricted in England, lonely at Holwell Farm – not surprising – and is very much conscious of today's lack of opportunity for exploration and getting away from the madding crowd. Told me that being a war baby, he was his mother's darling. He only saw his father during his rare leaves from the Army, and when he appeared in the home Bruce resented the intrusion. His mother, an unwise woman, doted, even dressed him up in her clothes for fun when he was a child of 6. In spite of this silly treatment he hates transvestism, but is inevitably homosexual, because of the circumstances related above. Said that homosexuality was nothing whatever to do with genes, or inheritance, but solely upbringing, and relations with one's parents. I don't altogether agree. He admitted it was odd how homos are on the whole more intelligent, certainly more sensitive than heteros. Said that in many primitive tribes the homosexual becomes the wise man, the healer, the oracle and often the leader; and is greatly revered. I asked what would happen if a white man descended and fell in love with the healer. Would the tribe regard him as a hostile Martian, or a divinity of wisdom and light, and their union as a mystic, wonderful blessing for them? All depends upon the tribe, he says. The healer would either be exalted, or instantly assassinated for his

---

* James Willoughby, 3rd Earl of Ancaster, 1907–83, landowner.

presumption. Bruce has gone into this question in his Nomad book.

In the evening to a concert at Dyrham of Renaissance music. Viol and lute, etc. Music most melancholy, tuneless, despairing, irritating in its self-pity, love-sick artificiality, like those Wyatt sonnets. Boring I find. I could not be moved by the music, and was only moved by the earnestness of the dedicated young performers, boys and girls who make these concerts their livelihood. There is something splendid in the unworldly way they marry themselves to these puny instruments. Because we were with Paul Methuen who is stone deaf, and 85, we were put in the front row, and had a close view of the performers. The tortured, anxious concentration of their faces was striking. They had faces beautiful because of their love of their music. The boys had hair shoulder-length, which did not accord with the absurd white ties and tails which it is still *de rigueur* to wear it seems. Ridiculous. No clothes can be less suited to music playing, or more calculated to make the performers hot. The young lute player with an angelic face, when one could see it through the hair, had trousers far too long for him, and a seedy look which was upsetting. I wondered if he had enough to eat.

Tuesday 5th October

Audrey telephoned to say that Prue* has another lump in her other breast, and fears it may also be cancerous; and is going to see a London specialist today. Poor girl! This is dreadful. She lost one breast two years ago. If the second is malignant what chance does she have? If she were to die it would be a disaster for those three boys now growing up, and for Audrey. Prue is a pillar of strength and justice.

I wish I had not left Edinburgh in such a hurry after my horrid experience ten days ago. It is still a most beautiful city, although rapidly being spoilt. It has not yet been totally spoilt like Glasgow which A. and I drove through on a Sunday morning from Ayrshire. Whereas Glasgow no longer has a single street intact – when I last visited, the city was almost unadulterated Greek

* J.L.-M.'s sister Audrey, 1905–90 (m. 1. Matthew Glenarthur, 2. A. Stevens): and niece Prudence (née Arthur), 1932–76, m. Edwin Winwood Robinson, 1921–85, of Moorwood, near Cirencester.

Johnson, pitch-black and mysterious and of one epoch, today it is
a mess – Edinburgh still preserves some unbroken Adam terraced
streets behind Princes Street. The great width of these streets gives
spaciousness and majesty to Edinburgh. Then the castle is proudly
perched on the dominant hill. Scott's memorial and the Parthenon
or whatever it is called are other noble features. But already
Princes Street has some despicable modern blocks of utter medioc-
rity. What horrified me was the Royal Mile leading to Holyrood
Palace. Here the old crow-stepped, tall sixteenth-century buildings, rather Dutch than British, are being torn down. This is
lamentable. But what behaviour of city councils is not lamentable
today? Inverness, never a particularly beautiful city, used to have
its own Scotch character, with those absurd nineteenth-century
baronial banks and palatial blocks proudly vindicating their Walter
Scott Scotchness. They are rapidly disappearing, to be replaced
with the usual cosmopolitan muck. Edinburgh of all the Scotch
cities has a peculiar smell, an acrid, fresh, half moor and peaty, half
sooty railway-engine smell which is invigorating and in autumn
exciting and nostalgic. When the bitter cold winds blow through
these high-sited terraces one can imagine the cosiness inside the
granite walls, the elegant living behind the glazed windows, the
welcoming lamplight through the fans over the solid Georgian
doors.

Thursday, 7th October

An embarrassing occurrence last night. Two days ago I rang up, as
I thought, the Anthony Sandfords at Poulton Manor, to ask if we
might call and see their house on our return from spending the
afternoon with Eliza Wansbrough.* A year ago he asked us to
luncheon and again for something else, and we were unable to
accept. Still I wanted to be polite and also to see his beautiful
Caroline house. A woman answered, said she was Mrs Sandford,
her husband was out, but when I gave my name, said she was sure
he would be delighted to see us after 5.30. Last night at 5.45 we
called at Poulton and the door was opened by Sandford himself.
'How nice of you to let us come,' I said jollily. 'We won't stay

---

* Elizabeth (Mrs) Wansbrough, daughter of Sir George Lewis, Bt., well-
known late Victorian solicitor.

more than half an hour.' He looked amazed. I said, 'Your wife no doubt told you I had telephoned.' 'No,' he said. However he was very polite, and showed us round this marvellously intact Charles II manor-house. It was all very satisfactory. When I got home I looked in the telephone book, and sure enough I had rung up a stranger of the same name who lived at Purton, Wiltshire. But not even the same initials. I had thought the wife seemed a little surprised, and when she said, 'You are welcome' in a sub sort of voice which I did not associate with the elegant and *racée* Mrs S. I knew, I wondered what the real Anthony Sandford could be up to. A. says I *must* take a pull of myself.

Eliza took us to Buscot, Gavin Henderson's* house open on Wednesdays. It is years since I was there. There were a few visitors, not too many, yet enough to justify the opening. House and grounds beautifully kept. There are some very fine things, Hope of Deepdene furniture and old masters, all well arranged. It's a joy to wander round by oneself in these civilized surroundings. Yet the house lacks charm, is stiff, and feels uninhabited, which it is. Nevertheless this is how great houses which are uninhabited should be. Better than when turned into loony-bins and reformatories. I must say *great* pictures such as the Rubens and Rembrandt rather bore. I hate burghers' wives in ruffs. And I don't much care for Pre-Raphaelites, insipid things. I hate Jane Morris's petulant face.

I am a great hater as well as a great liker.

Saturday, 9th October

I am constantly amazed by the historical ignorance of people who should know better, and by the anachronisms they commit. For instance, in the beautiful *Go-Between* film motor-cars dating from the 'thirties were allowed to appear in Norwich Close in what was meant to be Edwardian times. In the short excerpt shot at our house (Alderley) in May for *The Search for the Nile* film, the coachman's livery did not date from the 1860s, as was intended, but from the 1820s. Furthermore the director persisted, in spite of my friendly remonstrances, in making the coachman bring the carriage up to the front door preparatory to taking the chateleine

---

* Gavin Henderson, 2nd Lord Faringdon, 1902–77, Labour statesman.

out for a drive, at break-neck speed, the coachman whipping the horse in a frenzy. I pointed out that carriages walked slowly to front doors. I can remember this when I was a child at Ribbesford. Furthermore in a ludicrous way the carriage was halted with the horse's head before the door, whereas of course the carriage door should have been opposite the front door.

Yesterday going round Stourhead gardens with Kenneth Wood-bridge* we found that Graham Thomas,† who is a first-rate plantsman but with less feeling for or understanding of the eight-eenth-century landscape principles than Kenneth, has since our last visit planted individual specimen trees, horrid little Japanese maples, ailanthuses, weeping dwarf elms which Colt Hoare‡ would not have known, far less tolerated if he had known them.

The Stourhead problems worry me. For twelve years now I have been made responsible with Graham Thomas, and since 1968 also with Kenneth Woodbridge, for seeing that the gardens at Stourhead are brought back to an – I don't say the – eighteenth-century mode because in Colt Hoare's day they had been altered from Henry the Magnificent's§ baroque to a neo-classical aspect, which in turn they lost during the Victorian and Edwardian periods. Yet they look today just as Edwardian as when we began caring for them. This is owing to two things – Graham's indif-ference to the Georgian spirit, in spite of a good-natured readiness to compromise with me, and my feebleness in not sticking up for my principles more resolutely for fear of offending Graham whom I both like and respect, and because I am totally ignorant of horticulture qua science, of which he is a master.

Sunday, 10th October

Yesterday a very nice man from the Birmingham BBC came at tea-time to take tape recordings of me reading a few extracts from

---

* Kenneth Woodbridge, expert on eighteenth-century landscape gardens.
† Graham Stuart Thomas, b. 1909. Gardens Consultant to National Trust, rose expert and writer.
‡ Sir Richard Colt Hoare, 2nd Bt., 1758–1838, of Stourhead, Wilts., county historian.
§ Henry Hoare II of Stourhead, 1705–85, styled 'The Magnificent'.

Greville and Creevey's diaries for a radio film on – I am still not quite sure what. Some kind of history of Western civilization from the year nought to the present day. It is to be released in over twenty programmes. At any rate my extracts were very short, to be sandwiched between the commentator's chat, of which I was totally ignorant. So was the BBC man. Before he came I read out loud to myself a page or two from Creevey. I fancied I read well. I thought how easy this is, just enough expression, not exaggerated, in fact faultless. When the time came I found this was not so easy as I imagined. I was not the least nervous, only anxious not to mispronounce words and names or to miss them out, or to trip, some of the sentences being rather long. Because of this anxiety I emphasized in the wrong places, or read in a sing-song way, or did not put enough expression into what I was reading. After six attempts the matter became stale. I don't think I acquitted myself well in the end. But the man was very patient and friendly. When my words were played back I was dismayed by the affected pedagogic way in which I began sentences, rather twentyish too in a red-brick university sort of la-de-da. Shaming.

This man who is not young, about 47 with a beard, is critical of the TV side of the BBC, which he says is responsible for much harm in lowering standards and distorting truths. *Sound* is the poor relation, edged out of documentaries, and given ludicrously little funds for programmes. He thinks Sound may have to pack up altogether. He said that Archie Gordon,[*] my old friend, now head of the Sound Talks department, has got to the top through sheer indifference to criticism, courage of his own opinions, and refusal to make concessions in either his manner or speech (which is la-de-da *in excelsis*), or the things he says.

Monday, 11th October

Don Nicholas and wife lunched. Joanie Harford[†] to meet them. I made a mistake in not letting A. invite John Huntley of Boxwell to come too. But I wanted to talk to Don N. about our Highlands tour. Mrs however must talk to me tête-à-tête about irrelevancies.

---

[*] Archie Gordon, 1913–84, writer and broadcaster. Succeeded as 5th Marquess of Aberdeen, 1974.
[†] Joan Wylde, m. 1937 Charles Harford of Ashcroft, Glos.

As host I get landed with the wives, and in six cases out of ten couples the wives are uninformative. I overhear the husbands saying fascinating things to A. whereas I am left hamstrung. It is extraordinary how the English educated will not tolerate general conversation. Again at tea, the Baldwins having come over to discuss with me what is to be done about Monica Baldwin's problems, I overheard Bloggs talking about them with A. who knows nothing of the matter, while Elspeth regaled me with her intestinal rattlings. Whereas if only Elspeth had had the sense she would either have allowed Bloggs to talk to me, or she would have allowed the four of us to talk together about Monica. God, there is something maddening about the matrimonial assumption that husband and wife are, or may be considered interchangeable. How I sympathize with Vita who devoted as she was to Harold hated being described as Harold's wife, hated being called Lady Nicolson because she claimed to be a person in her own right, just as he was in his; even hated being asked about with him as though she was his Siamese twin.

Was reduced to a beastly mood by the evening. Mood not improved when A. said what a nice and interesting day she had had.

Then we dined at Moorwood. Prue as cheerful as ever; never once alluded to her illness, or allowed a suspicion that she was under the threat of a recurrence of cancer. I admire her courage. The three boys home for leave from Winchester. Nicky the second is about the most handsome boy I have ever seen. He is $16\frac{1}{2}$ but looks 18. A sidelong smile has taken the place of a rebarbative scowl. I talked after dinner with Ted, the father, about them in the way the old do the moment the children's backs are turned. He said that Nicky alone was an introvert, and might surprise them yet. He clearly is the intellectual of the three. I tremble for him on account of his looks. Will he become horribly pleased with himself?

Yesterday in the British Museum I was shown Mary of Modena's coffin plate. I handled it. Quite small it is, of copper, about 6 inches by $3\frac{3}{4}$ inches. '*C'est le corps de Très haute, Très puissante, et* [added as afterthought] *Très excellente princesse Marie Éleonor d'Est, veuve du roi Jacques ll, etc. décédée à St. Germain en Laye 7 Mai 1718.*' So small, so simple, so touching. It was decent and unobtrusive like the woman it recorded, and not meant ever to be seen or handled as it was by me yesterday afternoon. It was acquired by the

BM in 1876, and I think had been wrenched off the coffin by the damnable Communards of Paris in 1871. All the royal tombs and graves which had not been violated in the Revolution of the previous century, were then destroyed, and their remains thrown to the winds, having first of all been treated with every obscenity and indignity by the mob, that beastly, that iconoclastic, that loathsome vermin.

Thursday, 14th October

All my contemporaries seem to be ailing. Jack Rathbone who looked well in the chair at the MHA meeting came away with me to lunch. In the street he doubled himself up, practically squatting on the pavement. Back trouble, he said. He is all right in a sitting posture, but cannot straighten himself. I said how strange. With me it is always the other way round; I cannot sit with comfort. He gave his complaint an impressive name, but added, 'It's age', in a re-signed way. He told me that David Crawford has had a bad heart attack, Ran Antrim* will never be the same man since his last; nor Joshua Rowley; and that Rosamond is still ill. I telephoned her. She has not recovered from her attack of shingles six months ago. Her son Hugo is still suffering from his back. Poor Joan Drogheda is in screaming agony with shingles. I think one is lucky to be free from an ailment for a week. At present I have ear-ache, something painful whenever I touch the inside of my left ear, which now begins to throb; also a return of my arm eczema. A. undergoing tooth trouble. There is something horrid about old people con-stantly ailing. Something contemptible too. One feels they ought to be put down, ought not to encumber the earth. Doctors and nurses must feel impatient with the old. As if it matters whether they get well again, or go out, they must think. I used to think this, and must remember that the young today must think the same. Must remember.

Friday, 15th October

And Audrey admitted on the telephone last night that Prue has got cancer of the other breast, what Audrey calls primary, not

---

* Randal McDonell, 13th Earl of Antrim, 1911–77. Chairman of National Trust, 1965–77.

secondary which I should have supposed. This presumably means that the new attack is unconnected with the first. She is awaiting advice from the London specialist whether to have a hysterectomy too or only removal of the second breast. Anyway her courage is an example to all.

I am reading [R.A.B.] Butler's autobiography, because of the glowing reviews it received this summer. I find it intensely dull. He may be a civilized man, he undoubtedly is, but his personality which is not forceful is uncharming. I can quite understand why he was not called upon to be Prime Minister. He is not entirely a human being. He lacks a light touch, and has an intellectual superciliousness (rather like the late Bill Kennet),* and is po-faced. How one is deceived by the opinion of the majority. There was no dissent that this book was first-rate, and above the average politician's memoirs. The truth is that politicians, unless they are great statesman, which Butler is not, and unless they are something besides being politicians, like Wellington and Churchill, are not heroical. Butler is besides an ugly man.

Saturday, 16th October

I have been too severe. Read fifty pages more last night. Undoubtedly Butler has compassion, of a dried-up sort, and is a good man, caring for the human race rather than for individuals. Moreover the passage about his mother's declining years shows understanding, and love. His account of his first wife's death is perfunctory. Perhaps he is keeping a stiff upper lip. How much more sympathetic to be like Churchill, who when moved, cried: yet a very bad man.

Woke up this morning from a vivid dream, in which I had composed a most beautifully melodious tune, high-brow too. I was thinking that if only I had had musical training I would have been a popular composer, for tunes come easily to me. Then I thought how tiresome that I hadn't the slightest notion how to record this new tune on paper. How to score it. So I just went through the tune once more. It was divine. I thought 'I must at once rush to Lennox and hum it to him. He will take it down. The

---

* Rt. Hon. Edward Hilton Young, created 1st Lord Kennet of the Dene, 1879–1960.

world will be amazed by this new unmusical prodigy that I am.'
Alas!

Yesterday A. and I went to visit an old man at Doughton, called
Hoad, who had worked at Westonbirt in the Holfords' day. I
wanted to glean information about the house when the Holfords
were still in residence. These old men cannot be consecutive in
their memories, and jump from one thing to another. However he
said he went into service in 1923 as Saloon Boy, in charge of the
large central room now called the hall. He was there in 1926 when
Sir George* died, and until the place was sold remained as care-
taker. In Sir George's day there were 7 men in the house, 7
housemaids, a steward, butler, hall usher, and 6 in the kitchen; 60
gardeners, including keepers; only one chauffeur. Hoad was paid
£65 a year and given one suit of clothes. Every May to September
the family was away, and the servants were put on board wages
of 18/- per week, milk and vegetables free. He said these were
excellant conditions, and he was very happy there. All the servants
were happy and were well treated. At times there were 60 in the
servants' hall when visiting servants were present. The Steward
said grace, and meals were eaten in total silence until the Steward,
Housekeeper, Lady's Maid and Cook retired for pudding to
the Housekeeper's Room (known as the Pug's Parlour), when the
remaining servants were allowed to talk. There were no prayers at
Westonbirt. But there were prayers at Mr Wingfield's, at Ampthill,
he said. I knew this old gentleman of the old school, a charming
man. Here, Hoad said, the servants would wear their oldest shoes
so that when they turned round to kneel at their chairs, Mr
Wingfield would notice how worn their shoes were, and out of
the kindness of his heart tell them to get new ones at his expense.

Sunday, 17th October

The Somersets† and Diana Westmorland dined on Friday. David
was very tired and not well. Caroline, when he is out of order,
becomes fidgety. They were half an hour late for dinner. I think

---

* Sir George Holford, d. 1926. Last of the Holfords of Westonbirt, Glos.,
and Dorchester House, Park Lane, W1.
† David, b. 1928, and his wife Lady Caroline Somerset, then living at The
Cottage, Badminton, Glos.

David is a moody man, and very restless. One would suppose he was born with a handful of silver spoons sticking out of every corner of his mouth. Heir to a dukedom, rich, handsome, success-ful, courted, blessed with a heavenly and beautiful wife, and four children. What more could a man want, a stranger might ask? He has good health, strength, guts, and above all – charm, that often fatal gift of the gods. He wants amusing and interesting company. He wants peace of mind, and more time to read. He loves and needs reading.

Yesterday afternoon a woman came for an interview as house-keeper. She was half an hour late. During the wait I worked myself into such a state of nerves that I could easily have run away, or created a diversion, like setting the house on fire, in order to get out of the ordeal. I hate interviewing people, perhaps because I remember hating being interviewed, when I was searching for jobs in vain, years ago. One's *amour propre*, which only suppliants have, one's pride, one's sense of inferiority and of the interviewer's superiority, one's inadequacy, are too painful to be witnessed in others now. The lady came, was perfectly self-possessed, rather noisy, absolutely in command of herself, confident, and superior. My nerves evaporated within two minutes, and I found myself becoming first prickly, then a little indignant that she was so much at ease.

Monday, 18th October

Just as well I went to the 8 o'clock service, for the Vicar [Sparks] told Charles Ivemey, the people's warden, and me, the vicar's warden, that he was going today to St Luke's Hospital for invest-igation and possible operation. Seven years ago, he explained, he had half his stomach removed. Since then he has suffered recurren-ces of stoppages, etc. back and front. In the vestry after the service he went into horrifying details, which I could not parry, and the poor man was practically in tears. Finally he wrung my hand, and with a sob dashed out of the church. Ivemey was white with dismay because he had airily said to Mrs Savory, 'I am so sorry I didn't have the opportunity of a nice talk with your sister after last week's service.' 'She has since died,' Mrs S. replied, and burst into tears. We are faced with raising hundreds of pounds for the restoration of the south windows. The depressing fact is that whereas we few old people are busting ourselves to raise money, we are the last generation which will use this church. When we are all gone there will not be a soul to attend it. It will be declared redundant and either pulled down or turned into a squash court for the school, which by then will be a state school, if not a lunatic asylum. Of the old generation only the upper- and middle-class parishioners go to this church. The lower – not that there are more than one such family left in the village, and a few farmhands scattered around – don't go at all. I suppose it is the same the whole country over. The lower consider religion tosh. I wonder if, when they, *if* they ever become better educated, they will return to the churches. I doubt it.

Tuesday, 19th October

Anthony [Chaplin] telephoned at 9.30 to say that Gwladys died Sunday night at 7.30. She went out like a lamp, gently and quite without pain. Her last words had been, 'Everyone has been so kind.' Poor old thing. She was 90 and the cancer of the jaw had got a grip. It was all for the best as Clarissa said, aged 11, when her grandfather Lord Chaplin's death was told her. Gwladys said early this year that she was 'lookin' forward' to her ninetieth birthday party, and when that was over she would die; and she has.

Leslie Hartley came to dinner last night. Graham Thomas who is here for the night, and Derick Gascoigne were dining also, and Ursula who brought Leslie over. His is a terrible decline. He is enormous like a blown-up bull-frog who gnashes his ill-fitting false teeth. He tottered in, not knowing what he was doing. With him there came the most appalling smell of fish. I said to A., 'What can this ghastly smell mean?' She said, 'I know it only too well', for she had nursed old people in the war. Throughout the evening she sprayed scent at him, without his having the slightest idea why. At dinner he made no sense. His memory has entirely gone. He drank whatever was given him, vodka, wine, port, and more port, and appeared less drunk as the evening proceeded. For after dinner I was able to talk to him about books, while he sank from the sofa, with the cushion, on to the hearth rug. I am so fond of him, and his condition is very sad indeed. Why must one's friends ruin themselves with that 'nasty Bottle', as the Cardinal of York said apropos his brother, Prince Charlie?

Our domestic quandary has put me into a terrible state of nerves. When our nice but simple Mrs Mason announced for the second time that she could not stand us, and must leave, during the last attack of depression, we put an advertisement in *The Lady*. Then Mrs M. got better. The one applicant we selected called last Saturday, and telephoned yesterday evening, as she said she would do, to say she wished to take up the post. I stalled by pretending that A. was in London at Gwladys's death-bed, and could not let her know until luncheon time today. Ever since, and throughout the night, I have wondered whether to tell and how to tell Mrs Mason to go. Even motoring A. to Chippenham station just now I was undecided. When I got back here I asked Mrs M. to come and have a talk over a glass of Dubonnet. We talked, she said she liked being here when she was well, but that her illnesses were bound to recur. She would leave the decision to me, she said. Still I could not decide. Finally, to cut the interview short, I said it might be better for A.'s sake to take the other woman. And so we left it. I have since telephoned the other woman, and engaged her. It is finished. Have I made a great mistake? Most probably I have. I am worn out by the emotion of the whole affair. Sacking people is extremely painful, even when one dislikes them. When they are decent, it is worse.

Thursday, 21st October

I decided I ought to go to Gwladys's funeral, tiresome though it was in that I am leaving for Italy via London almost at once. I mistook A. when she told me G. wanted no mourning. In fact she said G. wanted no music. So I dressed in a light blue suit, and blue tie, and was so found by A. when she picked me up at Eardley's flat at 10.15. She was horrified and managed to find a black tie of Eardley's which I put on. We drove to Mortlake Crematorium. Anthony, Rosemary* and the few relations present were in deep black. As we walked into the Crematorium across a yard there was a strong sweet smell of burning wood and, I suppose, flesh, but I am not sure. Rosemary said perhaps it was burning leaves. But I don't think so. Ghastly these crematoria are. Queues of funerals, one after the other. The chapel, decently undenominational, was

---

* Rosemary Lyttelton, daughter of 1st Viscount Chandos. Married as his second wife Anthony, 3rd Viscount Chaplin, 1951.

decorated with hideous red and yellow chrysanthemums. G.'s wreaths and flowers were laid out in the cloisters for all to admire. When the labels were removed the flowers were sent to St George's Hospital. The service was better without music, i.e. the old worn record of 'Time like an ever-flowing stream' with which I am over-familiar. It was soon over, the coffin slid through the pickled oak doors.

We rushed back in the train to Stroud to hear Lennox Berkeley's newly commissioned piece for two pianos. Too late for the first half of the concert. A. and I went to a pub for a sandwich and drink, and arrived just as the interval began. Lennox told us that they had played his piece in the first half; so we missed it altogether to our chagrin. Heat in the concert hall stifling. I took off my jacket and, sitting in my shirt sleeves, vestless, was dripping. I am always amazed that other people never get as hot as I do. In the old days before central heating reached such a pitch in the winter one could rely on no houses being too hot. On the contrary the larger the country house the colder it would be. Nowadays one has no idea what to find. Small flats are often stifling. I suffer dreadfully from the heat, and prefer cold to heat.

I am off this evening to join John K.-B. in London for tomorrow we leave at dawn for Florence. Mixed feelings. Not looking forward to it as much as I should.

Alderley Grange, Wotton-under-Edge   *Monday, 1st November*

Returned last night, Sunday, about 8. The clock in England has been put back. I am so glad. To my surprise found a note from A. saying she had gone to Cyprus only on Thursday. Am very distressed. I returned earlier than I intended because I fancied she was at home fretting. Indeed her note says she was so lonely and wretched that she couldn't stay here alone any longer. I had exhorted her to go to Cyprus and stay with Mickie Renshaw,[*] but no, she had said she couldn't be bothered to go alone. And now. Had she sent me a telegram to Rome I might have stayed on in Italy, even gone south, into Calabria, for all the time away the weather was absolutely perfect. As it was, I left John in Rome. He

---

[*] Michael Renshaw, b. 1908, had a house outside Kyrenia, Cyprus. On staff of *The Times*.

was infinitely kind, accompanied me to the air terminal and was
evidently sorry that I had to leave. I must be truthful. I had had
enough in that my objectives (in search of Stuarts) for going to
Italy had not been wholly achieved. So many rendered abortive in
one way and another. For instance in Florence the Casa Alfieri on
the Lung' Arno was covered with scaffolding and straw sheets for
repairs. I got inside however and saw ceilings which Alfieri and the
Countess of Albany knew and saw. The Palazzo San Clemente in
which Prince Charlie and the Countess spent many of their
wretched married years had been taken over by Maoist students
and was therefore impenetrable, and the outside likewise obscured
by scaffolding. In Urbino, in the Ducal Palace, the rooms in which
the Old Pretender lived in 1719 were shut for repairs. In Rome I
had great difficulty in getting access to only four out of dozens of
the Cardinal of York's books, now stored in the Vatican Library –
'for safety'! The Stuart papers which the Library admitted to
owning could not be laid hold on. In the Vatican Treasury there
was no sign of the jewellery bequeathed to it by the Cardinal. No
one could tell me when or to whom it had been sold by recent
popes since Pius VII. Nevertheless my tour was not without some
successes. This time I was shown the royal rooms in the Palazzo
Muti, and the Cardinal's in the Rocca at Frascati, the portraits of
Alfieri and the Countess in the Uffizi which are not on exhibition,
besides a few other things.

The nicest thing that happened to me was at Falconara station
where John and I had an hour's wait between trains. I wandered
into the town to look for a paper. Found a yesterday's *Daily
Telegraph*, bought it from a friendly woman in a kiosk. Returned
to the station, and began reading it on the platform. Just as our
train was drawing in the woman ran up to me with the day's copy
of the *Telegraph*, seized my old one, and would not take money for
the substitute. Greatly touched.

Particularly when I am abroad I glance through the list of deaths,
and am always secretly disappointed when there is not one of
someone I have known. Not that I want my friends to die, the very
reverse, but I suppose like most sub-educated people I get pleasure
out of being able to mourn.

In Florence, the first Sunday morning, went to Mass, and
followed it through with great discontent. It was all in Italian, 'O
Signore tante grazie a Lei,' etc. Extremely distasteful and only less so

in Italian than when it is in English. I did not hear one single Latin word. Here as in every Italian church the priest faces the audience, and waves his arms in their direction when they are to respond. However I lined up and took the sacrament. I have never done this before without going to Confession, and I have not been to Confession for twenty-five years I suppose. I had no qualm of having acted wrongly, although were I still a Roman I would have to believe I had committed one of the mortalest of sins. All rot I consider. Now the following Sunday in Rome just before leaving for the air terminal I went to S. Maria Minerva where Mass was ensuing. Here I was intensely irritated by the modern rite which I could not follow decently, and started wandering, while half listening. Over a dismantled altar in the south aisle there were on a ledge some votive silver hearts in frames, piled in an untidy heap and others which had been taken out of their frames and chucked among dust and filth in a corner of the ledge. These little objects given by devout and either sorrowing or rejoicing persons far back were, like so many such tokens today, treated as rubbish, and waiting for the first methodical sacristan to take and throw away. One of these had CR in the middle of it. I debated, should I take it? Was it stealing? Yes? No? If I did not take it, it would soon be in the rubbish heap. I took it. No one saw me. I felt extremely guilty, and uncomfortable. The congregation filed up to take the sacrament. Clearly I could not do so this time. I walked out of the church with my tiny loot. Then it occurred to me to make some amends. I returned to the church. There was no box for money for the church itself, only for alms for missions, for which I have no sympathy. So I approached a young Dominican sitting in his confessional. '*Desidero dare qualcosa per la fabricca della chiese,*' I said, and thrust into his hands more notes than the heart I had stolen was worth. Before he had time to smile gratitude upon me, I turned and left.

Only once before have I stolen from a church. That was two years ago in Worthenbury church, Flintshire. In the Puleston pew I came upon a heap of Puleston prayer books and bibles with the Puleston bookplates and names engraved on them. These things had been chucked into the fire grate in the family pew, the backs of most of the bindings off. They too were thought useless lumber by the incumbent. Since these books had belonged to the family, I took away the two best preserved, one a Queen Anne prayer book, the other *The Proper Lessons*, with the name of Sir Richard Puleston, Bart., 1840, in gold tooling on the cover. Under the very eyes of my grandfather's memorial to his first wife.

When in the Vatican Library I handled the beautifully illuminated *Books of Hours* which had belonged to the Cardinal Duke of York, and studied minutely the pictures, and pondered over the years of skill, of patience, of love, of implicit faith which had inspired some old monk abounding in goodness, I thought, 'How can men fail to be Christian, when our religion has produced such testimony to the Truth?'

I went in the lift above the Sacristy in St Peter's to see an old Irish Monsignor, Denis MacDaid, one of the most wise and charming old men it has been my privilege to meet. He said Cardinal Heenan had lately been quoted out of context. He had not advocated the Pope selling all his Vatican treasure to give the proceeds to the poor. On the contrary he had said the Vatican treasures belonged to the world, and their total sale would only help the starving for a few months. How can newspapers be so wicked as to distort what men say? Apparently Heenan did suggest that as a gesture the Pope might sell one treasure, as an example to others. Pretty fatuous perhaps, but not philistine as I supposed he had been. My old Monsignor who was dead against the selling of treasure said, 'We can only teach people to help themselves.'

Sitting in the Piazza Navona on the pavement of my favourite restaurant, Mestre Stefano, waiting for John, sunning myself, an old whining beggar woman approached me querulously. '*Non piange! Signora, non piange!*' Mestre Stefano addressed her, quite kindly.

In Sant' Ignazio I noted the succinct inscription on a floor stone, '*Hoc sub Lapide / Ludovisae Familiae Principes / Conquiescunt.*' How admirable the '*Conquiescunt.*'

I no longer enjoy aimless sightseeing. I must have an objective in view. As soon as I had exhausted what I came to investigate for my book, I did not know where to turn. On my last day I wandered from one church to another not observing anything in the particular manner which is essential for profit. Whenever a guide shows me a room I cannot observe the room thoroughly because I am anxious not to keep him waiting, or am put out by his remarks, or embarrassed by his respectfully fixing me in a gaze and longing for me to go. This happened in the Palazzo Muti. Had I been left to myself I might have made notes, or at least absorbed more. As it was I touched so lightly with the tips of my eyes, that the impressions left on my memory are slight.

I did not tell John that I had stolen the heart. Perhaps he would have been shocked. As I left the Minerva church after Mass was over, '*La Messa e terminata*', the priest said instead of the age-long, lovely words, '*Ite Missa est.*' Why can't they leave things alone, damn their eyes, lovely things, like that phrase? Then the organ struck up. It played, 'John Brown's body lies a-mouldering in his grave'. What is the Catholic Church coming to?

Tuesday, 2nd November

In the Palazzo Ducale, Urbino, I was fascinated by what must be the earliest graffiti of modern times, the names of visitors carved with a knife on the soft marble door surrounds. One dated 1586 and several others round about that date. Perhaps the Palace was sacked then, for most of the names seemed to be German or Low Country, as if they were mercenary soldiers'. Some of the door surrounds are of a composition, neither marble, alabaster nor stucco.

I was struck by a change in Italian politics since my last visit in February. Maoism seems to be on the rampage if one may judge by the slogans on walls, not only in large cities like Florence but smaller ones, like Urbino and Pesaro, which we passed through; and the number of Italian young men in hippy dress with those wet, drooping Chinese moustaches, which Mrs Dentler in Florence assured me was the hallmark of Maoism. In Frascati I saw 'Viva Lenin, Mao,' etc. The majority of books in the bookshops, especially those catering for students, are puffing Communism in one form or another. If Italy goes Communist I shall never visit it again, even if foreigners are admitted as tourists.

As a corollary (I think) the churches are becoming increasingly puritanical and bare. Chandeliers have been removed. Side altars are stripped and *bondieuseries* scrapped. High altars are reduced in height so that priests may officiate from behind them, and yet face and be seen by the congregation. Mean little lecterns have sprouted each with a loudspeaker attachment. The priest's voice booms, or rather squawks and squeaks round the nave. You cannot get away from it. You may no longer pray. You must participate. All this is left-wing, insidious penetration into the mysticism, hitherto inviolate, of the Roman Church. Much in evidence this time are printed notices pinned to church doors advocating Christian brotherhood, illustrated by a clenched fist (very sinister) scattering seed (of what in God's name? Marxism?) in front of a plain cross, no longer a crucifix, over a map of the world, the seed falling upon South Africa. Another poster of two clasped hands, the forward and larger hand black, the rear and smaller hand white. All as clearly indicative as sunlight, indicative of the new leftish, defensive, apprehensive, godless, evil road the Church is being pushed along by secret Commies.

While abroad I was reading Leslie Marchand's latest one-volume life of Byron. He records that Byron on his first visit to Rome stayed at no. 66 Piazza di Spagna, in a lodging house nearly opposite Keats's house. It is still no. 66. I walked into the entrance passage under the baroque doorhead through which B. passed. A narrow, vaulted passage. At the end an iron Gothick grille, or double door. On the overthrow a roundel, inside which a cockerel. On the border of the roundel, as it were the Garter badge, the words in metal, 'English Dairy'. I asked John to visit next time he was passing. He thought it was after Byron's day because the door is of cast iron. I think too the lettering is later, or may be. But what a strange device to find.

Wednesday, 3rd November

Dining with the Gascoignes Monday night we talked of the Common Market. Derick said that every single businessman he knew was pro. In his and their opinion Britain was finished if it did not join. When I asked what about the Commonwealth, did it not present just as wide an area for trade for us as Europe, Derick said, 'You evidently don't realize that Canada, Australia, New Zealand and those ex-white dominions now look to America for trade; all their cars are American; they think in dollars, not pounds.' I had not realized this. So that, apart from the ideological reasons for a politically united Europe which have always appealed to me, the economic ones seem to be overriding. The only thing that worries me about the first is, are we as a nation likely to be drawn in the wake of Communism if other member countries of the Market, like say Italy, turn Marxist?

Last night I dined with the Chatwins at Holwell Farm up the Ozleworth valley. The moon was full, so I walked there with the dogs up the Ozleworth lane. I had a torch but it was not necessary beyond use as a signal for flashing at Holwell to warn them that I was on the way as I passed by before turning at Ozleworth lodge to double back to their house. The scene was serenely beautiful, absolutely quiet. A mist rose from the bottom of the valley and accentuated the height of the hill below Tresham. The moon scurrying through faint clouds illuminated the Newark woods on my left. The woods stood serried in bastions of silent strength. Unexpectedly, for I have not heard them before, the bells of Wotton church started pealing. The world was remote and my own. I have not experienced so Samuel Palmerish a scene for ages. I might have been plunged back into 1820, and this is how our neighbourhood looked then as the owner of the Grange would have seen it had he walked to dine with friends at Ozleworth Park which he doubtless often did.

Shelley's lines came ringing in my ears, 'And like a dying lady lean and pale / Who totters forth wrapped in a gauzy veil / Out of her chamber . . .' although this moon was not tottering, but scurrying like a boisterous well-fed cheeky cherub. Bruce could not continue them. I don't believe he has read a word of Shelley. He was not very nice to Elizabeth who cooked a marvellous dinner; he was very abrupt and discontented; whereas when he came to tea with me the day before he was all charm. I have seldom met a human being who exudes so much sex appeal with so comparatively little niceness. What does this boy want? He is extremely restless. He hates living at Holwell, wants continuously to be on the move, and is shortly off to South America. He has finished his nomad book, and I wonder how good it is. When the 'or' has worn off his 'jeunesse', how much substance will be left beneath?

Thursday, 4th November

Never has there been such a beautiful autumn. One golden day after another. I took the dogs across the field below and to the south of Foxholes Wood. Couldn't go very far because I was expecting the new lady, Miss King, to call and leave some of her things pending her taking up duties on Monday. The damp leaves from the hedgerows smelt more acrid than I remember for years, and the fresh cowpats sweeter. As children we loved the smell of horse droppings. We had a pony trap which we were allowed to drive along the lane to Evesham for shopping and to Bretforton to

tea with the Ashwins.* Audrey would drive, aged 12 or 13; Dick
and I, aged 8 and 10 respectively, were passengers. Miss Wood, the
governess, being overweight was not allowed by Mummie to join
us, and was obliged to bicycle, which she greatly resented. Whenever the pony did its business, which involved first a premonitory
raising of its tail over the crupper, then pouff, pouff, out would
come the fresh, green buns. We children, relishing the delicious
aroma, and entirely without any Freudian guilt or consciously
repressed sex instincts, would rush to the back of the trap, Audrey
even relinquishing the reins, lean over the door and inhale the
fallen droppings on the road. Miss Wood thought this behaviour
disgusting and reported it to Mama, who reprimanded us, not for
being disgusting – it never occurred to her that we were – but
for being unkind to the pony in that our action tilted the trap
backwards so that the shafts were raised in the harness, and thus
caused the pony discomfort. I am amazed now that such young
children could drive a pony trap along main roads, but we did, and
I remember often without the governess bicycling alongside.

Saturday, 6th November

Sally [Westminster] is like a good-hearted scatter-brained teenager.
The evening I got back from Rome, sooner than intended, she
telephoned, 'Oh, I thought you were both away.' 'Yes, I should
have been,' I answered. 'Why are you telephoning?' 'I don't
know,' she said. She had returned from the Wexford Festival
for three operas, and couldn't recall the name of one. However
I asked her to dine at the Hole-in-the-Wall, Bath. We ate mussels.
The next night she asked me to dine with her. Again mussels,
but wrapped in rich sauce on top of skate, that loathsome, tasteless
fish. Result that immediately after dinner I felt rotten, and had a
headache and could think of nothing to say. There were *longueurs*.

I was ill all night, had violent diarrhoea and sickness, and felt
that my guts were being torn out of me. Vomiting is a ghastly
process, but I must say after the third, or was it fourth retch of
terrible intensity I already felt better. But remained shaken, and
not totally and instantly recovered, as the dogs are after being sick.

---

* Ashwin family of Bretforton Manor, Worcs., squires from sixteenth to
twentieth century. Now gone.

Freda* engenders mysteries because she attracts confidences. All her friends ring her up about their troubles, which she delights in sorting out. This makes her endeavour to be extra-cautious not to disclose secrets. Nevertheless the sympathy she exudes for poor 'So-and-so' cannot be contained. It wells up in her and overflows willy-nilly. 'I can't possibly tell you,' and, 'It's too sad for him, or her,' is all that's revealed to the next ringer-up. He or she at once calls up another mutual friend who misinterprets and spreads the most inaccurate rumours of horrors that have befallen poor 'So-and-so'. This some-times brings the unjust penalty Freda suffers for having a kind heart. Everyone forgives her and she is universally beloved.

Freda telephones from London asking me to see her next time I am up – which is to be next Tuesday – because she has something very serious to tell me, something which Lennox feels I ought to know. Would give no indication over the telephone what it was. Was it about A. who might be ill or upset about something which she was concealing from me? No, she assured me, it was absolutely nothing like that: nothing about A. and was more mysterious than ever.

Our Mrs Mason is leaving tomorrow, and has been so sweet and gentle all this week, and so considerate that I am feeling sorry, and a brute. She registers no complaint at her treatment, no indications of hurtness, merely accepts her dismissal with unreproachful resig-nation. Poor woman, I sense that she feels this interlude in her life has been one more failure, and will tend to undermine her self-confidence, which is barely existent.

Sunday, 7th November

Isn't it better that we should all be forgotten? We are of course; even Winston Churchill, even Byron, Shakespeare will be forgotten when our civilization has passed, and a new one dawns after the atomic disruption of the world. There is something infinitely pitiable in the way human beings can't face up to their mortality. The rich buy themselves memorial tablets, which get destroyed by time or vandals. The ambitious make names for themselves, although totally un-deserving of immortality because most of them are second-rate. The deserving unambitious are too modest or too idle to produce anything which will keep their name before the public eye after they

---

* Freda Bernstein, b. 1923, m. 1946 Sir Lennox Berkeley.

have gone. I think of people like my Aunt Deenie, so good, simple, un-evil, unambitious, without guile, without intelligence, dead these nineteen years and totally forgotten. She has no memorial tablet, no gravestone. She left nothing behind her that is memorable, except a flickering, diminishing love in the hearts of Audrey, Dick and myself. Her contemporaries are all dead. There is not a soul beyond us three who even remembers that she existed. I suppose children are the best memorials, because in them and their children one never quite dies. In a hundred years' time not one soul will know that I existed, for my books will not be read. All I can be sure of is that had I never existed the future of the world, or should I say of our civilization, would not be quite the same for this paltry reason. However unimportant I may be, I have said something, uttered some word which overheard by another has even in an infinitesimal degree influenced his life, which has in turn influenced another's for good or evil. The fact that one has existed means that one has trod on and killed an insect which has deprived another insect or bird of sustenance, which has affected another bird or insect, and so on *ad infinitum*. In these attenuated hypotheses lies our chance of immortality. Nevertheless once this world has been destroyed I doubt if an individual's existence on it will have any remote bearing upon the existence of an individual in another galactic let alone another solar system. So there is no hope of immortality except through the grace of God and his word, if only one can have faith. Faith is essential to man's happiness, and all that counts. But who has unquestioning faith? Peasants used to. But they are dying out. God, what a prospect! I only hope that by growing simpler and better I may enhance my wavering faith. Yet I suppose one should not sit back and expect this to happen. Every good requires inexhaustible effort, and waiting for faith to come is not the way. Prayer, prayer, prayer the theologians will answer. Yes, but I have never known how to pray. I can only meditate, and worship, and communicate and thank. Is this enough?

Monday, 8th November

A. came back last night, having telephoned me at luncheon from Heathrow to say she had landed. A great relief. Although I am told to believe that there are fewer people killed flying than on the roads, I don't believe it. I never shall believe aeroplanes are safe until they can hover in the air like birds.

A. has an uncanny way of arriving at telepathic truths, or half-truths, rather near-truths. For instance, if I have invited someone she does not like to dine with me in London, without telling her, she will say, 'Haven't you seen So-and-So lately? Funny! I thought he or she was dining with you shortly', when in fact I may not have mentioned his or her name for months. When she saw the little heart I took from the Rome church – incidentally it is made of tin, not silver – she admired it, asked how and where I had bought it, and said, 'Such things can only have been stolen from churches.' She is a suspicious character, and hates things being concealed from her. Yet she will not understand that no one, certainly not a husband or wife, is obliged to tell all to her or anybody else; that husbands and wives are not one flesh, one soul, indivisible. This is just what I dislike about the married state, and shall never reconcile myself to. Husbands and wives do not, must not belong to each other. They are individuals. The very worst principle of all is 'conjugal rights', i.e. the obligation a husband or wife has to go to bed with the other – an obligation usually imposed by the husband. This totally repugnant notion fills me with such rage that I cannot speak rationally on the subject.

For twenty-four hours we have discussed whether or not to go to the Droghedas again for Xmas. Having written to Joan two months ago to say we could not manage to have the three of them here and having no reply from her owing to her serious illness, we decided it was a good plan for once not to go to Parkside. Then before A. left for Cyprus Garrett sent a telegram ordering us to go to them. A. hedged, said she must wait for my return. Garrett telephoned me last week. I made excuses. Today I have drafted already two differently worded letters to Joan saying No. Finally we decided that rather than cause bad blood with our oldest friends, we would go. And so I told Joan on the telephone this evening. It is a nightmare thought that I may have posted both the letters, each telling a different, involved lie. In fact I haven't. But if I had, what would have happened?

Thursday, 11th November

We had supper, as Joanie calls it, at Ashcroft on Monday. Charlie Harford* extremely cross and disagreeable, snubbed us whatever

---

* Charles Harford of Ashcroft, husband of Joan.

we said, looked daggers, and after dinner disappeared, not to be seen again. Joanie admitted to A. the next day that Charlie was disgruntled, that he enjoyed nothing, hated everyone, not just us, and did not add what she must think, poor thing, that he is impossible to live with. Usually blind people become equable, cheerful and sweet, and the deaf suspicious, cross and thwarted. And Charlie is not totally blind; perhaps he would be nicer if he were.

A. says she is labouring under a sense of doom, for no apparent reason. I am usually labouring under a sense of doom, which I can in no way explain.

Nothing is so pathetic as middle-aged, single women's little bundles. Miss King last week dropped a 'few things', to await her arrival on Monday. They consisted of tidy little baskets tied with string, an iron, a plastic contraption to hold newspapers, several brown paper parcels, and a plastic suitcase with fragile locks. Together we carefully deposited them in the harness room.

I had four shocks yesterday morning in London. In Brooks's Ralph Jarvis,[*] now a little, bent, hollow-cheeked old man. I only recognized him by his deprecating laugh. Quite cheerfully he told me he was suffering from a tired heart from which he could never recover. He wants an article done on the garden at Doddington as a memorial to Coney [his wife] whose creation it was. I told John Cornforth, who agreed, and suggested that A. should do it. I met Francis Watson[†] walking into Christies. Lined and the shape of his face changed from an oval to a circle, plump body, tiny steps and absurd. Am told he now has a boyfriend, since his ugly wife's death, who treats him abominably; and this pleases. Eardley says the Wrightsmans, his patrons, have quarrelled with him and dismissed him. Then in the London Library Patrick Kinross,[‡] thin, and blotched with dark blue spots. Freda [Berkeley] is worried about him, says he sleeps all day, cannot get on with the History of the Ottoman Empire, and talks of his will. Lastly John Summerson[§] approached me, with a rather sweet smile and wearing a beret on

---

[*] Colonel Ralph Jarvis, 1907–73 of Doddington Hall, Lincoln.
[†] Sir Francis Watson, 1907–92, Director of the Wallace Collection, 1962–74, and Surveyor of the Queen's Works of Art, 1963–72.
[‡] 3rd Baron of Glaschure, author, journalist and broadcaster.
[§] Sir John Summerson, 1904–92, architectural historian. Curator of Sir John Soane's Museum, 1945–84.

one side of the head. Has become an old man. I said, 'Only last week I was looking at the monument to Pius VII in St Peter's by Thorwaldsen. He always reminds me of you, majestic, handsome and holy.' Sir John was pleased. He said, 'I have not enjoyed a book for years as much as yours. Can't you write a sequel?' 'No, I don't dare,' I said. 'I expect you are right. It is not a thing that could be repeated.'*

Friday, 12th November

Christopher Chancellor is an odd fellow. He asked himself to lunch with us yesterday in order to talk to me about the Bath Preservation Trust, of which he is Chairman and of which he has made me a trustee. I admire his enthusiasm and drive. He cares deeply about Bath, and proposes that he, Philip Jebb† and I should ask the Minister of the Environment for an interview, at which we should beg him to set up a special commission and meanwhile halt further demolition of buildings in the city. Now the Minister has given consent for New Bond Street to come down, which is appalling.

I was not sure how much I liked Christopher, thinking him a faceless tycoon of a sinister sort. I now do like him. He talks non-stop without letting one express an opinion, in a monotone. His voice is low, husky and without emphasis of any kind. So after five minutes one's ear is paralysed and one cannot physically listen any further. He talks one into insensibility, not offensively, but insidiously like a Chinese torturer until one falls asleep, and in one's sleep might then 'talk' oneself. He is curiously indiscreet and outspoken when most people would be reticent. For instance when A. said apropos domestic help, 'You are lucky to have your secretary, that nice Miss —.' He said, 'She's a terribly stupid woman. We had her to stay out of kindness two years ago, and have never been able to get rid of her. When she came we were sorry for her because the friend she had been living with died. A Lesbian relationship of course. She hates men. Can hardly bring herself to address me.' And of his own daughter Susanna,‡ 'She's all

---

* *Another Self*, Hamish Hamilton, 1970.
† Philip Jebb, b. 1930, architect grandson of Hilaire Belloc.
‡ Susanna Chancellor, wife of Nicholas Johnston (Nicky), architect.

right now. But until she married, she was a great worry to us. Sleeping with every man she met, and a great trial, and no pleasure to us at all. Then she got the job as reader to Percy Lubbock. He civilized her, and taught her to love literature. Now she is intellectual, and I believe exceedingly nice. She had a bedroom next to Percy's, and heard him talking to himself at nights. For the first fortnight the gist of his talk was, "Oh God, how on earth am I to get rid of this woman? God help me to find a means." Susanna was determined to stay, and did until she left to get married. Percy was then broken-hearted.' Needless to say his strictures upon his daughter's youth are totally without foundation.

Monday, 15th November

One of the alarming aspects of motorway travel is trigger-happiness. When I am bowling along in my tiny Morris at 70 mph, it feels like 30 mph. When another car comes up alongside, or I am passing another, I feel impelled to behave as though I were in one of those fun-fair dodgems, which one drives into others and bounces off for the fun of the thing. On the motorway I lose all sense of speed and danger.

Tuesday, 16th November

We stayed the weekend with John Fowler.* On Sunday morning he came into his garden room, which I call the Cardigan Chamber because he built it out of proceeds of the film about the Charge of the Light Brigade. I was sitting in the window with the sun behind me shining on John. At once I realized how ill he is. His face has become puffy and round, instead of oval, and his colour is mauve and grey. He talked about his house and garden which the Properties Committee is considering next month, so he says. It is his intention to leave it to the National Trust which already holds covenants. He says that if his terminal illness is long and expensive he will be obliged to sell the place to pay for the treatment – 'for nothing, not even the preservation of the Cottage will induce me to go to a public ward' – I agree – therefore the Trust will not get it; but if, as he sincerely hopes, he is carried off quick, then they

---

* John Fowler, d. 1977. Interior decorator of historic country houses.

will get the place, without contents which he is leaving to friends, and it ought to be no liability because it is so lettable. I promised to press the Committee to accept. And I do think it is acceptable on account of the little Gothick façade and the lovely formal garden John has made. If this were not my honest opinion I should be torn by conflict between duty and friendship.

He told me all about the recurrence of his cancer this spring. It has attacked the glands, has become Hodgkin's Disease, and is being kept at bay by drugs, notably cortisone, which is making him so fat. Says he does not want to die, but yet is prepared for it. Poor old John, he has tremendous courage.

When yesterday I got back from Crickhowell with Tom Rolt* to look at a small property, Llangattock Court, covenants over which are offered to the Trust, A. greeted me with the announcement of Miss King's departure. She gave notice in the morning. Bloody woman. Said she simply hated the place and the work, having too little time to herself. Considering that when she came she asked to have more to do than Mrs Mason had, and when we told her there was no need for her to work after she had cleared away the luncheon things, she expostulated and complained that she would be unhappy and preferred to come downstairs in the evenings, we agreed joyfully. After the first two days I noticed that she had become abrupt, and bad-mannered. What is the matter with these people? They are all, always, discontented. Nothing pleases them. They contradict themselves, and lie, and are savages. So she is off. And now I have got to call on Mrs Mason in Bath this afternoon and eat humble pie, which I don't mind eating, and beg her to return. She won't, of course. Oh, the horror! Writing and what it entails is utterly impossible when one is put out in this sort of way.

Wednesday, 17th November

The whole question of our leaving Alderley has arisen again because of this tiresome woman giving notice. For some months it had been happily dormant. But it does seem as though we shall never get a single woman to settle, and we cannot afford more

---

* L.T.C. Rolt, 1910–74. Expert and authority on industrial monuments; engineering historian.

than a single woman, nor do we want a couple again. A. secretly
wants to move to London in spite of protestations that she prefers
the country. Anyway she has taken a small flat for herself which she
is furnishing and decorating. London has changed so much for the
worse since we lived there over ten years ago that I couldn't bear
to live in it again permanently. Yesterday I went to Bath to plead
with Mrs Mason to return, ineffectually. She was strictly polite but
clearly does not wish to return. I would not in her place. But she
made maddening remarks like, 'I am enjoying a well-earned rest',
so that I could have shaken her. If she did return she would
madden me again with her tragedy-queen manner.

Thursday, 18th November

If a crack of any window is left open in come the tits, beastly little
birds, which invariably sit on the lamp-shades, and leave marks
which are indelible. I wonder why they come in at this particular
season after the fly plague has abated. Presumably in pursuit of
some insects seen through the window panes. Unless it is us,
insects they see through magnifying eyes and like the look of.

I drove our daily help Mrs Margery to Wotton this morning.
She has gone for a fortnight while her tarty daughter is having a
baby. She laments the departure of Miss King whom she much
likes working with. Says she cannot understand why she is leaving.
I asked, why? Well, says Mrs M., she says she doesn't like the way
she is spoken to. I have heard this sort of thing before. 'But I don't
see as how,' etc., she went on in her gabbling, uncontrolled way,
'and I don't mind, I always gets on well with you.' I should think
so too in the circumstances we have had to put up with.

Went to tea with Audrey. She looks ghastly ill, having had a fall
in her attic, all alone; is black and blue. A tragic little figure. I
telephone Prue who says worry is the cause. Of falling in the attic?

Audrey quite solemnly tells me she attributes her present troubles to retribution by the Almighty for her having put down two
of her eight cats. She is haunted by guilt for taking away their lives.
I said modern God is no longer Jehovah of the Old Testament.

Friday, 19th November

A. was invited by Anthony [Chaplin] to choose some memento of
Gwladys in Chelsea Square this week. Gwladys had been her

mother-in-law for nearly forty years, had never broken with her after A.'s divorce from Anthony and marriage to me. A. had constantly visited her, had her to stay here and treated her like a mother in spite of Gwladys's horrid treatment of her in the early years. Yet Gwladys left A. nothing in her will. So A. went to Chelsea Square, expectant of something. In G.'s bedroom Anthony had laid out a handful of trashy things, little cheap boxes, etc. which he clearly did not want. A. was invited to choose one of these. She couldn't bring herself to take one. Then she saw a piece of china on the dressing-table which wasn't too bad and which she associated with Gwladys. 'Oh,' said Anthony, 'that is quite valuable. It must be worth at least £15.' So A. came away with nothing.

I became fond of old Gwladys. She was a period piece, and for brief spells amused because of her goosiness. But she was a desperately stupid woman. One of her distinguishing qualities was disloyalty. She was always quarrelling with some member of the family, taking sides with one against another; not unlike my poor mother. An Edwardian trait, I fear. I may have inherited it to some extent. The root cause is not fundamental evil, but stupidity, in allowing the mood of the moment to oust reason. It is lack of forethought, lack of control; also the knowledge that the victims are vulnerable.

Saturday, 20th November

At dinner with the Somersets Caroline said her friend Niarchos, the Greek, spoke odd English in an inaudible voice. He was very touchy, quick to take offence, and tiresome. He said to her what she took to be: 'I say, your breath smells beastly.' C. was very cross, turned on him and replied, 'Well, if it is, I can't do anything about it. So you must take it or leave it.' What he had in fact said was: 'I saw your best friend lately.'

When the women left the table David, Peter Quennell, Derek Hill and I talked about the everyday things which people throughout the ages take for granted and don't write in their diaries, such as going to the lavatory and how much and where they wash themselves. Even Pepys, Peter said, doesn't mention how often he washed and what with. He did mention that he had a place of easement on the leads of his roof in one house, and in the cellar in another. In the eighteenth century grand people living in the country sent to London for washballs. David said, 'I never wash at all. I have two baths a day, but I never wash.' He is the cleanest, sprucest man I know. I said one did not have a bath in order to wash but for relaxation, that one washed much better without a bath. All one needed was a washbasin and a bidet. The latter is essential but the English still for some idiotic reason consider bidets funny. In my youth they thought them immoral. I wash myself thoroughly after I have soaked in the bath. It means standing up and soap-washing neck and ears, rather perfunctorily; then chest, under the arms, stomach and groin, and lastly legs. With a sigh of relief I return to the water, and lying wash the toes, and scrub the finger-nails with a brush. In the height of summer on the Mediterranean I don't need a bath. I stand upright and naked, and slosh about in front of the basin.

Sunday, 21st November

After Communion this morning, standing in the cold outside the church door, the Vicar [Sparks] gave me such an elaborate description of his bowel trouble – how he had a wire cage put inside him seven years ago, how blockages occur, what the blockages consist of after a week's non-evacuation – that I felt faintly ill. I preserved a sickly smile of interest. Now had it been David giving me these gruesome details I should not have been disgusted, for his descriptions would have been hilarious.

A. said how stale the wafer was this morning, she could hardly swallow it. It tasted of gloves. I had truthfully not thought of such a thing. I don't consider whether it has taste or no, I don't look upon it as food. A. then asks, do I look at the Vicar's fingers? No, I say, I try not to; but on the whole they are clean, or were when I last looked. I say I wish the C of E did not have communion in both kinds. At 8 a.m. I don't fancy Wincarnis, and take the tiniest sip. The Vicar does wipe the chalice in a perfunctory way. Nevertheless I don't like it, although in theory I strongly approve of the communal cup. One must in fact look upon the whole ceremony from the spiritual aspect, and ignore the physical. That is what I try to do. Easier said piously than done with a good grace.

A. telephoned my nephew Simon asking him if he wanted to take away the remaining Sheraton chairs I promised him. He already has taken three. No, he said, thank you, 'I have sufficient accommodation.' How can this boy have learnt these ghastly expressions? It is not middle so much as lower class. Not even shopwalkers talk like this, but waiters on the trains – 'Will you commence with pamplemousse, sir?' and 'Have you had a sufficiency of sweet?'

At Eny Strutt's I talked for a few minutes with Peter Lubbock.* I have known him for many years, but never well. If I had seen more of him I like to think he might have become one of my best friends. I am greatly drawn to him. He is infinitely sympathetic, sweet and good. A nice man.

A. found an advertisement in the *Wotton Gazette* under Situations Wanted by a gardener-handyman with three children. Suspects it may be our gardener Mr Margery with or without the missus. The terrible truth is one cannot trust anyone today. One is suspicious of them all. They have no loyalties, no morality, no gratitude, no decency – all those virtues for which *one* is so pre-eminently conspicuous. They think only of themselves and of money, and more money, and employers are 'they', to be rooked, tricked and deceived. It is a sad state of affairs. After the dozens of experiences we have encountered since we have lived here these past ten years, no bad treatment will ever surprise us again. A. says nothing; and nothing in the way of a let-down by her greatest friends will come as a shock to her. She is so disillusioned. But I find this attitude a bit too cynical.

I went to the SPAB annual meeting in the Banqueting House, Whitehall, to have another look at that glorious room and to assess the principal speaker, Peter Walker,[†] Minister of the Environment. Hugh Grafton [SPAB chairman] speaking from notes acquitted himself extremely well. He has greatly improved as an orator, and has acquired confidence. I suppose becoming a duke helps. After one and a half hours I left before the end. On going down the stairs I stopped to put my overcoat on ('top coat', Eddy Sackville called it). A handsome, smartly dressed lady called out to me and flung her arms round my neck. It was Diana Menuhin.[‡] She had a rich Mercedes waiting outside the door in Whitehall, with a smartly liveried lady chauffeur who called me Sir. Diana gave me a lift to

---

* Peter Lubbock ran a small and select travel agency.
† Rt. Hon. Peter Walker, MP, b. 1932. Minister of State, Department of the Environment, 1970–2.
‡ Diana (née Gould), ballet dancer, wife of Yehudi, now Lord Menuhin.

Paddington station. She is affected in a professional sort of way. She is very funny, but awareness that she is going to be funny sometimes makes it difficult for me to be as amused as I ought to be. Takes the edge off the response. She looks splendid, tall, thin, distinguished. We both agreed that the Minister made a speech of clichés, typical Tory complacency. He reiterated all that the Government had done for the amenities, and what a beautiful world he was going to make for Britons to live in. I longed to shout 'Use your eyes, man. You have only got to see how the country diminishes day by day, and what is left gets fouler and fouler. More and more old buildings disappear, or are polluted by diesel fumes or are whittled away by traffic and motorways.' Diana says she bombards Walker with desperate pleas for the Government to safeguard the Witanhurst estate adjoining Hampstead Heath. She demands interviews with local mayors, and vamps them. 'They all pinch my bottom', she says.

I said the Banqueting House looked better than I had thought. Diana said that was only because it was now dirtier than when it was first decorated six years ago. It is painted stone colour with white half columns. I think this is right, but the green gold 'paint' is abominable. I admired the four huge brass spiders, modern I suppose, but very suitable and handsome. Hugs and effusive messages of love to Alvilde from Diana who swept away in a haze of furs and scent into the night.

Thursday, 25th November

To the Bath Preservation Trust annual meeting in the Guildhall, at 8. o'clock. It went on for two and a half hours. The huge room was packed. The issue was a resolution that the Buchanan Tunnel scheme should be rescinded. Passions were aroused. The resolution was passed, but the Chairman pointed out that it did not commit the trustees, who on the information obtained would decide and pronounce their statement pro or con. There had never been such a large attendance before. Christopher Chancellor a bad chairman, couldn't be heard, and lacked determination. In fact I was surprised that such a man could have been the success he was said to be as Chairman of Reuters and Bowaters.

Several people spoke with rage in their hearts; one young man, a confessed Communist, talked arrant drivel, quite irrelevant to the issue. 'Damn the elegant buildings of Bath. It is the people's needs that are the issue, and not the privileged people either', with venom. I thought to myself, with Miss King's troubles in my mind, is the world today mostly evil, or just stupid? I went away having decided for evil. Then this morning Miss King having packed and said good bye confessed to me that she was going to a doctor to discuss her 'instability'. She said the impulse came over her to speak her mind and she regretted it immediately after; that it was absurd she could not settle; something was the matter with her she did not know what. I did. She is a lonely, crotchety old spinster going through what Tony Gandarillas* would call 'the time of her life'. We shook hands, and I felt sorry for her. Yet I am glad she has gone, for she has done mischief.

Now I decide that the world is mostly stupid. Reading the papers and the way in which the marchers outside the House of Commons injured policemen and their horses, and smashed Members' cars, I am certain that these people's motives *are* evil. So was that young anarchist's last night. They are anti-everything, positively destructive and so evil. I have no sympathy for them at all. Let them burn.

Saturday, 27th November

Mairi Bury† is staying. She is very sweet indeed, and rather lonely and touching. She is only 50 and has endured hardships – divorced, widowed, having lost her mother on whom she doted and Betty Batten her closest friend with whom she lived for the past ten years. We talked of Londonderry House days and the part her mother‡ played in civilizing the first Labour Government. Mairi has all Ramsay MacDonald's letters to her. He was definitely in love with her; she not at all with him, merely fond. She did a great service to the country in the 'thirties. We said someone ought to write her life and Lord Londonderry's, together. Who? I thought Philip Magnus. Mairi thinks it ought to be someone who knew her

---

* Don Antonio de Gandarillas, d. 1970, Chilean attaché in London during the 1939–45 war and after.
† Lady Mairi Vane-Tempest-Stewart, b. 1921, youngest daughter of 7th Marquess of Londonderry. Married 1940–58 to Derek Keppel, Viscount Bury. Lives at Mount Stewart, Co. Down.
‡ Hon. Edith Chaplin. Married 1899 7th Marquess of Londonderry and d. 1959.

mother, whose strong personality was evanescent. Neither Edy nor Lord L. left diaries, and only a few letters, so there is little of the written word to go by. I don't know how biographers can claim to be accurate about subjects who left no written words.

At the moment I have stopped reading for the Stuarts, and am struggling once more, and for the last time, with my novel.* I have cut almost 50 pages out of 370. But this is not enough, and I must cut out more. I cannot do what Norah Smallwood quite rightly counsels, namely put Parts 2 and 3 into the same key as Part 1. Nor so far have I given telling episodes about Star which will unfold the relationship between the twins. Norah complained that there was too much explanation, too little incident. As I cut so I am appalled by the jejuneness of the excisions. Then I realize that the parts I decide to leave in must be just as jejune. Am I wasting precious time on something which will never be printed?

Why too is my style stilted and pedantic? I should always bear in mind that prose should be written like conversation; and conversation never be spoken like prose.

Sunday, 28th November

I told Mairi the following tale. When years ago I was staying at Florence Court with the late Lord Enniskillen, an old and delightfully eccentric Irish peer, he told me that as a young boy he was staying at Mount Stewart with the Londonderrys. One afternoon the Lady Londonderry of the day took him for a drive in her carriage round the estate. Trotting along the country roads they came upon a peasant's cottage seemingly on fire, with smoke issuing from the door and windows. Lady Londonderry stopped the carriage and sent her footman from the box to ask if they could help put the fire out. The footman returning at leisure said: 'It's quite all right, m'lady. They're only smoking a whore for his lordship.'

Mairi said that her grandmother, that Lady Londonderry's daughter-in-law, herself a daughter of Lord Shrewsbury, the premier earl of England, always considered her marriage with Lord L. a *mésalliance*. She would refer to Mount Stewart as 'my little villa by the sea'. She had a half-sister, illegitimate daughter of her father, whom she employed as head housemaid at Wynyard (County

---

* *Heretics in Love*, Chatto & Windus, 1973.

Durham). This half-sister gossiped with the other servants so much about Lady Londonderry's amours that she had to be dismissed. At Mount Stewart today Mairi has a cousin working for her in the house. The cousin's mother, illegitimate daughter of Lord Londonderry, married the coachman. Mairi remembers the mother whom she used to refer to in the presence of her father as 'Charlie's Aunt'. The late Charlie Londonderry was not amused.

Monday, 29th November

It is very ridiculous how self-conscious the English are. I speak for myself. Facing an audience of 400 in the Bath Guildhall the other night I blushed to the roots of my hair when Christopher Chancellor introduced me, a recent recruit among the trustees, as that well-known author, etc. I hate any reference to myself favourable or unfavourable, at least in my presence. I feel it to be a derogation from good taste. Instead of holding my head high with a vacant, but self-contained expression, I looked at my feet and frowned. All wrong. Poor Christopher said when the meeting was over that during it he kept asking himself why, after half a century of hard work with responsibility of a high order, did he now gratuitously expose himself to anxiety and abuse for no financial reward.

Tuesday, 30th November

Sunday evening we went to Eny's to hear Penelope [Betjeman] give a lecture about Turkey and India – Injer she calls it. She is a good lecturer in that she addresses the audience as she might speak to a single person tête-à-tête, with interjections: 'Drat the blinking slide', and 'You know the name as well as I do. Come along now. Hurry up, just tell me.' And 'You're hopelessly slow,' etc. Her trouble is that enthusiasm leads her to go on and on, and she can't stop. Professor Hewer and wife were there, and stayed for dinner afterwards. I liked them. He is an eminent botanist, a handsome 70, dandyish, with exquisite manners and a trifle insinuating. She tall, handsome, with a presence. Again went on about my book. Says it's a classic, and so forth. Which makes me worried that I cannot repeat the performance: I mean with my novel on which I am working. I simply cannot re-assume the light-hearted tone of Part I, try as I may. It will not come out. All I am able to do is to cut, cut and cut. And still what is left is dead, dead, dead.

Thursday, 2nd December

Only wax, is Dr Adamson's verdict. So again a reprieve. Dr A. is a charming Scot, with an amused and twinkling eye, gentle, shrewd, keeping his opinions to himself. Would I have liked him for a father, or would I have thought he was laughing at me, and been wounded? I feel it is wrong my going to him for small ailments for nothing (he being on the Health), whereas if anything serious strikes me I rush to Rettie in London – and pay. But since I have always had to contribute to the Health Scheme I have every right to visit Adamson. I merely feel I ought to do something for him in return. He is so nice. And as good a physician as Rettie I daresay.

I notice how the semi-educated constantly attribute base motives to their neighbours. For instance, on the tiresome Wotton Planning Committee of townsfolk, if Mr So-and-So applies for planning consent to build a new porch on to his house, the knowing members will say, 'I think this is a try-on. He happens to be going bankrupt, as some of us well know.' And some of us break into a chorus of smiles. Or, 'Mr Stokes (the farmer), he hasn't yet paid for the land he wants to put a bungalow on. And since he already has one cottage and only one worker, I guess he means to sell the new one to a stranger for a profit.' What they want one to understand is how 'in the know' they are, rather than how malicious they are being, for on the whole they are a kindly lot, and would go out of their way to help a friend, or even acquaintance. The human wish to be considered cleverer than others is strong. I am influenced by a contrary wish, if anything, and people who don't know me accordingly consider me stupider than I am.

Last night I read the book on F.L. Griggs* which Harry Horsfield lent me weeks ago. He was Harry's wife Lily's brother-in-law. Griggs married her sister. I had not before realized what a great etcher he was. His landscapes, better than his pictures of buildings, at least secular buildings, his content with poverty, his generosity, make me feel humble. His adoration of England, the England of

---

* F.L. Griggs, 1876–1938, of the Chipping Campden school of artists and craftsmen. Etcher and print-maker.

smocks and hayricks, was touching. Poor fellow, in his youth this still was England.

The dreadful things that happen to one in real life are worse than those in dreams. Last night I dreamt that I had to climb up the high wall of a cathedral. I began upon the carved wooden west door. There was not enough to grasp in the way of carving and the lintel stuck out above me. How was I to manoeuvre around it? The problem was agonizing, the fear of the height, ever increasing, as I somehow managed to climb. I was frightened and miserable. Yet not as desperate as I would be if confronted with this ridiculous situation in real life. The reason I suppose being that even in my sleep I was to some extent aware of its ridiculousness, its Alice-in-Wonderland meaninglessness, which remained unquestioned.

Friday, 3rd December

I can sympathize with the truly deaf. Now I am taking drops of oil in my ear to loosen the wax for the doctor to extract tomorrow. Consequently my left ear is deafer than before. Deafness does not cause total, blissful oblivion, but curious noises inside the ear, resonances and stabbing pains, noises which would not be engendered were I not deaf. Long echoes down empty corridors, and in my case sudden loud poppings during the night which wake me from sleep. Eliza Wansbrough has told me of these experiences, which she suffers every day and night of her life, and I have never taken in before.

Whereas I think F.L. Griggs's etchings of secular buildings are harder and less romantic and feeling than his landscapes, his churches and religious edifices on the other hand are soft and deeply devotional. They show what a devout man he must have been. Why when we lived at Wickhamford did we not know people like Griggs and Jewson, instead of those idiotic, arrogant, stupid good-timers with their contemptible standards of what was right for people of their class to do and say; their abysmal ignorance of art and intellect, and their pride in ignorance? Answer: Griggs and Jewson would not have wanted to know us.

How uncomfortable the houses of artists among the Griggs generation. The bare rooms of the Bussy villa, Le Souco, at Roquebrune come to mind. Admittedly Simon was a French peasant, but Dorothea upper-middle-class English. The skimpy curtains not reaching the tiled floor; the lack of rugs and carpets; unshaded electric light bulbs; bath like a pig's trough. Complete lack of cosiness. As though they saw a virtue in pigging, which in truth was arrogance of an intellectual sort, almost as offensive as the good timers' hedonism because puritanical. Puritanism is worse then hedonism. And high-thinking coupled with plain living worse than no-thinking coupled with sybaritism.

Griggs's etchings bring back to me the nostalgic cosy beauty of Broadway and Chipping Campden and the Cotswold villages of my boyhood in the 'twenties. How more wonderful still they must have been in the first decade of this century when totally unspoilt by the commuters and the alien retired. I relish the memory of winters in these little villages, the smell of wood smoke, the empty streets, grass growing down the humped middles of the roads, animals straying, the inhabitants all belonging and knowing one another, the hounds wandering among all, the clip-clop of horses and occasional bulb horn of some old-fashioned motor-car. Oh the bliss departed! Every sortie by car was an adventure. My father putting the Minerva into reverse half-way up the Fish Hill, and our just reaching the top one cold, frosty afternoon on the way to the Knox children's party at Springhill. I suppose we skidded downhill later in the dark, but I don't remember this.

Wax it may have been in the left ear. Yesterday Dr Adamson syringed it with warm water five times. Result, total deafness in it ever since. I can't hear anything at all. A bomb exploding would not be heeded. So long as this condition does not last, it interests me. For with this partial deafness the other senses become blunted, or muffled. For instance, I can't smell as acutely. I have always found that without wearing my spectacles I do not take in what is said to me so clearly. Cannot concentrate. Yet in the darkness I concentrate rather better than in the daylight because, I suppose, there are no visual distractions. So it would be, presumably, with total blindness. The creaks of my neck joints, the crunching of my teeth make resonant noises in my head now.

Friday, 10th December

Dick and Elaine* stay the night. This is their first visit to England after nearly two years in Cyprus. Both very well and happy. They

---

* J.L.-M.'s brother Dick and sister-in-law Elaine (née Brigstocke).

went to see the Haines's at Wickhamford and were so depressed by
the surroundings and the gloom of the village that they wonder
how they managed to live there so long. They would not return
to England permanently for anything in the world. They see more
people (and people are their chief recreation) in Cyprus than they
ever did at Wickhamford. He is the same old, lovable, simple,
happy, amused Dick in an accepting philosophical way.

Saturday, 11th December

Have received a cutting from *The Times* relating that at Sotheby's
a week ago a ring which had been given to Byron by the choirboy
Edleston at Cambridge has been sold. Byron was wearing it at his
death in Missolonghi. It has been bought by Murray's for £450, a
lot of money, but I would willingly have spent this amount for
such a treasure. On the other hand, quite proper that John Murray's
should have it. The ring was apparently acquired by B.'s (and
subsequently Disraeli's) gondolier, Tita, and has been sold by Tita's
great-nephew, a Canon in the Church of England. Byron wrote a
poem about this ring. If he wore it at his death so many years after
Edleston's death this romance must have meant more to him than
the infinite number of other affairs of his susceptible heart. Indeed
he hinted at it. He was more romantic than cynic.

Dr Adamson gave one further spray into my ear, and out jumped
a rock the size of an old threepenny bit in diameter.

Harry Horsfield has written to me that his brother-in-law Fred
Griggs had the highest opinion of Samuel Palmer's painting, which
is evident enough in his etchings; that New Dover House in
Chipping Campden, which he built and worshipped, was completely gutted about six months ago by an incendiary whom the
police have not discovered. 'Poor Fred, the house which broke
him, and killed him in fact, has now gone.'

Sunday, 12th December

Bill Raines, living in Hillesley, is the most Gloucestershire of
Gloucestershire yokels left. He is actually a few years younger than
me. He works as journeyman-gardener for the Gascoignes. He is
sexton, grave-digger, earth-stopper. He told Derick Gascoigne
that he attended last year's earth-stoppers' dinner at Badminton, an
annual event. 'The Dooke of Boofore he made us a short speech

and wishes us all a Merry Christmas. When he left what do you think we 'ad? A stripper. She took off all her clothes, down to the last stitch.' Thus permissiveness comes to Gloucestershire.

I spent this afternoon with members of the Bath Preservation Trust being shown on the spot exactly where the proposed tunnel will go and which buildings will have to be sacrificed. It is extremely difficult to make up one's mind whether all this tremendous work will be worth the effort and damage. Because where old buildings will be spared their proximity to the new through-road will render them uninhabitable. Thus the terraces on London Road will have a road on both sides of them instead of one side as at present. I was horrified by the poor condition of the houses at the back from where one can see their roofs all tumbling in. The trouble is that the artisans will no longer live in Bath, preferring the suburban estates with modern houses and gardens. None of them wants any more to live in a bustling town. But if only the streets were made residential and traffic-free then surely people would return to live in Bath. What with the appalling destruction lately of the nice little streets of small, neatly stepped terrace houses, and the laying waste of large areas like Southgate (within one week bulldozed to rubble), and Lansdown, and the now proposed destruction of New Bond Street, I despair for the survival of Bath. I am sure it is doomed.

Monday, 13th December

There is really no one whom I like kissing or being kissed by on the mouth. I notice that certain women will try and do it to me, old retainers, viz. Mrs Haines and Irene Staveley, who make for my mouth a bee-line which I endeavour, usually in vain, to parry. In sophisticated circles no one does this. All my women friends put their faces aslant to mine barely touching; usually first one cheek and then the other is proffered. To kiss, say, Eliza Wansbrough or Diana Westmorland in any other way would be unthinkable. Very few men kiss me, only some very old friends, like Raymond, Eardley, Desmond S.-T., then with token rather than actual embraces. I remember Emerald Cunard greatly embarrassing Field Marshal Wavell at dinner at the Dorchester by asking, 'Field Marshal, do you like kissing on the mouth, or where?'

Met Debo in Heywood Hill's shop yesterday. She said Nancy is taking such a strong drug that whereas the pain is kept at bay her temper is badly affected. N. got extremely angry when Debo suggested that she ought to buy a house and live in London, railing against England and the English until D. thought she was out of her mind. But she says we must remember that the cause of her tempers is the drugs. Says they are not a cure, merely pain-killers.

Thursday, 16th December

Dreamt that I was climbing a rope-ladder against a very tall mast of a sailing ship on a rough sea. I had to get to the mast head, or crow's nest. That was bad enough. I looked round and there behind me was darling Fop. This made things worse because Fop could not possibly get down a rope-ladder, and how on earth was I to get him down from the crow's nest if indeed either of us ever reached it. Most of my dreams are of heights. I have always supposed I shall meet my God in an aeroplane.

The Lennox Berkeleys had their silver wedding party on Tuesday. About forty people to a stand-up dinner. Many old friends, yet I did not enjoy it. I never enjoy parties of this sort. I have no small talk – precious little big talk either. I only went because A. said I must. However I did enjoy the entertainments because I didn't have to make conversation. These consisted of, firstly, a piece for four hands, commissioned by Burnet Pavitt,[*] composed by Lennox, and played by Lennox and Burnet. Very charming it was too, in the Poulenc manner. They were encored and played it a second time – a waltz. A. said afterwards that it was light – which explains why I liked it. Then John Betjeman read a short poem he had composed for them – too light by half. Paul Dehn[†] read a sonnet he had composed. Arthur Marshall[‡] gave two recitations, one the funniest I have ever heard, of Queen Wilhelmina broadcasting to the British people in the war in broken English. And John Julius Norwich[§] sang to his guitar, plangently.

There is no doubt the Berkeleys are greatly beloved by a host of friends, and Freda was very moved by the testimonies to their love.

[*] Burnet Pavitt, b. 1908. Managing director of Roche, 1948–73, and director of the Royal Opera House, Covent Garden, for twenty-five years.
[†] Paul Dehn, 1912–76, poet and author.
[‡] Arthur Marshall, 1910–89, columnist and broadcaster.
[§] John Julius, 2nd Viscount Norwich, b. 1929. Writer and broadcaster.

After she and Lennox had been toasted Freda dragged in Babs (their daily help) whom she and we toasted much to everyone's delight. Babs wiping away tears of joy.

Sunday, 19th December

June at the Berkeley's party told me she and Jeremy [Hutchinson] had recently dined at Chequers; ever since her marriage there had been coldness from Mr Heath. She had sent him a message through a mutual friend on the eve of her wedding. After all, she explained, he had never so much as held her hand, far less breathed a word of love. The Hutchinsons motored to Chequers from London. There was a small dinner party of musical friends exclusively. I asked if Heath was cosy. No, for he shuns all conversation, all intimacy. He is terrified of talk which is not about national or international topics. But he was proud of Chequers and showed them the Nelson and other relics. They saw his bedroom. June said she supposed that this was always the Prime Minister's bedroom. 'No,' he said, 'it was certainly not the last Prime Minister's. I wouldn't do a thing like that. I couldn't.' He and Wilson do not just dislike, they detest each other.

Monday, 20th December

At luncheon with Elspeth Huxley[*] she said what worried her deeply was this. We, Gt. Britain, were repeatedly letting down those people to whom we had serious obligations, simply because we were weak and had no army, no gunboats to enforce their rights. Since the last war we had done this all along the line in Africa; now we were likely to do so again in Ireland. Harold Wilson's proposition for a United Ireland was a major instance of this amoral policy. We would be handing over a million reluctant Protestants to the South against their wishes, against their very beliefs. But I said, this action could only result in a devastating civil war of the very worst kind. Elspeth said, 'You have always agreed with us [Elspeth and Gervas] that over-population is the cause of most of the world's ills. We have realized for years what the general public are only beginning to understand. That is a healthy

---

[*] Elspeth Grant, b. 1907, writer of fiction and travel. Married 1931 Gervas Huxley, who d. 1971.

sign.' 'Yes,' I answered, 'in spite of this, in spite of the awareness of pollution dangers, pollution increases yearly, more and larger oil tankers are built, and more and more spill oil into the sea; and then that damned Concorde . . .' 'Yes,' she said, 'only a fool could be an optimist.'

Dined at Badminton. David away. Cecil Beaton staying. He has much aged, very white in face and hair, and scalp covered with light red blotches. A slight paunch. He has lost his old exuberance, but is mellower, and has for me great charm and sweetness.

Cecil said he could not see more of Jamesey [Pope-Hennessy]. He took him to the theatre a month ago. James kept screwing up his eyes, focusing them on something unseen while making the most excruciating faces, and stretching out an arm in a mad fashion. Was distant and nagging. Kept on pitching into Cecil, and expecting him to admit guilt for the malpractices of our ancestors 200 years back. 'Well,' said Cecil, 'the truth is I feel no guilt whatever for the fact that in 1771 my ancestors may have been slave traffickers.' He is sure James was 'high' and doped. 'Why,' he asked, 'must he write books on such boring subjects?' (as slaves).

As we left the dining-room I overheard Michael Briggs[*] say to Daphne Fielding[†] 'Can you believe it, he actually said that if he had to begin his life over again he would not correct anything he had done before? He doesn't think he has made a single mistake in his life.' I said: 'Are you referring to Nicholas Ridley?' 'No, Robert Heber-Percy.' Then Daphne said as she went through the door that she too regretted no action of her life. I was amazed. Cecil stood, and just looked blank, which told me what he too was thinking.

Cecil then went on to say that Robert Heber-Percy was one of the wickedest men he knew. He was a bad father, a worse friend. He had got Faringdon out of Gerald Berners by most questionable means. Somebody interpolated 'Oh merely the legitimate wages of sin.' 'Sin!' said Cecil. 'If you call it so; once only between 6 and 6.30 with his ears back.' That Robert refused to allow Gerald to leave even a clock to his oldest friend; he grabbed the lot while Gerald was alive to make quite sure.

---

[*] Michael Briggs, businessman and aesthete, of Midford Castle, Bath.
[†] The Hon. Daphne Vivian, writer; m. 1st, 1927, Henry Thynne, 6th Marquess of Bath; 2nd, 1953, Xan Fielding, war hero and author.

Cecil does nourish some hates in his life still. I suppose that anyone who has once done him an injury is never forgiven, like Anne (Rosse)* of whom some truly horrifying caricatures exist. Or has he an objective view of right and wrong? In other words, is he a good man? I can't make out. Charming, disarming as I find him, he is the archetypal twentyish man. One must not forget that. And the 'twenties mean cynicism.

Wednesday, 22nd December

A.'s love of giving exceeds anything I have known. At Christmas she must give at least 100 presents. From mid-November she spends days and nights tying up parcels in Xmas paper. She gives presents to her friends, their servants, the girl who brings the fish, and the man who brings the laundry, the postman, the dustman (£2 each, one from her, one from me). I simply hate Christmas, and everything to do with it, except the message. I don't like getting presents. I remember my father saying to my mother, 'I never get a present I want, except from you'; whereas, poor man, he had to dole out tips to all and sundry like every paterfamilias. I have reached that age and situation.

Every single night I am woken up about 4.30, occasionally later. I have dreams, nightmares, and then lie half-awake, aware that something is wrong, but unaware what is wrong. One would suppose that after years of this experience one would quickly realize what was wrong: but no. And then the dreams – always of worry, frustration, fear, as if one did not have enough of these torments during waking hours. It is strange how our subconscious lives are governed by the dictates of the bladder. And the bladder affects presumably the behaviour of the adjacent sexual organs. Why in God's name were they put so close together? Kept apart, distinct, each would in all conscience cause enough mischief, without their both ganging up. The only animal known to me that also dreams is the dog. This is another link which binds us together in sympathy – a shared pain and sorrow.

The ridiculous march of events, or non-events, takes place every night until I am awake enough to rouse myself, get up and stumble down the five steps to my bathroom. With care, that is to say by

---

* Anne Messel, d. 1992, wife of Michael Parsons, 6th Earl of Rosse.

not allowing my attention to be drawn to anything *en route*, I can, on returning to bed, fall asleep again fairly soon, the elusive tranquil sleep I always am longing for but which invariably turns out to be a battle. But if I have been unwise enough to open or shut a window, even pat Fop in his armchair, I become wide awake and do not fall asleep before it is time to get up. Then I hear my little tortoiseshell clock on the shelf beside my bed give its silvery strike of 8. I immediately turn on the news from Radio 3 and listen to the summary. I get out of bed, and stroke or have a word with Fop who by now may have jumped on to the bed. I draw the heavy wine-red curtains and drowsily descend the five steps to the bathroom again, carrying the wireless with me.

Thursday, 23rd December

To the strains of Couperin and Rameau conducted by Raymond Leppard, that charming musician, whom I know but superficially, and wish I knew better – I shave, cutting myself whenever the blade is a new one. Before the glass I feel awful, sway a little as though I had a hangover, whereas the previous evening I drank one glass of wine. Nevertheless I sing in accompaniment to Rameau and expulsions of wind accumulated during the night from lying horizontally (as if one could lie vertically) in bed. In winter I like to keep an ear open for the school bus which descending from Tresham slows down before reaching the corner to pick up the Alderley schoolchildren. Since it is high in the chassis I try to duck to prevent the Tresham children getting a glorious glimpse of me standing half-naked and scraggy with soap on my face. Having shaved and washed my teeth (I am inclined to eat digestive biscuits during the night) I soap my neck and ears. Sometimes Fop comes down to the bathroom with me, flop, flop, flop, he makes a clumsy noise, and when I return up the steps he whines because he is too frightened to risk slipping on the polished boards, so I have to lift him. Strange how after all these years he never thinks ahead, 'If I go down I shan't be able to get up; therefore I will be sensible and stay in the bedroom to which Jim must return in ten minutes.'

Back in my bedroom I think swiftly – what do I wear today? Nothing is happening, no one is coming, therefore another old pair of trousers, the yellow corduroys, yesterday's dirty shirt and a polo sweater to cover it up, thus avoiding the necessity of choosing a tie.

Hastily I pull back the bedclothes to air them, ruffle the pillows and, carrying book and papers, descend the main stairs with Fop in wild excitement because he longs to go out and to greet Chuff who meets him in the hall. A mutual examination of pudenda ensues and they part company, satisfied. By 8.35, seldom before, I am ready for breakfast.

Friday, 24th December

The stairs are the greatest joy to me, indeed are the part of the house I admire the most, so spacious and generous. The stairwell is huge for the size of the house, which when rebuilt in the mid-eighteenth century was a smallish middling sort of house. Before the two downstairs front rooms were extended about 1810 they were exactly the same size as the central stairwell. The actual staircase is of oak, with turned and twisted balusters, three to each tread, and has a comfortable handrail. Ramped at the newel posts the handrail swoops switchback-like down to the bottom, where the balusters swirl round in a curlicue. The dado echoes the height and rampage of the handrail and balusters.

The first flight from my bedroom is of seven steps. For a long time this perplexed me because the little stair from my bedroom to bathroom on the same level as the flight is of five steps. Then I realized that the five steps are of course steeper. The main staircase treads are broad and shallow. I can trot up and down them without watching my feet, without making any effort, and feeling as though my feet were happily winged like Mercury's. How many stairs can one say so much for? Besides I love the plaintive creak they make as they resist the rubber soles of my shoes. I run my sensuous hand along the handrail which fits it caressingly. I could write about the merits of this staircase for ever.

Wednesday, 29th December

Our Christmas with the Droghedas at Parkside, Englefield Green, much the same as in past years. Present-giving, effusive thanks, cries of gush as we unpack expensive parcels which we don't always want, much over-eating of too rich food, walks in Windsor Park – which I do like – ending on the third day with frayed tempers on the part of the overstrung Joan who picks little quarrels with Garrett, who in turn bends over backwards to make amends for nothing wrong he has done, but she likes to make him suppose he has done. Derry looking almost Byronic having lost weight, and picturesque with thick, bushy dark hair and a white face. He and I on Christmas morning stride down the Long Walk back from St George's Chapel to Parkside exchanging harmless confidences. We wonder why Parkside, which is a nice, white, once-Regency house with pretty things inside, good taste, is yet without much character, and like any Ascot tycoon's villa. It does not seem lived in, has no knick-knacks. The rooms have that vacancy which rooms have when used for company and not by the family.

Thursday, 30th December

At Lyegrove June [Hutchinson] said her great friend – I forget the name – swore that when in her teens she used to lie in the same bed with Prince Philip, a bolster between them. They would talk for hours. She was much in love with him. He would not transgress the bolster for he was, he told her, destined for Princess Elizabeth. When we said we did not believe it June said that only the young were capable of such restraint, such Tennysonian chivalric idealism. It is true.

Friday, 31st December

We lunched with the Tom Rolts at Stanley Pontlarge. I expected a more interesting house than the two Tudor cottages knocked into one. Its single feature of interest is the remains of an open-halled roof, only visible from the attic. The Gordon Russells* the other guests. He now an old man, rather slow and not v. communicative until he talked to me about the condition of York Minster foundations, which he says are those of a Roman temple. York is the first Saxon cathedral to have been built on Roman foundations. His father was the original proprietor of the Lygon Arms, Broadway. I remember him, a nice, respected, rather deferential publican. His knighted son is a distinguished craftsman and cultivated gentleman. Lady Russell clever, and rather tart.

Having made a resolution that I would finish my novel by the end of the year I put it down yesterday. I can do no more to it.

---

* Sir Gordon Russell, 1892–1980, designer, founder of Council of Industrial Design and creator of the Russell Workshops, Broadway, Worcs.

1972

Alderley Grange, Wotton-under-Edge   *Saturday, 1 January*

Thirty years ago today I began my diary which I continued for some eight years, then broke off. The resumption last July was to be for six months only. I shall continue for another six months.

Reading in bed last night Gérin's life of Emily Brontë, I was struck by Emily's knowledge of passion without apparently having experienced it. I think after all that those who have never experienced passionate love can easily imagine it, and having read deeply can know it even better than from the actual experience. After all the desires are there, and because not realized become no less poignant, rather more so. It is unfulfilled love which intensifies passion. The terrible storms of emotion which passed through that remote Yorkshire parsonage must have left an indelible impression on the house. I wish I could visit it out of the tourist season, alone, the only visitor. Or have the impressions been driven away by the numbers of shuffling feet?

John Chancellor* drove over from Hunstrete [House] three days ago with the twenty-two volumes of the *DNB* which I had always wanted to have and which he said he could as a bookseller procure for me at cost price, viz. £60 instead of the £90 which is the retail price. I shall feel permanently indebted to him.

Monday, 3rd January

On New Year's Day was Communion service which I alone attended. The Rector read a long lesson about Circumcision, it being the Feast of that event. As we walked away down the church path he said, 'Well, Jim, a very happy New Year to you.' I nearly replied, 'And a merry Circumcision to you, Rector,' but refrained.

We had the Somersets and Loewensteins† to dine. They seemed to enjoy themselves, yet I didn't, unreservedly. Why? I like them

---

* John Chancellor, son of Sir Christopher, b. 1927. Married 1959 the Hon. Alice Jolliffe. Marriage dissolved.

† Prince Rupert zu Loewenstein, b. 1933, financial adviser; and Josephine Lowry-Corry his wife.

all: I love Caroline and admire David who is extremely entertaining as well as the most elegant, best dressed man in Europe. But
tonight talk was about people, few of whom I had heard of. No
topics discussed.

Tuesday, 4th January

Two of the three Robinson boys came to luncheon. We asked
Joanie Harford to join us to help with the ordeal. It was the very
opposite of an ordeal. They were both absolutely charming. They
are interested in everything. Have perfect, easy manners, are not
the least gauche or awkward. Are already men of the world. Henry
is 18, Nick 17. Nick is better looking than words can describe, tall,
good figure, carries himself erect. He has dark hair, cut short above
the shoulders like a Bronzino youth's. Is earnest, with great love
and knowledge of birds and nature. Is writing a thesis for his A
level on David Cox. I telephoned Audrey to congratulate her on
her grandsons and she asked, 'Did Nick tell you what his ambition
of the moment was?' No. 'It is to go to Rome with you.' I told A.
this who said, 'Let's take him tomorrow. I would like to adopt
him.'

Winifred Gérin's life of Emily Brontë is first-rate. What a
tragedy, those last six months when Branwell, Emily and Anne all
died. And what a totally unfathomable mystic Emily was. Who or
what was her God, her guiding star, her light and life who visited
her from outside, and who deserted her at the end? What was the
real cause of her dying within three months, less than three? Was
she in love with Branwell?

Cheered this morning by a letter from Norah Smallwood saying
she is glad I wrote and she will gladly re-read my novel. But she
will first of all give it to another to read and form a fresh, unbiased
opinion before she tackles it.

Wednesday, 5th January

My only long-term criticism of the two boys, and hardly criticism,
is that both have that fashionable cockney accent which is so odd
in children of their upbringing, Winchester of all correct schools
too. I think it is a pity. Why do upper-class boys have to speak like
the lower classes? Do they do it on purpose, in submission to the
classless age, in protest against their elders? I don't think so in this

case. I think they hear it spoken all around them, and imitate it like parrots.

While beginning Proust's *Captive* in bed last night I also listened to the 11.30 News. It was a great shock to hear the announcement of Gerry Wellington's death. I said out loud involuntarily, 'Oh dear, oh dear!' and felt truly sad. For a moment let the book fall to my lap, and thought about him. Then picked it up and resumed. Thus we take note of the passing of our oldest friends who have meant much to us. Because of their old age we accept it hardly with demur, thinking, 'Well, it is not quite my time yet.' This sounds hard and unsympathetic. But for the past few years Gerry had changed into a querulous, unhappy, indifferent old man; and I don't believe wanted to see anyone. Indeed this morning I still feel fairly sad.

I recall staying with him at Stratfield Saye in 1943 a few weeks after he succeeded his nephew, killed in the war. We spent a morning unpacking ormolu wall brackets in the cellar. They had been ordered by the first Duke of Wellington in Paris and never unpacked. We fumbled with the knots of string tied by long dead fingers over a hundred years ago. Gerry was thrilled with his inheritance. No man was better qualified to inherit a dukedom. Not a wholly estimable character, for he was selfish, unforgiving and cruel; he nevertheless was the best companion in the world, highly informed, and great fun.

Thursday, 6th January

Gerry had the memory of an elephant, and never forgave an injury, intended or supposed. When in 1937 I and George Chettle[*] of the Ministry of Works together compiled a list of the 300 most important country houses in England and Wales – an absurd undertaking I knew at the time – we rather naturally did not include Stratfield Saye. Gerry expressed discontent. In those days he was a valued member of the Historic Buildings Committee of the National Trust. From time to time throughout the years he referred obliquely to this omission. He never trusted my judgement thereafter, and I know bore me a slight grudge, notwithstanding his kindness and hospitality to me always. His misgivings endured.

---

[*] George Chettle, chief inspector of Ancient Monuments Department, Ministry of Works.

Another source of embarrassment was that whereas I often stayed with Ted Lister at Westwood during the 'thirties – I do not remember whether he first introduced me to Gerry – Ted resented the fact that we became friends. He unjustly accused Gerry of 'friend-snatching'. I learnt from Ted, to my dismay, that he and Gerry had a row over this and were never real friends again. I was the totally innocent and ignorant cause of the friction between these two elderly, cultivated, yet in a sense infantile old men. *Hinc illae lacrimae!*

I counted the list of books read during 1971. They amount to 142, not of course including articles, or parts of books, but whole books. No wonder Agatha Christie dissented when I said few people read as many as 100 books in one year. 'I always do,' she protested. 'I read over 200.' I wish I could remember half of my total.

Saturday, 8th January

At the Bath Preservation Trust committee we voted on the Bath tunnel issue. The strange result was that the old trustees were in favour and the young ones against the proposal, they protesting that it was bound to cause much harm to the amenities of the city. I would have supposed the contrary to be their opinion.

In bed read my diary of January 1942,* the year in which I began it. How immature I was then in spite of my 33 years, how censorious and absurd. I have forgotten so much that happened to me. Yet I find it difficult not to believe, irrationally perhaps, that all the experiences of my past life, good and bad, the books read, the thoughts thought and the things (not deeds) done have not been to some purpose to be gleaned in a later time. In other words I cannot believe that all the million things that have happened to me are for nothing, and will be wasted. There must be an accumulation of my stored knowledge and experience for somebody's purpose hereafter, if only it will be sifted by the Almighty.

Sunday, 9th January

To tea with Eny [Strutt] at 4.30. She is just back from her daughter Nicole Hornby's,† full of complaints at the way Nicole bullies her. She was very ill all Xmas with influenza, and looks frailer than

---

* Subsequently published as *Ancestral Voices*, 1975.
† Nicolette (Nicole) Ward, m. 1928 Michael Hornby.

ever. Her arms above the wrist are like two thin pencils, and she was so doubled up on the sofa that she was practically invisible, yet her voice as powerful as ever, and her mind. To our surprise she did not seem the least bit upset by Gerry's death, but was delighted that his son Douro telephoned her every day, and was coming today to tell her all the particulars of the death-bed scene. Talked a lot of Gerry and went through all his bad points as though he were some public figure whom she did not know; whereas he was her greatest friend. This is the merciful palliative of sorrow which old age brings.

The last time we stayed at Stratfield Saye we were taken to church. On leaving the family pew Gerry said, 'My coffin will rest exactly beneath the place where I sit in this pew. I like to think of it.' The church was beautifully restored by him at enormous cost, I think £25,000, which he raised by selling a Breguet watch.

This morning ringing the church bell at 7.30 I felt it getting out of hand; the rhythm got all wrong, and the bell stopped. Try as I would I could not get it going again, so gave up. I thought the rope must have come off the wheel, and told the vicar. After the service he tried it, and it started at once. The professional's knack not yet mastered by me. There were four of us at Communion, A., Rachel Savory and Mrs Mallinson. We were out by 8.30. I much dislike early services in the winter.

This morning it was still dark. In consequence, or rather in anticipation, I slept extremely badly. Half-way through the service the rooks outside set up a tremendous clamour, which lasted five minutes and abruptly ceased. They were waking up. Having woken up they shut up. The other birds were singing as I walked down the church path while dawn was breaking.

Monday, 10th January

At Great Maytham House [Kent] this morning – quite a sweat getting there by Kemble station's 9 o'clock train to Paddington, and changing at Charing Cross for Staplehurst station which re-minded me of my visits to Vita at Sissinghurst. I can't get enthusi-astic over this cumbersome Wrennaissance pile in spite of Lutyens. Assembly of Mutual Householders – Alex Nunburnholme* wearing

---

* Wife of 3rd Lord Nunburnholme (who d. 1974).

purple plus-fours, plastic boots, a long, tatty, loosely knit jersey, and around the neck on a long chain what is called a zodiac badge, like a large half-chewed lump of toffee. In this disguise the wearer looking astonishingly handsome. When I told her aunt Gwladys [Chaplin] how charming and intelligent she was G. said, 'Impossible. She is only a captain's daughter,' adding, 'and of a very small steamer.' How could G., being herself the daughter of a Hull shipowner, have the effrontery to be so snobbish?

Before dining with Patrick Kinross I telephoned A. in the country who said that Eny had told the new Duke of Wellington he must get me to write an appreciation of Gerry for *The Times*. This has caused me much bother. First, I had to think whether I could find anything fresh to say, then telephone the Duke, then telephone *The Times* editor, who said no one else had written one and he could not possibly guarantee publishing one from me. In this uncertain state of mind I went to Patrick's. Alone with him who is not too well, looks aged and grey and feels sleepy all day and cannot write except with great effort.

Got a secretary in the MHA [Mutual Households Association] office to type out what I dictated about Gerry. Not pleased with it but Alec Clifton-Taylor* with whom I lunched was a great help, pointing out mistakes of fact and style. We ate in a glass summerhouse in the back garden of his house in Clareville Grove, with rain pattering on the glass roof, bitterly cold and cheerless. He disappeared down a hole into the basement and brought up food: very good liver pâté and brown toast, cold meat and mashed potato, of which there was not enough, pineapple, and coffee, too weak. He is going round the world next week on a lecturing tour. A dear old, mothy, musty, cheerful, happy, fuddy professorial creature, with appalling taste, infinite knowledge of buildings, and his heart firmly set in the right direction. Thence I taxied to *The Times* to deliver my much overworked notice, which may after all not be published.

Tuesday, 11th January

When I was greeted by George Rettie, my doctor in Harley Street, I said, 'After all these years I do think we might call each other by our Christian names. Don't you agree?' I don't think he did agree,

---

* Alec Clifton-Taylor, 1907–85, architectural historian and broadcaster, chiefly on cathedrals and churches.

although too polite to say so. Yet it seemed absurd to go on writing, Dear Lees-Milne and dear Rettie, or dear J.L.-M. as he did last time. I then informed him that I thought I had a fistula, whereupon I was put on a couch and examined. After that operation I don't suppose he feels any more inclined to call me Jim. Fistula will, he assures me, disappear in time. Nothing to worry about.

John K.-B. and I went to *The Changing Room*, a play by David Storey. Oh dear! The scenes are three, all in the changing room of a Yorkshire town, where a Rugby team change before the match, change during the interval, change after the match. The audience has the doubtful pleasure of seeing them at various stages stark naked. But with one single exception (I am being generous) the fifteen are flabby, unathletic, middle-aged, ill-favoured men, and it is no pleasure to see their wobbly flesh and ugly pudenda. These are not aesthetically pleasing parts of a man's anatomy. Anyway they are a sort of appendices which ought to have been got rid of, along with the umbilical cord. In this play every adjective is substituted by the word bloody, no one makes an utterance that is not wholly banal, there is no dramatic action, yet the boring, plebeian, crassly stupid characters do emerge at the end of the play in a way which is masterly. How to explain it? I could not bear to see a repeat performance.

Wednesday, 12th January

At the breakfast table John said, 'I love Mozart more and more. He is the greatest of composers. His music is sacred.' Having made this pronouncement he switched on the radio, and there was Mozart. We both put down our spoons beside the grapefruit and listened. We were both reduced to tears. I am seldom moved to this extent, not at breakfast, over eggs.

The Fergusson* boy came to tea at Brooks's. He has left Sherborne School now. He is undoubtedly clever. Bespectacled, with a thin face, bushy hair, he speaks with such a low voice that I hear little. But what he has to say is worth listening to. I had to say you must speak up for I am rather deaf. It made no difference. He has got an exhibition at some Oxford college. I suppose he thinks it

---

* James (Jamie) Fergusson, now obituary editor, *The Independent*.

worth while seeing me from time to time. It is good of him if he really does. He is my second cousin once removed. Then dinner at the Hamish Hamiltons* which I hated. Boiling hot so that I could not drink more than half a glass of vin rosé. Chitter-chatter with Yvonne. A. enjoyed every minute. It was 12.30 when we left.

Thursday, 13th January

Since it was pouring this morning I telephoned for a mini-cab to take me to Paddington. A Negro driver rang the doorbell. The inside of the cab was redolent of that sweet stink which Negroes exude and which does not please me. To my horror the driver took me miles out of the way while I was not looking, beyond Shepherd's Bush and on to some motorway. Was I being abducted? Actually we got to the station in time but the long route was quite unnecessary and very expensive. When I questioned it the man in a surly way assured me he knew what he was doing.

Friday, 14th January

As I drove up to our front door [at Alderley] I noticed the first snowdrops of the year, too early, for the weather is far too mild. One little bunch under the drawing-room window nearest the porch. A small, clustered bunch, the buds not yet unfolded, upright glistening white nipples sprung from a green, protective button, and others as yet unborn, the white streaks just beginning to burst from the green sheathes, forming a striped design rather like a Tissot skirt, only in miniature. The incredible whiteness and purity of the flower. It does give a promise of better things to come. It is a marvellous flower, on a par with Mozart for inducing tears.

I am immensely impressed by a passage in Proust's *Captive* (in English of course) where Proust comments on the Vinteuil sonata performed by Morel at the party given by Charlus in Madame Verdurin's house, the party which brings about Charlus's downfall. Proust wonders how such a tremendous work of art can be brought to birth by so much evil. The score was pieced together by the cleverness of the lesbian friend of Vinteuil's daughter, who was the cause of Vinteuil's death through grief over his daughter's liaison.

---

* Hamish (Jamie) Hamilton, 1900–88, publisher, and his wife, Countess Yvonne Pallavicino, who d. 1993.

The sonata is first performed by the unsurpassed artistry of the violinist Morel, himself a totally vicious man, and at the instigation of Charlus whose motive was to strengthen his unnatural passion for Morel. In other words all the participants in the story are supposed to be bad people. Thus good comes out of evil. This is a theme for a novel indeed.

My appreciation of Gerry has appeared in today's *Times* after all. It is not too bad, and I daresay his son and Eny and other friends may not think it laudatory enough. Anyway a great effort on my part was not wasted.

A person cannot deceive others about his origins. Alec Clifton–Taylor said he had little opinion of poor Bertie Towers. 'He pretends to be grander than he is. He pretends that his house is an old manor-house of the Towers. He buys ancestors.' I don't know if these strictures are justified for I barely know Bertie Towers. But if they are, what an ass the man must be. He ought to know that others will see behind his façade. It is easier to know whether a man has ancestors than it is to know his age. How extraordinary that people can so deceive themselves. I believe it is the romance in men which leads them to fabricate illusions about themselves; it is something not reprehensible, but foolish.

Saturday, 15th January

The *Ecologist* paper has come out with a strongly worded declaration, signed by some thirty distinguished scientists, and Peter Scott, to the effect that the population/pollution problem is so grave, so urgent that the signatories may even found a new political party. In my totally ineffectual way I have been labouring on about this very subject, only to be considered a crank. Now letters are written almost daily to *The Times*, and everyone who thinks at all realizes that the future of the earth is literally at stake. The Conservation Society is quoted every week. And when this society of cranks was founded ten years ago and I was on the founding committee, I was actually invited to be the principal speaker at its first annual meeting. Now established scientists like Professor Fraser Darling* are its speakers and Presidents of the Royal Society, to boot.

---

* Sir Frank Fraser Darling, 1903–79, ecologist.

Freda Berkeley asked John Julius Norwich if *Another Self* had been considered for the Duff Cooper award. J.J. said it was, and some of the judges wanted it but were prohibited by the rule that no autobiography qualifies. Well! So the prize goes to G. Grigson* who gave me my only bad review.

At night I can see from my bed, while reading, Fop on his armchair by the door, beneath the tapestry. He reclines his long neck on the right arm, with his sleepy head lolling over it, his eyes screwed up, ears back, looking so peaceful and adorable that sometimes I get out of bed in order to kiss his forehead.

Monday, 17th January

Poor Freda telephoned at breakfast in great anguish because Nicky the youngest boy and A.'s godson has run away. Didn't want to go back to school. Patrick [Kinross] told me last week that on his sixteenth birthday he had his first woman in Patrick's house, in the bedroom of his servant who was away, Patrick half-amused, half-annoyed, but said that Freda knew all about it and was pleased, just as any Continental mother would be. Last week was Berkeley week too, every night there being a performance of Lennox's work, and high tribute to him in the *S. Times* by Desmond [Shawe-Taylor]. Freda so concerned about Nicky's truancy that she could not even speak of Lennox's swimgloat.†
Poor Berkeleys! they are still in the throes of Michael the eldest boy's affair with a girl who has been sent to a home for drug addicts. The three boys are nice boys, but they have been brought up too indulgently.

Tuesday, 18th January

It is extraordinary to think that someone died yesterday, in 1972, who wrote a best-seller in 1890. Daisy Ashford, authoress of that divine book, *The Young Visiters*. It was not however published until 1919 when she was a middle-aged woman of 40. She had lent

---

* Geoffrey Grigson, 1905–85, poet, critic and anthologist.
† 'Swimgloat', a word coined by Logan Pearsall Smith and much used by his literary group, meaning a state of joy experienced by someone who has had a success.

the manuscript to a friend for her amusement. The friend recommended it to a publisher. It sold nearly a million copies and brought a fortune to the authoress. Such an easy and satisfactory way of setting oneself up for middle and old age and acquiring immortality. All the effort at the age of 9.

Thursday, 20th January

Keith Steadman said, dining at Sally's, that he was trying to look at pictures and works of art with his own eyes and not through the eyes of others. I said that my trouble was that I seldom saw them at all. I did not look into pictures enough, and merely derived cursory impressions. Even my own belongings I don't know properly and could not describe them in detail, because I have not looked at them. We agreed that to do what Keith has set out to do may be laudable, but is almost impossible, and I think not necessarily desirable, because we ought to be guided by our qualified understanding of the artists' minds and motives and the periods in which they moved, before venturing to appreciate their creations at all. Without this knowledge our opinions are as worthless as Margery's would be were she asked to give hers on Michelangelo.

I lunched with Eny alone today. She has got a tape recorder and is going to talk into it about her youth in Holland and England before 1914 and some of the people she knew well like Arthur Balfour and 'Jackie' [Admiral Lord] Fisher. I advised her to make a list of the things she wishes to talk about and get her grandson Charlie Hornby (whose idea this is)* to do the same. He must think what questions to put to her in advance. Otherwise she will not know how to begin, or stop.

Eny now very sad about Gerry, and feels great remorse for being so unkind the last time she was with him. When told of his death she imagined she was glad and that it was high time he went, for he had become so cross and disagreeable. Now she realizes that for forty years he was her very best friend whom she had always loved. As she spoke she cried, a thing I did not know she could do. I was moved. I tried to assure her that she had no cause to reproach herself; for when she rebuked Gerry she meant to snap him out of

---

* Charles Hornby, b. 1939, second son of Michael and Nicole(tte) Hornby.

his terrible depression and hatred of everybody-and-thing. I left with her the letters I had received, including one from Field Marshal Templer* asking permission to quote from my tribute in the address he is giving at G.'s memorial service, and asking for any further suggestions what to say.

Friday, 21st January

I remember when a child that there lived a little way behind Ribbesford up the Heightington lane an old woman who had never been in, or seen, a train. Yet Bewdley station was only 2 miles away and the line to Worcester ran just behind the cliff in front of Ribbesford House the far side of the river.

Monday, 24th January

Eny (aged 89) to whom A. said, 'The new motorway is wonderful. I motored from Warwick Avenue to Alderley [110 miles] from door to door, in 1½ hours only,' replied, 'Oh, but people do it in one hour.'

Tuesday, 25th January

Quite a satisfactory day. We reached Cadogan Square car-park by 11.30. I went to the Tate and spent an hour at the Hogarth exhibition. Lunched at Brooks's and to the MHA where I took the chair at a tiny committee, Design and Development. At 6.30 A. called for me in the Fiat and we drove to Covent Garden. Garrett [Drogheda] had forgotten that he did not have the royal box. Nevertheless he managed to get eight seats in the dress circle and to entertain us all to supper in the lower room under the box. *Pelléas and Mélisande*, which I thought I was going to dislike. On the contrary was much moved by its dreamy, tragic flow. Yet I deem Debussy to be largely responsible, albeit unconsciously, for start of the music rot, just as Picasso is largely responsible for the painting rot. In beautiful Pélleas I detect symptoms of the aimless, untuneful rubbishy cacophony by way of most opera today.

---

* Field-Marshal Sir Gerald Templer, 1898–1979.

I sat next to Loelia [Lindsay].* Mrs Heinz (baked beans?) very jolly, said that John Foster† read extracts of my book to a house party at which she was a participant. She said, he was the best reader she know. 'Now you've simply got to follow up this book, James, and not rest on your laurels,' she advised me, a bit late in the day. While she was talking I was thinking of John Foster when I last watched him on television interviewing that bitch Bernadette Devlin. It was embarrassingly clear that he was greatly attracted by her physically. I know that lecherous look men assume when they lust. Loelia contradicted me when I surmised that Winston Churchill was a chaste man. Far from it, she said, and she mentioned Wendy Reeves. Yes, I said, that was merely an old man's fancy, nothing physical. 'Don't you believe it,' and she told this story. Lady Churchill and Daisy Fellowes were discussing the infatuation in the South of France while Sir Winston was sleeping. 'What can he see in her? She is common, vulgar, and hardly pretty,' Lady Churchill was saying. At that moment Sir Winston opened an eye, and said, 'She is more desirable than either of you two,' and fell asleep again.

Wednesday, 26th January

Spent the greater part of the day at no. 21 Portman Square in which John Harris‡ has set himself up with the RIBA collection of drawings. Here in these lovely surroundings he is quite independent. He sits in an upstairs, first-floor room with curved angles overlooking the back garden. The room is hung with portraits of famous architects and with busts of Wren and Inigo Jones. The telephone rings and John very graciously agrees to give audiences. He has just returned from India and Japan, I mean a fortnight ago, whereas last week he flew to America to see Mr Mellon§ for whom he acts. Another telephone call, and he explains he has to go to Buckingham Palace to see the Queen. I am sitting humbly in his room the while, looking through Westonbirt papers and letters.

---

* Hon. Loelia Ponsonby, 1902–1993, wife of Sir Martin Lindsay, Bt., of Dowhill (m.1969), and previously of 2nd Duke of Westminster (1930–47).
† Sir John Foster, 1903–82, QC, MP. Fellow of All Souls, Oxford.
‡ John Harris, b. 1931, architectural historian.
§ Paul Mellon, American millionaire and art collector.

J. has got far from Geoffrey Houghton-Brown's antique shop in the Fulham Road on his undoubted abilities. He deserves all the tribute and glory he has won.

Friday, 28th January

Saddened but not distraught to read the announcement of Bridget's [Parsons] sudden death. Freda Berkeley saw her at the Duff Cooper prize-giving on Monday which surprises me for I thought she was immobile, and she was dead on Wednesday. Thirty years ago her death would have been a cruel blow, but now, no, for she had died some years ago to me and most of her friends. When I think of the awesome, positively amorphous lump of flesh which had been that bright vision, identical with Desmond [her brother] whom I dearly loved, I rail against time. I was, in the war days, semi-in love with Bridget who to me was an incarnation in the strangest way of Desmond. Both were in my mind when I wrote my novel. It is dreadful how one can be unmoved by the deaths of those to whom one was deeply devoted in years gone by.

Saturday, 29th January

Such an extraordinary day. At 10 I telephoned Doris Solly* to ask if I could see over Hector Lees's house tomorrow, Sunday, instead of Monday, the viewing day as I had mistakenly supposed. She said viewing day was today, Saturday. So Eardley staying here gallantly said he would accompany me. We jumped into the car and by 12.45 reached Congleton where we snacked in a pub. Called on Doris Solly, Hector's first cousin who lives in a glorified villa outside Congleton. She, a dear little brown mouse, kindly conducted us to the gate of Hector's house, a middling Victorian pile in a park, called The Moor House, Biddulph. To our dismay the roads around all blocked with cars. We had to walk through the park. Never have I seen such crowds. E. could not face it and having struggled into the hall left, saying he had claustrophobia. The smell of human flesh ghastly. I couldn't even get up to the bedroom floors for the crowds. Almost impossible to see the things

---

* Doris Solly, née Lees, and Colonel Hector Lees of Alkrington (1900–71), cousins.

displayed. However I left a few bids for some family things, including Lewis Carroll letters – to Cousin Connie I think – which I shan't get. Now why these immense crowds for Hector's house? The numbers frightening. Is it because they are drawn to see how the lesser gentry lived, and to see, handle and covet ordinary things made by craftsmen in the last century for the most part, and several earlier? The Moor House is not a stately home. Eardley said the reason is probably the television programme, *Going for a Song*, which that old ass Arthur Negus* conducts. I think he is probably right. On our way home a fullish moon was sailing on our left. We drove at a spanking speed when half an hour later I noticed the moon was sailing on our right. It is true we had crossed, as I thought, a roundabout, but turned too far. We were in fact driving back the way we had come.

Monday, 31st January

I wish I could remember which of my Lees forebears it was of whom my father told me the following story. (The trouble is that when one is young one does not bother to listen; is bored by parental anecdote.) Anyway he was a direct ancestor. He had a ne'er-do-well friend to whom he lent a largish sum of money which was never repaid. The friend then, to everyone's relief, went across the Atlantic to America. Years later my (?) gt-gt-grandfather received a solicitor's letter, or deed, entitling him to several hundred acres of land which the friend had in recompense bequeathed him. The land was on Long Island. My Lees grandfather was so enraged at not getting back his money that he threw the document in the fire.

Today bitterly cold, and snow. The flakes tumble noiselessly down. Before shutting of windows this evening the blackbirds made the hell of a caterwauling, but no other birds or cats were preying on them. Can they be mating in this freezing weather?

Thursday, 3rd February

The Irish are unmitigated philistines as well as barbarians. I felt sick last night watching on television the crowds burning the British Embassy in Dublin, that beautiful Georgian house in beautiful Merrion Square. Beautiful because built, not by them, oh no, but

---

* Arthur Negus, auctioneer, antique dealer and broadcaster.

by the English Ascendancy who built, chiefly in the eighteenth century, all the architecture worth looking at in their benighted country. The venom with which they threw petrol inside the house and jubilantly cheered the destruction made me loathe them. The whole business in Ireland is sickening. I telephoned Midi after I had watched and she said the Irish were less civilized than the most backward African tribes. She said, 'I wish we would leave the country to cut its own throat.' But I said what about your nephew Raymond O'Neill* at Shane's and our friends like the Rosses at Birr, and the Beits at Russborough? She said it would be too bad, 'but they must leave the country and sacrifice their houses and estates. After all Shane's Castle was burnt down in the 1920s. Let it be burnt again. And as for those people who have gone to Ireland to evade taxation in this country, this is a gamble they must take.' Midi is as vitriolic about the Irish as I am – she born O'Neill too. I think it was Tennyson who said, if he had his way, he would tow the whole island into mid-Atlantic and cut it up into small pieces.

It is utterly incomprehensible how foreign countries can blame England for the loss of the thirteen lives in Derry, when the Civil Rights march was contravening the law forbidding it, whereas for years now our soldiers and the police and innocent persons have been butchered by the IRA without protest from the Church and government in Eire.

Friday, 4th February

One mustn't curry favour with the young by tending to agree with their views when one honestly doesn't. It can be a temptation, even when they are not attractive. Last night at the Bath Preservation Trust meeting I sat next to young Joan Smithers, whose heart is in the right place although her body smells horribly. She feels violently, as I do, against the philistinism of the Bath Corporation, but goes too far. Unwashed and filthy clothes.

Mary McNeile has died. A dear, gentle, kind woman, married to that sarcastic brute, my Eton housemaster, Archie McNeile. While I was with Desmond Parsons† for the last time – he then dying at the age of 27 – I told him about McNeile's death. This was in

---

* Raymond, 4th Lord O'Neill, b. 1933, of Shane's Castle, Co. Antrim.
† Hon. Desmond Parsons, 1910–37, brother of Michael Rosse.

1937. He said, and his eyes brightened. 'This news really does make me feel better.' I remember being shocked. Mary Arbuthnot was at a girls' coming-out place in Dresden with Mama who was fond of her. Hence my being sent to her husband's Eton house.

Saturday, 12th February

In Brooks's before luncheon Everard Radcliffe[*] appeared. I had not seen him since his fall over the staircase at Rudding [Park] and severe illness that followed. He said he was waiting for Peter Chance[†] who was lunching with him, in order to discuss the sale of all his wonderful possessions. He is definitely selling Rudding [Hall] and, so he maintains, everything inside it in one clear swoop. Arrangements had been made by him to give or leave the place to the National Trust. Instead he made over everything to his son Charlie who was brilliantly clever and whom he adored. But Charlie dying at the age of 21 left it all back to him again. So Everard has had to pay death duties or capital gains, which he already had to do lately on his father's death, and is in consequence ruined. Such is the legislation in this egalitarian country. E. is a tragic figure, prisoner-of-war pursued by th'abhorred shears.

After the Trust meetings on Wednesday I went to Chesterfield by train; was met and driven to Chatsworth for two nights. The following day spent at Sudbury. Three Mitford sisters, Debo, Diana and Pam staying at Chats. Together they seem very affected until one gets 'into' the Mitford swing and then it's difficult to get out of it. When I left on Friday morning Debo said, 'Diana is a saint nowadays, definitely a saint. I am the first to admit that previously she was anything but.' I do not forget her pro-Nazi sentiments. But then Tom Mosley has definitely changed from the bombastic pseudo-Mussolini to the calm, wise, elder statesman. Diana told me that somebody was writing a life of Tom Mosley and that they were giving him help. Then she said with a seraphic look, 'He is inserting that disobliging piece you wrote about Kit.' All I did was to make a face. I was not going to excuse myself. Thought it best to change the subject. Did not want to cause

---

[*] Sir Everard Radcliffe, 6th Bt., 1910–75.
[†] I. O. Chance (Peter), 1910–84, chairman of Christies, 1973–6, and chairman of the Georgian Group, 1968–80.

further offence by having to say that what I wrote then was what I felt then. Time is not always the enemy.

A. telephoned me at Chatsworth on her return from staying with Nancy in Versailles with bad news of her. Diana said, 'I look upon you as a brother.' What heavenly forgiveness.

She had flown from America the day I arrived at Chats. One American said to her, 'What did your father *do* to produce such brilliant children?' Diana said he did nothing. 'What job did he have?' 'Oh,' said Diana, 'he didn't have one. Englishmen don't work, you know.' Tom Mosley told her she should not have said this. She should have said that her father, because he was a landowner, was a farmer.

Debo wants John Fowler to be made a knight. I think this a very good idea, and he deserves it. It would give him pleasure too.

I never get over the Chatsworth Weather Report Book, entered every single morning in a meticulous copybook hand, on the sideboard in the breakfast room. The temperature, the condition, fog, how much sunshine, frost, rainfall of the past twenty-four hours. Even throughout the war this book was scrupulously entered, although none of the family lived in the house.

Wednesday, 16th February

Plunged into acute depression by the political situation. The electricity supply in the country can only last another fortnight. Already we are strictly rationed, and the current is cut off for hours each day. Yet the miners refuse to return to work pending negotiations by the enquiry set up and the offer of an immediate increase of £3 per week. What I cannot understand is why they are allowed to picket other industries and prevent supplies being admitted. I suppose it can't be stopped because there are not enough soldiers or police, and even if there were their presence would invite civil war. In fact defiance of authority and law-breaking are so prevalent that the government dare not enforce the law. A jolly state of affairs we are reduced to.

Last Monday I attended a luncheon given by the Bath trustees to Professor Colin Buchanan.* For an hour he answered questions. I raised the final question which was greeted with laughter, the

---

* Professor Sir Colin Buchanan, b. 1907, planning consultant.

laughter of derision. I said I would like to know from Sir Colin why he thought Bath must not be allowed to become a dead city. I would like to see Bath become as dead as a doornail. Then the people who now move to the periphery to live in new estates might return to the centre. I would like Bath to become purely residential for retired people and workers in Bristol. The rejoinder I received was, 'If I had pressed this view the Bath Council would never have employed me.' I said, 'Bath ought to become another Venice or a large Broadway for tourists and residents.'

Saturday, 19th February

Had to meet the architect at Pythouse [Dorset] on Thursday to consider his proposals for making two additional apartments, neither of which schemes could I approve. The one involved making a new window and a raised attic storey on a wing, the other cutting up the charming library with its recessed arcaded bays for shelves. The silly fool of a young man has no clue as to the importance of this house, and no appreciation whatsoever of Georgian architecture. Doesn't even realize that plate-glass windows in this Georgian house are wrong. It was strange while upstairs to see a closed door with a card pinned to it and the name Miss M. [Monica] Baldwin. This was her room until a week or two ago, from which she wrote me so many letters. The house secretary asked if I wanted to go inside. I said yes, and he got the key. It is no more than a cell, and although quite empty except for a plain frameless mirror on one wall, yet gave an indication of her character, meticulous, tidy, conventual and scrupulously neat. But the atmosphere inside this little cubicle was tense. I felt a contact with her which I can't explain. It is all the more mysterious that we have never met.

With these repeated blackouts when the electricity is cut off for hours at a time we are reduced to candles. How beautiful the golden light they shed. How mysterious and solemn the flickering shadows they induce. While we walk up and down our stairs the big shadows of the banisters move against the white walls of the hall softly and across the portraits fearfully. Suddenly a white face is looking at you, then retreats into shadow again. I find reading by candlelight difficult, and A. finds it impossible. How did they manage in old days? Those over 30 didn't. Couldn't.

Tuesday, 22nd February

Yesterday I noticed the first daffodil out on the lawn in front of the house. It is full out but looks solitary, lonely and already perishing. It must regret its rash delivery for it is bitterly cold in a sleety way. We have had an unhealthily muggy winter hitherto and everything is far too early.

A prospective lady housekeeper came yesterday afternoon for an interview. The conversation and ritual are always the same. Please come into the library we both say. Did you find the way all right? Idiotic remark because otherwise they wouldn't be here. After asking the same questions we receive the same answers. Yes, I don't mind dogs, so long as I am not expected to take them for walks. No, of course not. I don't mind a little cooking; I'm not cordon bleu. Thank goodness, we think but do not say. Where have you been? At Mrs So-and-So's for six weeks, Mrs X's for five months, Mrs T's for three months (they have never been anywhere for long). And why are you leaving Mrs So-and-So now? Because I never have five minutes to myself. Am never off my feet. I have to take breakfast up to ten people in bed, nurse Mr So-and-So who is incontinent, wash him, dress him, take him for walks, etc., etc. 'If I may interpose' (a favourite expression), 'I would like two days off a week for hunting.' 'Yes, I would bring my own horse. And then if I may have my two step-children for weekends. They're no trouble.' The moment the applicant has gone we telephone the So-and-Sos. They say, 'Don't quote us,' and after a pregnant pause add, 'Don't touch her. She drinks, is a thief, is bone idle, complains ceaselessly.' Actually yesterday's lady we quite liked and she seemed to want to come to us. Looking out of the window she said, 'What lovely lilies of the valley you have.' 'They are snowdrops – actually.' 'Oh, is that what they are? I love the country and country things. What a lot of books you have. Have you read them all?' 'Yes, all.' 'And do they require dusting?' Pause. 'I see you like antiques. I like antiques too within limits.' Oh God, the boredom of the conversation.

In bed last night I read from Tom Rolt's remarkable book, *The Clouded Mirror*, the following quotation from Traherne: 'It is no blasphemy to say that God cannot make a god; the greatest thing that he can make is his image, a most perfect creature, to enjoy the most perfect treasures, in the most perfect manner.' In a flash I thought I understood by this statement why we Christians have to believe in a personal God. Because a human being however seldom he is a perfect creature, is potentially divine. If this creature of flesh and blood and with a mind has potential divinity then he can only rank with God. There can be nothing superior to him. He is God or a part of God; and this is what saints presumably are. What an elevating thought, and a sobering one too, that man has the equipment, is given the latitude to become God, and so seldom exercises it, so seldom takes up the opportunity, but rejects it wittingly, knowingly. Written on paper like this it seems impossible that anyone should be either so stupid or so wicked as not to want to be God, given every chance. Yet how few, if one person in a generation, achieve this. Now, in another flash, my intimation that God is a personal God has gone again. I can't see why he should or could possibly be such a debasing thing. I wish a theologian would explain to me in a simple shown-to-the-children manner.

Saturday, 26th February

Jack Rathbone told me that Desmond S.-T. left his motor outside their house in Regent's Park for two hours after dark. He noticed that there was a workman's hole in the road with a rail and lamp to prevent motorists and pedestrians falling into it. When he returned to his car he found that the rail had been removed and the oil lamp thrown through the windscreen, smashing it to smithereens but luckily not setting fire to the car. As Jack said, No further comment is necessary.

Pat Gibson* told him that Jo Gormley,† the Miners' Trade Union boss, said to Pat that if he had been able to offer the miners a £3 rise when they first asked they would have accepted it. Instead of which they ultimately got an enormous rise after bringing the country to the brink of disaster and engendering a bitterness which will last for a generation, if not longer.

O'Neill, the nice man who looked after the Droghedas at the Royal Box at Covent Garden, is dead. He had a motor accident in

---

* Lord Gibson, b. 1916, chairman of the National Trust, 1977–86.
† Jo(seph) Gormley, 1917–93, president of the NUM, 1971–82. Created a life peer, Lord Gormley, in 1982.

the Cromwell Road. My first reaction on learning the news was how sad, such a decent fellow, and the second was, 'That puts an end to my embarrassment wondering whether each time I am invited to the box I ought to continue giving him the £1 tip which I foolishly made a precedent years ago, and indeed whether it is even enough.' What a beast I am. Joan [Drogheda] says he had taken to the bottle and was frequently extremely drunk. She rang up his mother-in-law to condole and received the reply that she could not care less.

A pretty girl got into the tube opposite me. She was wearing an enamel button with the words, 'It is wrong to eat people' on it. What can it mean? Allow people to eat you? Some leftish slogan I can only assume.

We stayed two nights with the Graftons at Euston. What a good, decent, public-spirited, high-principled pair they are. She with her duties on the juvenile courts, her family, Household and royal waitings. He with his endless committees and chairmanships. Billa [Harrod], likewise staying, says he never refuses an invitation to address an amenity society. Feels impelled by an irrepressible urge. He is great fun to be with and has a wry, not un-sly humour. Yet disapproving of course. Architecturally Euston is a mess. Made so by the clumsy way his father demolished three-quarters of it. The family portraits make a superb collection.

I ponder, do I like pornography? In literature, honestly hardly at all, because I find the written word unexciting, on the contrary boring. But in photography I am afraid Yes, so long as it is not vulgar, or subversive, which may sound a strange adjective. By this I mean that I don't approve of obscene photographs calculated to corrupt, or lead to violence; those which merely titillate the appetites and are of beautiful people strike me as harmless. If the participants are ugly and the actions vile then I am revolted. Do I write contradictory cant?

Monday, 28th February

Elspeth Huxley says 'Of course there must be millions of earths similar to ours in the Universe, and with life on them.' She sees no reason to look upon our earth as important; and considers its ultimate destruction to be of little moment. No bad thing it seems. Our earth is like an apple being eaten by maggots. The maggots increase by devouring the apple which then falls to pieces, hollow and empty. The maggots then die for lack of sustenance. The sun sees to the remains. This is happening with us.

I am finishing the last Proust novel, thank goodness. It is a great struggle to keep the attention fixed. Sometimes I feel on the verge of inspiration to write a work of genius myself, such is the effect Proust has upon me. But the wave disappears without my quite realizing what the inspiration is about. The trouble is that difficult though Proust be he has expressed practically every thought that has occurred to me, with a thousand others besides.

I think at times of my callow unkindness to Mama during the closing years of her life, with much remorse. I recall walking with her from La Meridienne to Roquebrune village and her making what I considered heavy weather in climbing the gentle slope under the archway. Now I puff when I have jumped off the sofa and run upstairs for something. On returning to the sofa my heart thumps and I am breathless. It is difficult to summon sympathy for others when one is feeling well and normal. When Harold [Nicolson] was in his dotage I did feel profoundly sorry and distressed to see him in that condition, and even humble that I, so far his inferior, should be all right; yet I did not sympathize to the extent of not forgetting his dreadful misery by the time I had left Sissinghurst and was back in the train to London and having a jolly evening with friends.

Tuesday, 29th February

Motored to Aynho [Northants.] to see what exactly the proposed new flats for the Mutual Households Association will involve. If they threaten the architecture of this house in any sense then I shall veto them, for luckily I am chairman of the small committee concerned with the fabric of MHA houses. On the way just before Barnsley I gave a lift to an old woman who was standing on the road verge waving an umbrella. It was raining. Although after my experience in Edinburgh last September I vowed never again to give *anyone* a lift I couldn't refuse this old creature. Well, she stank. Never mind. Then she said I have a dreadful cold; can you lend me a 'tissue', the first time I had heard the use of the word in that context. No, I said, thinking she meant my handkerchief. Then she spun a hard-luck story and asked for the loan of £2. I never lend money, I said. Oh, but I'm sure the Catholic priest in Cardiff

would have lent me £2 if he had been at home last night when I
called. But he wasn't in, I said. Since she was going to Oxford I
was able to drop her on the main road when I turned off for
Burford. Again she asked for money. Eyeing the crook of her
umbrella with some apprehension I handed her a pound, for which
she was not the least grateful; and was rather cross in fact. Next
time I doubt whether I shall give a lift even to an old woman.

Friday, 3rd March

Before I left for London on Wednesday *The Times* telephoned.
Would I write an appreciation of Violet Trefusis[*] who was dying?
This I did not know. In fact she died that very day. The editor said
that Patrick Kinross had been asked and refused. When in London
I asked Patrick why. He said he never knew Violet in the old days.
Neither did I. The following day there was a short obituary notice,
so I again asked the obituary editor if an appreciation was really
necessary. He said Yes and considered she was a figure of sufficient
importance to merit one although he knew absolutely nothing
about her. I am trying hard to get out of this for I did not know
V. very well, or really like her. She was the most opinionated,
self-praising person, very mischievous and even cruel. It will be
amusing to learn to whom she has bequeathed her possessions. She
adored teasing us all with promises. The last time we were at the
Ombrellino she told me she would leave me the Prince Regent's
snuff box. But I supposed this was nonsense. Her chief claims to
fame cannot be included in an obituary[†], namely her elopement
with Vita, and her appalling conduct towards her friends. What in
her favour? Wit, yes, and puns. Could be very funny. Vanity
engaging. 'Do admire my shoulders.' She was a romantic, living in
a world of her special fantasy, a sort of Ronald Firbank world, like
Daisy Fellowes. People who lead fantasy lives are not usually
estimable, but given to deceit.

At *The Flying Dutchman* last night. Joan Drogheda in the royal
box. Act 1 most tedious. I was sitting with Rosamond [Lehmann]
in the annexe box. She kept whispering, 'When will it end?' I said,

[*] Violet Trefusis, 1894–1972, daughter of Col. the Hon. George and
Mrs (Alice) Keppel, novelist and resident in Florence.
[†] J.L.-M. was writing this in 1972.

'When will it begin?' for as yet there had been no incident and the Dutchman was rambling on with a boring soliloquy which was insupportable. 'Get a move on,' I felt like shouting. The second and third acts were however enjoyable. Senta was a Swede called Caterina Ligendza, with a splendid voice to raise the roof. A very beautiful woman like Diana Mosley. So alike that all my inhibited love for Diana when I was 19 and she 17 surged within me. It is interesting how an operatic performance can revive emotions experienced nearly half a century ago, albeit less dramatically. Unlike Diana's her clothes were awful. Debenham & Freebody's said Ros.

David Carritt* was there. Very pleased with himself. Much to be pleased about of course. Can be funny, but too consciously so, too perky and sharp. A show-off. I shall never forget the first time I met him at old Lord Bearsted's Upton House when he was an undergraduate. He burst into the house like a whirlwind, rushed round all the rooms, knew where each picture hung although he had never been to Upton in his life, contradicted Lord B.'s attributions in the catalogue, gave his own opinions (which, to make matters worse, were correct), made us gasp, and swept away leaving us like broken huts after a tornado.

Saturday 4th March

Eardley found himself outside the window of Mr Fish's smart man's clothes shop three evenings ago. It was 5.10 p.m. He thought he would be bold and go inside this shop for the first time in his life, 'but I dread being mocked by the trendy young men. Shall I? Shan't I?' Summoning great courage he did. Hardly inside when Mr Fish himself appeared; clapped his hands and announced, to the assembled customers: 'Gentlemen, in twenty minutes this shop will close, for ever. You may take away anything in the shop for £2, but I can't accept cheques.' Eardley had £16 in his pocket, and came away with eight most beautiful silk shirts, labelled £14 each. He staggered off to a picture gallery in the same street. There were two millionaire dealers who asked him what he had been buying. Eardley told them. They immediately dropped their coats and umbrellas and dashed to Mr Fish's where they bought the remainder of the goods not yet snapped up by the other customers.

---

* David Carritt, 1927–82, art historian, critic and founder of the Artemis Gallery.

Eardley is going to be 70 this autumn. When I came back from the opera at midnight and told him about Ros's dress and how put out the dear old thing was by being eclipsed by Joan, in spite of her sweet way of pretending to be indifferent, he rolled off the bed with laughter. While I was brushing my teeth in the bathroom he continued roaring. No one I know roars like Eardley. No one I know is happier.

Sunday, 5th March

The same cannot be said of Ros whom I found most depressed. I said to her, it is a terrible thing to realize that adventure can never happen to one any more. One used to go out to dinner with that faint, sweet anticipation that possibly one might meet someone with whom one might go home, even to bed, and with whom one might have a lasting affair. She sighed and said, you still might darling. Not on my life, I answered. She said she had no one in her life, now Jim Mossman was dead, whom she deeply loved. 'Of course I love my old friends shallowly,' she said, 'but I am not in love with any of them. Whereas you are still capable of falling in love, aren't you?' 'Yes, I am capable,' I said. 'But that's all.'

Rory [Cameron] has written to A. from Cap Ferrat that he is wretched because of his French lover leaving him and feels as though his inside were filled with concrete. A. is not the best person to elicit sympathy from in this particular case. 'How could he? That dreadful creature too.' I thought he was a dreadful creature when I met him at Rory's two years ago, an ignorant, second-rate peasant. But that is beside the point. R. loves him and is utterly miserable. Like all people deeply in love he is mad, and not responsible for his feelings, or actions. Nevertheless he makes a mistake in telling all his friends, male and female, about his prostration.

Tuesday, 7th March

I said to Brian Gascoigne* that the spring still upsets me – that detestable spring as Constantia Fenwick† called it. He said it upset him too; that it reproached him. I said, presumably because you feel, here is this old earth which has rejuvenated itself, and is ready

---

* Brian Gascoigne, b. 1943, second son of Derick and Midi Gascoigne.
† Constantia Fenwick, wife of Ralph Arnold, publisher and biographer. She d. 1993.

again, whereas you, etc. He said, yes, that's the reason. He must be about 25 or 26. He wears his hair below shoulder length. It must infuriate poor old father Derick.

Thursday, 9th March

Driving to the station on Tuesday up the Tresham lane we saw a rainbow of spectacular beauty. In fact it was a double rainbow, the outer arc being – like the inner – complete, although fainter. The inner bow was the clearest thing I ever saw. Moreover it was quite close, for at one moment the northern end started at Newark Lower Lodge and the southern dropped into the valley below Tresham village where the cowslips are and where I walk in the spring with the whippets. For a minute it stood still, then retreated in that elusive manner of rainbows and suddenly, like the Cheshire cat, vanished. The sun was full out behind us, and ahead was a purple-dark storm cloud. Eardley, to whom I recounted this experience, said that the arc is the mirrored outline of the sun in the sky, and not of the earth's circumference.

Went last night to the Handley-Read collection of Victoriana at the Diploma Gallery. The hideousness and stuffiness of the furniture and ornaments beyond belief – sheer lodging-house, and no wonder both Handley-Reads committed suicide last year. Their house was apparently stuffed with these ghastly things to the exclusion of everything else. I wonder if the admirers of the style honestly find beauty, or merely amusement in it. I am too close to the Victorian age to be capable of swallowing Burges, Godwin, Teulon & Co., or I should say of detaching for disinterested assessment their artefacts, and their architecture, from antimacassars, dundrearies, woollen combinations and all frowstiness. Yet when it comes to Tudoresque Westonbirt, about which I am writing articles for *Country Life*, I can rhapsodize.

Having returned home from London I was struck by the scent of flowers as by a smart blow. Jasmine and freesias, grown by A. in pots in the hall. She is a marvel the way she produces, as though by wave of wand, exotic profusion.

Listened in bed to Raymond Leppard* conducting Haydn's *Creation*. Between the movements Raymond spoke to a commentator

---

* Raymond Leppard, b. 1927, conductor, harpsichordist and composer.

about Haydn who is his hero, his genius. I thought this man – Leppard – is one of the most attractive personalities in the art world I know. But I wish I knew him better. He is extremely sensitive, totally without bombast and show-off, deeply sincere, dedicated, humorous, generous with his information and highly intelligent. Jim Mossman told how sincerely he loved him. Merely listening to his voice and the diffident yet confident way in which he spoke about Haydn induced a thrill, a need to find out more about Haydn for myself. Now I understand why people can profit from lectures, for the personality of the lecturer may set them off on rewarding trails which a book may not do (or contrariwisely can put them off for ever).

Saturday, 11th March

Winterspring Lane behind the village is bright with glossy, shiny celandines, their little heads peering through the long dry grasses of the steep banks. The first I noticed were on the last day of February, surely a record and the consequence of an extremely mild winter. Now it is bitterly cold with cutting wind, the usual accompaniment of March.

Penelope [Betjeman]* telephones to say they are leaving Wantage and she doesn't know where she is going to live. Says John will never tear himself away from London and will die there in harness; that he hates going away for weekends and so seldom comes to Wantage (I did not tell her he was staying with us next weekend – and with Elizabeth [Cavendish]) and he would rather she took a small house miles off, possibly in the Welsh Marches where he could retire for months on end. It is extraordinary how people deceive themselves. Poor Penelope, surely she must realize that John does not want to live with her permanently. And surely she must know that on the contrary he goes off weekend after weekend with E., and to his Cornish house for weeks at a time. I suppose it is pride which makes women cling to delusions of this sort rather than face the truth. Yet P. is eminently sensible, and likes her independence.

---

* Hon. Penelope Chetwode, 1910–1986, daughter of Field Marshal Lord Chetwode, m. 1933 John Betjeman. Traveller in and writer on India.

Monday, 13th March

There is a grossness in drinking which I dislike. And I can't pretend that I don't. Robin [Fedden] stayed last night, arriving at 7.15 from Chippenham where I met him. In the course of the evening he drank half a bottle of whisky, one bottle of red wine, two glasses of port and one of brandy. Not only is it extremely expensive for the hosts but uncivilized in that it means he can have no palate for good wine, which is wasted on him. It also means that we don't crave to have him to stay again in a hurry. Yet I am fond of Robin, greatly admire his intelligence and ability, and envy his stamina. This morning he was down to breakfast at 8.30 fresh as a daisy (which is also tiresome). How does he do it?

Wednesday, 15th March

It is an extraordinary spring. Three days ago it was perishing, with a violent east wind so that for the first time this winter I took out my old Chinese fox fur-lined coat. Now it is boiling hot. There were swarms of bees this morning about the blue-and-white striped crocuses. A thrush has built a nest in the usual place on the wall to the left of the garden house. A. says it may not lay eggs for another few weeks. Why then build so early?

Robin says the reason for the prevalent violence is that there has been no war for over a generation; that even during the nineteenth century there were wars within the Empire in which the young could let off steam against the natives, viz. Zulus. He complains that all the young dress to look like refugees. Robin is a good dandy.

Thursday, 16th March

Dining at the Robinsons sat next to Mary Anna Marten.* She has some strong appeal. I don't know that she is strictly beautiful although her head is very splendid: piles of raven-black hair, and she carries herself and moves like a queen. Has a whimsical smile, is earnest, intense and intelligent. She talks with uncompromising politeness which is always a little disconcerting. Puts one in one's place. I am intrigued.

---

* Hon. Mary Anna Sturt, m. 1949 Commander G.G. Marten, MP.

Friday, 17th March

Am asked to write an article on Bath for *The Times*, a full page, illustrated with photographs specially taken by Tony Snowdon. I rang him up at Jeremy Fry's* where he is staying, to consult. He had spent the day going round Bath, seeing for himself the recent devastation and meeting the Mayor, Planning Officer, Chancellor of the University and the bag of tricks. He said, 'I hope this line is not bugged. But Stutchbury is a fiend, and Casson has no taste whatever.' Then went on to say that Adam Fergusson,† who is writing the pendant article to mine about what Bath is doing to itself today, criticized Stutchbury‡ for not mentioning the work of Colen Campbell in Russia, if you please, in his boring book on Campbell. 'Boring the book is, I agree, but Campbell never worked in Russia that I am aware of. Are you sure you don't mean Charles Cameron?' 'God!' Tony exclaimed. 'Jeremy agreed with us too about this,' then turned to Jeremy who came on the telephone. 'Have we really made this mistake?' 'Yes,' I said, 'it seems you may have.' Then went on about something else. Their two voices sounded much alike on the telephone. 'Who am I talking to now?' I asked, bewildered. 'Charles Cameron,' came the answer. 'Now it's Campbell speaking.' 'Stutchbury here,' I said. The conversation ended rather foolishly.

Last night at dusk from the front door there rose above the poplar trees the new moon with the old moon in its arms (Shelley?). The outline of the old moon was clearly visible like a great opal or dark grey pearl, very faintly rimmed with a tiny thread of gold. Venus was blazing away next door. As it grew darker the old moon's outline vanished. I do not remember experiencing this before.

Saturday, 18th March

John Betj. and Eliz. Cavendish to stay the weekend. I met them at Kemble. John now shuffles instead of walks, such short shuffles that he scarcely raises his feet. It is a habit, he admits, but it is a sad one. We tease him about it. Cruel, I hope not. Feeble [Elizabeth

---

* Jeremy Fry, inventor and entrepreneur.

† Adam Fergusson, b. 1932, writer and conservationist.

‡ Howard Stutchbury, Bath city planning officer. Author of *The Architecture of Colen Campbell* (1967).

Cavendish] and I walking with the whippets round the valley below Winner Hill and Foxholes saw hounds the other side of the valley. A still and beautiful afternoon, we could hear the voices of huntsmen clearly, that high-pitched, querulous note. She said, 'That's David Somerset's voice, swearing at someone or something. I could never be mistaken.' Half an hour later, back in the house I heard his aeroplane buzzing us overhead. I ran out to the front and waved my paper. I saw David's profile clearly as he circled over us a second time. He and Caroline and Jeremy Fry dined. Enjoyable evening. Jeremy left first because tomorrow morning he is flying to Bangladesh at dawn. I saw him off to the door where he embraced me on both cheeks. I said, 'Don't forget the clock goes forward an hour tonight. One hour less sleep.' 'God,' he said, 'I never knew that, and would have missed my plane if you hadn't told me.' We talked, the rest of us, about drugs till midnight. Caroline and David smoked one evening, not a reefer, but a whole marijuana cigarette each. She said she had no heightened sensations at all. She heard David say, Take off all your clothes. Which she did. He was then sick.

Sunday, 19th March

Olive Lloyd-Baker* at luncheon today said, apropos hereditary privilege, 'An ounce of heredity is worth a pound of merit.' 'Gosh! that's good,' John Betj. said. 'Did you invent that?' 'Yes,' she said, 'just now.'

Tuesday, 21st March

I asked John if he ever saw Lionel Perry† these days. He recited:

> 'Literary Lionel while sitting in his den
> Was visited by lots and lots of homosexual men.'

My love for J.B. is very deep. I am sure that hundreds of his friends like to believe they are the chief confidant and the one person with whom he is most happy. I don't kid myself to this extent. But I am sure that I am one of his fairly intimate friends. With him confidences pour out, fun, folly, tears, wisdom, recitation, reading

---

* Olive Lloyd-Baker of Hardwicke Hall, Gloucester, a neighbour.
† Lionel Perry, Irish landowner and old friend of John Betjeman.

of extracts from the *DNB*, *Burke's Peerage*, shouts of laughter, jokes about Irish peers, his friends, fear of the after-life and God's retribution, total disbelief in the whole thing, genuine deep devotion to the Church, hatred of Papistry, what a mixture. What torments he suffers, what enjoyment he extracts from life. I wish he were not so physically collapsed. He has a huge paunch, which means shrunken everything else, and the shuffling! He and Feeble no longer keep up a pretence that they are not totally and permanently attached. She does not ever seem to get bored, or irritated by his ceaseless fantasies. Just worships him.

Walking to church he said, I wonder what the bell-ringer will look like. I said boy bell-ringers must be plain, spotty and wear spectacles. Yes, he said, 'Men don't make passes at boys wearing glasses.' We were mistaken about the pimples and spectacles. Our bell-ringer was a very pretty little boy with a cream complexion. After Matins Gilbert Wheat the Headmaster buttonholed John who was made to go to Rosehill [School] for coffee. The boys came up with autograph books. J. is pursued wherever he goes. At Westonbirt during the afternoon I took him inside. In the library the girls were poring over their books. One with flaming red hair and wearing blue jeans was lolling lasciviously across a table. She sent him into ecstacies. These thrills and what he calls letchings are sheer fantasy, I presume.

A. must be moving about. The most restless of mortals, she has to run. While we were watching the telly she got up, dashed to the kitchen, tripped on the loose rug in the passage and fell flat on her front. It was a dreadful thing to witness. I picked her up. She was shaken. Last week she bent down over a pot of some plant and the stake went into her eye. She is accident prone. Yesterday she fell off her ladder in the garden. One day she will injure herself badly. It worries me. It is very, very dreadful to me to see her off balance so to speak. She ought never to be hurt or injured. I can't bear the thought.

Wednesday, 22nd March

The spring weather is divine, we are both well and are leaving tomorrow for our first stage of a fortnight abroad. I ought in all reason to be happy. Instead I am sad, sad, sad, as though teetering on the edge of an abyss.

Thursday, 6th April

I write this with my new typewriter. It feels very heavy and strange in spite of the assurances given me by the nice Mr Griffith in Bath who induced me to part with my old one. 'Which is quite worn out,' he said. 'Whereas this', he said, 'really is a man's machine.' 'But I'm not really a man,' I felt like saying, but refrained.

We got back yesterday from France. We stayed two nights in Paris in the St James and Albany, very old-fashioned and *gemütlich*. For the first time I felt happy in Paris, although I still maintain that Parisians are disagreeable people who revel in the discomfiture of foreigners. We lunched with Nancy in Versailles. On arrival found her lying on her sofa, dressed, with one leg bent up. There was the old radiance in her face as we entered. It soon evaporated. She did not seem to be interested in anything we said to her. It was difficult to decide whether she wanted us to drivel on, or shut up. I wondered if more interesting friends would get a better response from her. I was conscious that I was little use. Nor was poor A. much better, although she tried like mad. Nancy was quite ready to be cross with her, and at times sharp. She told me she was never out of pain and when drugged her pain was only less than when she wasn't. She said the drugs would kill her and were already affecting her mind. This was apparent to me for she forgets, and repeats. She is thin as a wraith and her face is parchmenty and yellow. I am sure she is very ill, and that she knows it. I felt dreadfully sad and sorry. Diana [Mosley] with whom we walked away from dining with Geoffrey Gilmour admitted that it would be better for Nance to die now, because she herself knows there is little chance of recovery and the sisters are certain there is none.

Sacha de Manziarly's* father was a Russian. He told Sacha that when his father was a young man some friends, asking him to visit them in their country house, said in all seriousness, 'Our house is most conveniently placed for you to stop with us on your way by train to X. It is only a month from the station.' This over Sacha's dinner – blinis, i.e. puffed pancakes, caviare and cream, Russian, simply divine.

---

* Sacha de Manziarly was in the French Resistance movement during the war. French consul-general at Los Angeles.

No sooner had we arrived at Montpellier than poor A. developed bronchitis and had a high temperature. There was a very cold wind blowing and when I met her by appointment for luncheon in a restaurant the first day of our stay there, having been researching in a library, she said, 'The wind this morning pierced me through and through. I shall catch bronchitis.' Sure enough the next day she did, and was in bed. She was very flushed and coughed incessantly. I was alarmed. Eventually I motored her to Rory [Cameron]'s on Cap Ferrat. This was the best thing. In Le Clos she could be cosseted.

In Montpellier the hotel lift was dated 1898, the sort of lift Proust would have used. It was like a mahogany bird-cage, the sides partly of engraved glass. The woodwork part was architectural, with cornice and consoles and dentils. It was operated by a rope.

Everywhere in France one sees written up Liberté, Egalité, Fraternité. The truth is that the first is undesirable, the second impossible and the third derisory.

On my return no word from Chatto & Windus. Very depressed accordingly; so I have today written to Norah [Smallwood] asking if I may expect to hear from her. So henceforth I shall dread the post.

Have typed out and sent to *The Times* my article on Bath. Not good. Doubtless they will ask me to alter or rewrite.

Friday, 7th April

This morning at breakfast a letter from Chatto & Windus. Well, I say to myself, there is nothing to be gained by deferring the opening of it. And at least the envelope doesn't contain the returned typescript. So I open it gingerly. Norah has accepted my novel and offers me terms. Also sends the reader, D.J. Enright's* comments. Blessed be God for being good to me. And about time too.

Saturday, 8th April

I thought I would go to Easter Sunday Mass at the little church in St Jean, Cap Ferrat, which I know so well. The notice board said 10 a.m. which was confirmed by someone I asked. I went in, took

---

* D.J. Enright, b. 1920. Poet, on the staff of Chatto & Windus.

a seat because I was early, and waited. As though a tidal wave had come from the harbour the congregation poured in. The church was packed. The Mass was totally unrecognizable. It might have been an Aztec rite for all I knew. The priest rushed about the sanctuary like a jack-in-the-box, talking to all and sundry, giving instructions to the choir-children, pulling their hair and feigning to box with the boys amid hoots of zanyish laughter. The congregation were handed stencilled sheets of ghastly hymns of the most banal and sentimental sort. These were sung unceasingly. A servitor approached the altar rail and spouted prayers like a muezzin, all in French. Meanwhile the priest conducted the children's choir with windmill waving arms. Several gentlemen approached the altar and read extracts from epistles and gospels. There was no reading the gospel from the gospel side of the sanctuary, or standing up by the congregation. We all embraced. Not a word of Latin throughout, of course. I was utterly at sea, and irritated. I left in the middle of this travesty.

When I took Robin Fedden to Great Chalfield Manor last month we were very disturbed by the down-at-heel look of the place. In the old Fullers'* day it was kept up beautifully, even during the war. Now the moat is choked with weeds. No water visible. The rooms inside dusty and unkempt. Half are unused and dust-sheeted. Fabrics in tatters. Mrs Floyd, recently widowed, is the Fullers' daughter. She is as nice as her parents, which is unusual in children. She loves the place, but lives in one tiny room only, for she has no servants of any kind. The same old story. And this family is not exactly poor. Just cannot find staff.

Monday, 10th April

April is a bloody awful month. One looks forward to it all the winter. It invariably disappoints. The world bursts with buds and glory, and one can only enjoy it through closed windows. As I write a tempest descends; rain lashes the window panes. But yesterday was a day of dreams. Unaccountably the gale which had been blowing from the north-west ever since our return, abated. It was a still, sunny day. I motored through the misty morning to

---

* Major and Mrs R. Fuller, donors of Great Chalfield Manor, Wilts., to the National Trust, 1943.

HC at Hawkesbury and was the only person in the church, apart from one old man, the sidesman. I felt sorry for the nice young parson, Ian Marchant, an ex-naval officer. If there will be no other day this month like yesterday then April has been worth waiting for, bloody month though it be. I walked home from Ashcroft where we lunched with the Harfords. Never seen so many primroses as there are this year. The shady side of the valley sparkling with them. Bluebells beginning to unfold. And by Lower Lodge to Newark a blue smoke of little speedwell. I met Miss Mary Huntley* and her married sister on my walk. They said that when they were children at Boxwell the speedwell was unknown. When it came it was called the Cheltenham Foreigner. Miss Huntley has lost all her teeth but two fangs. Joanie Harford said she had a terrible motor accident. She ran head-on into her niece's car in the drive at Boxwell. Both cars a write-off. This somehow so typical of the Huntleys who live an utterly isolated life at Boxwell as they have done since Henry VII's reign, going nowhere, knowing no one, content with their own family life in a heap together, hugger-mugger, old mother, son, daughters, son's children and now their wives, all apparently in the same rambling, old, untidy, featureless house, where any treasure might be spotted by a stranger if only he could get inside and be given a free hand. Even the accidents they meet with are on their own territory. Their long territorial descent, their dim distinction make most of us feel interlopers. Which we are.

Thursday, 13th April

John [Kenworthy-Browne] took me to a film at the Curzon which I realized was a good film but which I disliked. Called *The Last Show of Something or Other* it was set in a provincial oil town in Texas. The squalor of the shacks and the inhabitants, the total, absolute lack of culture and refinement turned my bourgeois stomach. It upsets me that such societies can exist in Western countries. J. says this is the wrong way to look at such a film, and he is probably right. Certainly I was appalled by the message that sex was the exclusive recreation of these people. J. thinks me very puritanical and he passes no moral judgements on works of art.

---

* Mary Huntley, sister of John Huntley whose family has owned Boxwell Court, Glos., since Henry VII's reign.

On Tuesday I went to Chatto & Windus and was greeted by Norah [Smallwood]. She is an immensely impressive woman. Extremely intelligent, obviously most capable; knows her own mind and would never compromise or be weak, yet is always polite and charming – to all outside the office I mean. She looks delicate with an absolute scone-white face. After some preliminary compliments she passed me on to Enright, the poet, who having read my typescript, went through it with me, or rather pointed out a few, not too many, lapses of style. When these are pointed out to me I invariably agree, and am left with little confidence that the rest is all right. I start wondering how many lapses there must be which he has overlooked.

Everything very early this spring. The amelanchier tree is nearly full out. Took the dogs for a long walk below Foxholes and round towards Tresham. Within my favourite secret cart-track before Tresham is reached, where the west bank is steep, the ground was carpeted with flowers – primroses in profusion and violets, the bluish and the white kind, large and small, celandines, wood anemones. I do not remember seeing such a profusion of wild flowers in England for years. We crossed over the road at Tresham and continued into the Ozleworth valley, across the fields. One field is under corn, but I managed to walk round the edge. A still, sun-patchy day of great beauty, the air crisp.

Monday, 17th April

Clementine Beit telephoned in a rage about the rumour circulating that the IRA demanded and received a large ransom from Alfred. Since their return from South Africa they have already been asked by twelve different people if the story were true. Clem said that at such a tricky time for English residents no more mischievous rumour could be put about; that there was not one vestige of truth in it; and that the IRA, if they heard of the rumour, might now act upon it. I quite understand their embarrassment. I said that we had heard of it from one or two sources.

Ian McCallum* just told me that poor John Fowler's garden house has been burnt to ashes, with all his cherished things, all his

---

* Ian McCallum, 1919–87, curator of the American Museum, Claverton, near Bath.

architectural drawings, and best furniture (with the single exception of his eighteenth-century commode), and his silver, this most
treasured possession all. There is absolutely no explanation how
the fire started. Last Saturday he was woken up at 6 a.m. by a smell
of burning and had to watch the holocaust. When rescuers
reached the garden house they could see the interior blazing but
intact. The moment they broke the windows there was an explo-
sion and John watched his priceless French chairs dissolve into
fragments.

Wednesday, 19th April

Bluebells are awash in Foxholes Wood today, which is again
unusually early. Looking at the dandelions now full out and in
their infancy I thought that if only this flower were rarer instead
of being the commonest weed in Europe – commoner far than
dog's mercury – it would be considered a marvel of beauty. No
flower is more royal than this wide head, one mass of blazing
curling flames like the sun. To think of this living flame of heat
and golden fire punctuating the cool green grass. Unfortunately its
leaves are very unworthy, very coarse and plebeian.

Ian McCallum tells me that Roger Hinks's* diaries are at last to
be published by Jock Murray; or rather the four million words
have been condensed by their editor to one volume. Ian says that
Roger kept the diary all his life. There is no sequence apart from
chronological, for it is not concerned with events, nor with gossip.
Hardly any reference to personalities, which is a surprise for he was
an extremely spiky, chippy man who could be devastatingly rude.
I found him alarming. He was exceedingly ugly (which probably
contributed to his chippiness), with a stiff, starch, pursed-lip, prissy
manner. The last time I saw him he said to me, who was rather
pleased with a new suit I was wearing for the first time, 'You are
mutton dressed as lamb.' But he was aggressively intellectual. Ian
says the diaries are in fact freely written synopses of all the books
which he never wrote. The best extracts are those written when
he was unhappy in capitals which he disliked living in, Athens and
Paris. Then he retreated into himself and wrote from the heart.

---

* Roger Hinks, 1903–63, art historian and British Council representative
overseas. Diary writer.

Presumably where he was happy and liked the society he went to parties instead. Ian says he was a marvellous friend, loyal and generous. I said to Ian, 'I assume that he was in love with you.' 'Yes,' said Ian, 'I suppose so. But because I made it clear from the start that I could not reciprocate, our relations were always on the happiest footing.' Happiest for Ian no doubt.

Years ago Honey Harris* and Roger were supposed to be in love. Gerald Berners wrote:

> 'There was a lady loved a swine.
> "Honey," said he. "Hinks," said she.'

The crown imperials are out in the garden, the crimson ones. I have just been to shake them, and the tears fell on to my hand. I do this every year in memory of Mama, rather like lighting a candle to her. For I shall always remember her joy when I explained once that the reason for their tears is that they were the only flowers which did not bow their heads to Christ on his way to Calvary. In self-imposed penance and remorse they have wept ever since. Mama was much impressed with this story.

I often wonder why it is that the old look forward so greedily to the newspapers, or the radio news, considering that their lives will soon be over, and future events must concern them so little, whereas the young are indifferent to the news. During the war my parents listened to the radio news five times daily and infuriated me by rushing into the house to turn on. Usually both fell fast asleep half-way through, and always before it was over.

Friday, 21st April

Today poor Papa's birthday. He would be 92 if alive. One writes 'poor' of the dead as Queen Victoria did, unwittingly.

Yesterday my *Times* proofs of the Bath article arrived only just soon enough for correction considering the railway go-slow. It reads all right but dully, and the editor has cut out my short diatribe against the Corporation. He did warn me that my piece was to be historic and non-controversial, so I can't really complain. I merely wanted to insert a dig. The go-slow provoked

---

* Honey Harris, unmarried daughter of Sir Austin (banker) and Lady Harris.

Georgia Sitwell* to say on the telephone that she feels like any
pre-1939 colonel about the working classes. When she telephoned
I happened to be reading the fourth volume of Osbert's autobiography. This induced me to remark how marvellous I was finding
it; that I considered it undoubtedly one of the great prose works
of the century. The remark riled her, for she said, 'This makes me
jealous on poor Sachie's behalf. Do you know he can't even get his
last book published. Have you ever heard of such a thing?' I think
it a bit silly to resent some friend praising Sachie's brother, whom
he adored, but I understand her feelings. I suppose I made a gaffe
mentioning Osbert. The trouble with Sachie is that he has written
too much, has over-written himself; and publishers are bored with
him.

Saturday, 22nd April

At Abinger's† request I asked John Betj. if he would give an address
in Westminster Abbey in July to mark the 150th anniversary of the
death of Shelley. He said No, for he did not like Shelley. Said he
agreed with Tennyson in declaring that Shelley was not worth
Keats's little finger. Life like a dome of many-coloured glass
staining the white radiance of eternity – made no sense at all. All
that rot about the Skylark. Besides he was silly as a man, and
wrong-headed. Leigh Hunt was a far better poet. So I have had to
disappoint the Keats-Shelley Committee. J.B. said Anthony Blunt§
was a great Shelley fan. Would he not do? Or the Poet Laureate?*
But the latter had already been asked and declined because of poor
health.

Sunday, 23rd April

Now that I am a churchwarden I take the bag round at the 8
o'clock service when Ivemey the people's warden is absent in the
school holidays. Although I piously look away in order not to see
what each member of the congregation puts into the bag, I know

---

* Georgia Doble, d. 1980, wife of Sir Sacheverell Sitwell, 6th Bt.
† James Scarlett, 8th Lord Abinger, b. 1914, chairman of the Keats-Shelley
Committee.
‡ Anthony Blunt, 1907–83, art historian and Communist spy.
§ The Poet Laureate, 1967–72, was Cecil Day-Lewis, 1904–72.

right enough exactly what each does put when I come to count the money after the service in the vestry. That is the worst of village communities. One knows one's neighbours far too well. A reason why I am always reluctant to be on too intimate terms with them unless they are old pre-Alderley friends like the Gascoignes.

At Paul Methuen's* exhibition in Bristol yesterday afternoon A. and I both lost our heads. I bought two watercolours of Vaux-le-Vicomte and Villandry for £90 and she spent £200. On the way there we each said, 'Now whatever happens, I am not going to buy a thing.' The old man was very pleased with the success of the show. Many old friends like Robin Darwin,[†] Teddy Croft-Murray,[‡] all of whom bought; Teddy bought one painting of Cold Ashton Manor for the British Museum.

Monday, 24th April

Lunching at Michael Astor's[§] at Bruern [Abbey, Oxon.] yesterday was Boofy Arran,[¶] as jumpy, nervous and funny as ever. He reminded me of incidents that happened years and years ago, of how Harry d'Avigdor-Goldsmid[||] wore such tight trousers that his enormous parts were protuberantly in evidence. I said that Johnnie Churchill and I always laughed about this, and when we met, were wont to say to each other 'Do you still dress on the left, or the right, Sir?' which tailors used to ask their clients in those days. I take it that left-handed people may dress on the right. Boofy also reminded me of the evening when the three of us dined together and went by prearrangement to a brothel with a red light over the door in the little Georgian square beside the Hyde Park Hotel, next door to Kathleen Drogheda's house – now all demolished.

---

* Paul, 4th Lord Methuen, RA, 1886–74, artist and landowner.
† Sir Robin Darwin, 1910–74, painter. President of the Royal West of England Academy.
‡ Edward Croft-Murray, 1907–80, keeper of Prints and Drawings, British Museum.
§ Hon. Michael Astor, 1916–80, son of 2nd Viscount and Nancy Viscountess Astor, MP. Patron of artists, writer and chairman of the London Library.
¶ Arthur (Boofy) Gore, 8th Earl of Arran, 1910–83, parliamentarian.
|| Sir Harry d'Avigdor-Goldsmid, 2nd Bt., MP, 1909–76.

When we got there Boofy and I got the giggles and escaped, leaving Harry. Next morning we telephoned Harry to apologize for letting him down. His reply was, 'It didn't matter at all. I had the three of them.'

Tuesday, 25th April

Received a letter from Nancy to whom I thought I had written a jolly one to congratulate her on her Légion d'honneur. As I expected she says it is the sole honour she ever coveted. Then launched into rather spiky remarks over A. having suggested a nun to sleep in the house at nights. 'A *nun* of all people!' she having previously said how much she found nuns sympathetic. Then pointed rebukes of my complaint about the ruination of the environment. If I had read as many books as she upon the miseries of the people in the nineteenth century – not so long ago – I would realize what vast improvements in social conditions have taken place. And *tant pis* the ruination, in other words. All beside the point. She has become querulous and takes against old friends and her family. All excusable because of the dreadful pain. But oh dear.

Less than a fortnight ago, about ten days I guess, in walking through the Newark woods I passed a sheep beside the path. It had recently died. Its eyes were wide open, and for a moment I wondered if it were still alive. Yesterday on the same walk I was horrified to come upon it again. But the carcase had entirely gone except for the ribs which I first noticed like the miniature skeleton of an upturned boat. Before I had time to look away I noticed the animal's head, which on the contrary was wholly preserved, the black face and nose and horribly grinning mouth. Involuntarily I gave a shout of revulsion and rushed on. I thought afterwards that if some ill-intentioned person had pursued me with that head and thrown it at me I would have died of a heart attack. I would not touch it for £10,000. But I would not admit that I had turned down the offer for such a reason.

Chatto's write me very nice letters and are most helpful, suggesting titles, and what lines might profitably be altered or left out. I have never received such help or interest from any publisher, and I have had many – Batsford, Faber, Wingate, Rainbird, H. Hamilton, Hamlyn – never such constructive, intelligent comments.

Wednesday, 26th April

Funny how on every fresh cowpat are to be seen reddy-brown flies guzzling happily. I never see these flies anywhere else. Curious to live exclusively on excrement. Coprophagous. There is a politician who resembles them, but shall be nameless.

Little Chuff in jumping a stream this afternoon, stumbled and fell, covering himself with mud. He did not seem to mind, and did not injure himself. But I minded very much. It made me dreadfully unhappy to see him out of step, so to speak. All my compassion and love for him rose in my throat, and I felt wretched. Such a thing would not have happened even a year ago. The age of these two dogs saddens me. I love them more and more and more, the companions of my walks and thoughts, never intrusive, never argumentative, always so good, understanding, obedient and unwilling to disoblige.

How cows and bullocks dislike dogs. They congregate and rush, stampeding upon them from the furthest ends of fields. What impels them to do this? In what does their dislike consist? They don't object to me.

Saturday, 29th April

Actually began writing my Stuart book yesterday, having spent the earlier part of this week roughing out the section on James II. Already I see that this is going to be a long book. Length can only be justified by readers' interest in the theme (how to ascertain?) and the way in which I compose. When I have done the James II part I must seriously consider and decide upon the approximate length the book is to be.

Joan Drogheda telephoned in the morning ostensibly to tell me that the Alan Hares* are pleased to give us supper after her concert next Monday. But since she had already told me this I was waiting for the real reason. It was that Garrett, having returned from America, has received over 200 letters congratulating him on receiving the Garter, but is tremendously sensitive about whether or not his old friends have written. Had either A. or I written? She, Joan, knew how absurd we would think this, but she hoped we

---

* Hon. Alan Hare, MC, b. 1919. Chairman of *The Financial Times*, 1978–83; and Jill Gordon his wife.

would write. I assured her that both of us had already written.
How odd that Garrett should be so sensitive. Rather sweet of him
in a way. That ridiculous Order.

Monday, 1st May

The Times printed my letter prominently on Saturday. I hope and
believe it will demolish Hugh Casson[*] who on Wednesday took
me to task (he mistook Adam Fergusson's article for mine) for
nagging and not understanding the problems in Bath. He made the
fatal error of admitting that many mistakes had occurred and that
many more would undoubtedly occur. In other words that many
more beautiful old streets would be pulled down. What an admission!

Jimmie Smith[†] who stayed the weekend is a dear man, of a
sweet nature and passionately interested in all that takes place in
the world of music and the arts. But as a guest he is hardly
civilized. He breaks things, and when he sits on a chair the
cushions split and fall to the floor. He rucks the rugs up, he lets the
bath-water overflow. He makes the most awful gurks and noises,
and he ceaselessly chews his thumb. Rather he puts his fist inside
his mouth and lets saliva course down his chin. Mrs Lancaster[‡]
says, 'I do wish Jimmie would find what he is looking for,' as he
fumbles for bits of food inside his teeth and plate, which never
seem to fit.

Wednesday, 3rd May

The Hubert Howards[§] lunched here on Monday. A. put herself out
in preparing a return for their frequent hospitality to us at Ninfa
and in making the garden presentable. But at this particular moment the spring flowers are over and of course the roses and
clematis are not out, and there is nothing for them to look at. It
was moreover bitterly cold, so the garden visit was over in five

---

[*] Sir Hugh Casson, KCVO, b. 1910, architect, artist and author.
[†] Hon. James Smith, b. 1906, governor of the Sadler's Wells theatre and
director of the Royal Opera House, Covent Garden, Trust.
[‡] Nancy (Mrs) Lancaster. Woman of faultless taste in decoration of houses.
[§] Hon. Hubert Howard, 1907–87, and his wife Donna Lelia Caetani,
daughter and heiress of 17th Duca di Sermoneta.

minutes. Lelia Caetani is extremely dignified, and handsome, and polite, but stiff and difficult to talk to on account of her shyness. Is diffident. Does not call herself Princess Caetani but Mrs H., and in Italy is referred to as Donna Lelia. Hubert is a man of wide interests, culture and reading, and has a correct sense of humour. Easy to talk to and full of charm. But these old Catholic families always put me on my guard, for with all their seeming tolerance and gentle mockery of others of their persuasion, they are underneath *très dévots*, and nothing, nothing will allow them for one minute to let you think they are the same as the majority of mankind. They have a subtle, inner arrogance, which will rise to the surface with a scratch. But I like Hubie Howard immensely. Quiet, gentle, very patrician.

Then we rushed up to London for Joan Drogheda's concert in the Euston Road, or rather her playing of some six piano pieces between recitations by Dadie Rylands and Peggy Ashcroft.[*] The audience, not very full, was a packed one. All friends of the Droghedas. I don't like this sort of Mayfair gathering. We found ourselves sitting next to Christian Esher;[†] so beautiful and sympathetic. Were taken by the Droghedas to supper afterwards with the Alan Hares at Hampstead. Long meal in a stuffy London dining-room, with low ceiling, very hot. Alan Hare's nice wife professed herself an admirer of my last book. I sat next to Peggy Ashcroft who repeatedly asked where and when we had met before. I told her it was with Rupert Hart-Davis before she married him in 1928. It couldn't have been after because they were together only for a fortnight. I asked her if she was ever tempted to weep when reading poetry of pathos. Never, she said with a look of one deeply shocked. Only when listening to others reading. She said that when asked to read verse with Lord Pearce[‡] she declined because he admitted that he was sometimes reduced to tears. She could not be associated with a reader so amateur. I felt ashamed that when the last time I was reading poetry with John Betjeman and he asked me to read Patmore's ode to his dead wife, I was reduced to tears and had to stop. Quick to tears goes with

---

[*] Dame Peggy Ashcroft, 1907–91, classical actress.
[†] Christian Pike, wife of Lionel Brett, 4th Viscount Esher.
[‡] Rt Hon. E.H. Pearce, Lord Pearce, KC, b. 1901. Lord of Appeal in Ordinary, 1962–9.

quick to cruelty; and is Teutonic and reprehensible. When you are close to Peggy Ashcroft she appears beautiful; but on the stage plain. Never undistinguished, however. She is every inch the professional and I noticed that while others were performing she sat with complete poise, hands folded, elegance and ease. Dadie sprawled. She told me she was very left-wing, and asked if I was. No, I said, very right-wing. She said Heath was evil. I said he was nothing of the sort; nor was Wilson, whom she disliked for not being radical enough, evil. She trails a coat; is fanatical in her political views, marches against the Industrial Relations Bill and any other assertion of national, traditional fitness. Tiresome these women are and impossible to have intellectual commerce with.

Thursday, 4th May

At a meeting of the Bath Preservation Trust last night several people referred to my article and letter to *The Times*. The last, they said, has effectively demolished Casson. Afterwards I had supper with Michael and Isabel Briggs* at Midford. They are enchanting alone. A most intelligent, civilized and amusing couple. Isobel, who in company holds herself in like a spirited horse on the curb, when she decides to release herself sparkles at a spanking gallop. She has no small talk which makes her dinner-table companion nervous until he knows her. She never says a foolish thing. How I love them for the contribution they make towards a tolerable world.

Friday, 5th May

A full and busy day. Writing in the morning at my new book, interrupted by Elizabeth Chatwin asking me to protest to the National Trust against letting nearby Fernley Farm to a notoriously anti-environmental farmer. This involves my telephoning the Trust regional office. I correct proofs of my *Country Life* article, telephoning to their London office. At 2.30 the editor and photographer of *Gloucestershire Life* comes to photograph the garden with A. and me walking self-consciously down the lime alley. We ply them with information and coffee. I write letters, including one to

---

* Isabel Colegate, novelist and wife of Michael Briggs.

Chatto about the latest title proposed for the novel – *Heretics in Love*, a quotation from Donne: and suggested by nephew Nick. A freelance journalist telephones; he has done so for the past three years, always in May, to ask what is the book I have on the stocks. Reluctantly and cautiously I have to tell him it is a novel coming out in January next. But I refuse to tell him the title – not yet settled – or the name of the publisher – I don't want Chatto harassed at this early stage – or the story. Love I say, all novels are about love. Is it sex? he asks. It is romantic love, I reply. It is *not* pornography. I don't belong to the generation that writes porn. Was not brought up to do such a thing. Inwardly I tremble what they will say when the book does emerge. They will probably only think something and say nothing. I detect down the wires a mystified young man, disappointed by the vagueness imparted.

Then I take Oenone [Luke, granddaughter] for a walk in Fox-holes Wood. She is thrilled to see so many bluebells. The ground is carpeted with them, like an ocean. We hear the first cuckoo of the season in the distance, away across the valley in the Newark woods. Then we come upon a pair of foxes, which the dogs chase. They were a mere twenty yards within reach, a huge dog fox with bottle brush, and a vixen. Mercifully the whippets soon returned, unscathed. In the evening to three plays given by the Wotton-under-Edge players as part of the week's Wotton Festival in the Town Hall. Two of the plays were drivelling, the third, Shaw's *Great Catharine*, splendidly acted by Howard Mann the green-grocer who ought to have devoted his life to the stage. He gave a truly professional performance of Prince Patiomkin. He is a tragic figure, tied to Wotton and the little shop which he hates, by a tyrannical, philistine old father. Howard Mann goes to Rome for his holidays and takes photographs of Bernini fountains, reads voraciously, is a gentle and enlightened solitary in a small, provin-cial town, a square peg in a round hole. And the citizens of Wotton all say how clever Howard is; he is made for better things. Now it is late. He must be 55.

Saturday, 6th May

The BBC telephoned at breakfast time to announce their presence in Bath, and would I please come immediately to walk round the city with them and explain what has happened to it recently. 'I am another gadfly,' the voice said, which endeared him to me. But I got out of it by putting him in touch with the director of the Preservation Trust, far better qualified than me.

Sunday, 7th May

In the early morning before it has melted, the dew lies in large crystal drops on the flat grey-green leaves of the alchemilla, exactly like the drops in Dutch flower paintings. On no other leaves do the drops lie in such an enticing, heavenly manner which brings to mind Shakespeare's descriptions of the jewellery of Cleopatra. David Cecil* in a television talk last night said that Shakespeare was so engraved upon our literary minds that the English novelist still could not create a heroine other than of the alternative kinds he did, i.e. the yielding, soft kind or the masterful kind. No other sort has yet emerged.

Monday, 8th May

Just after sunset last night A. and I listening to the birds singing like mad, blackbirds and thrushes, remarked that nowadays we never in the morning heard the dawn chorus. When we first came here I frequently heard it, but now never. Perhaps the birds have changed their habit, and sing instead in the evening, a dusk chorus. Perhaps we are both stone deaf in the early morn.

I picked a handful of cowslips for A., putting them beside her bed. But neither of us could smell them. Are flowers losing their scent? When I picked them in the fields skirting the disused Tetbury-Cirencester railway line I could just smell them faintly. But indoors, no. I fear it is we who are losing our olfactory senses which are still horribly acute when it comes to nasty smells. Must ask the children if they can smell this bunch. Perhaps the scent diminishes when cowslips are brought indoors. At the best of times it is a very elusive one.

John Harris came down for the day to look at a cottage of the Harfords at Ashcroft for renting. Was dressed in a beautiful smart suit from Blades, money no object. Good for him. He can be rough, yet is extremely diffident, never boasts of his golden store.

---

* Lord David Cecil, 1902–86. Professor of English Literature, Oxford University. Biographer and man of letters.

Thursday, 11th May

The brilliance of the bluebells growing out of the emerald-green grass, glimpsed unexpectedly as I motor through the lanes, is for the north almost indecent. The strong contrasting colours are tropical and not what one expects in a land of dismal greyness. I marvel at it. Dismal greyness is of course a foolish description of England, for on most days of the year subtle colours, Turneresque, can be found in the distance if there are hills about, and always in Scotland where it rains even more. But oh the monotony of leaden skies in an English summer.

Listened last night to a performance of Bartók's 3rd Piano Concerto, and remembered my attitude to Bartók only a few years ago. Then I considered his farmyard noises, as I found them, insupportable cacophony. Now I find his music nothing of the sort, and often tolerable. Sometimes boring; no longer shocking. One ought to be cautious before dismissing relatively new works of art. It's rash to express strong opinions when one is ignorant. And yet one's untutored intelligence, one's sense of fitness, are constantly outraged. And when is one being taken in?

The news generally is appalling, and without hope it seems. Strikes, utter bloodymindedness on the part of trades unions, agitators everywhere, students rioting all over the world because Nixon has, quite rightly, laid mines across the North Vietnam harbours to prevent Russian ships pouring arms into that country. Labour victories here, and signs everywhere of the world going completely Communist or worse within another generation. Labour now advocates rationing what they call the rich in houses. As though taking Boughton and Drumlanrig from the Buccleuchs, because they also own Bowhill (poor devils, the responsibilities), will benefit anyone, least of all the homeless poor.

Saturday, 13th May

A prolonged nightmare that I *had* to jump from an aeroplane with a parachute. The anticipation seemed interminable, the days on end deliberating how I would acquit myself. The jump was inevitable. That was understood. What concerned me more than terror of the physical leap was my honour, which is strange. Because if I were confronted today with the predicament, my honour would not be a consideration at all. This goes to show that I was dreaming, not of today, but of thirty years ago during the war, when in the Army such a decree was quite possible and there was no way out of a command. I suppose most dreams are backwards so to speak, seldom present and never forward.

Francis Lennox-Boyd* told me during the war how he had been jumping with his company behind enemy lines. They jumped quickly from the plane in succession. As the man immediately in front of him leapt he said loudly, 'Fuck!' He had forgotten to attach his harness properly, and fell to his death like a stone. Poor Francis was killed parachuting a few months later.

Last night at 10 I watched the sunset from the front door. The sky was still darkest violet, not yet black. Through the shimmering poplars behind the lawn the horizon sky was orange. Above, Venus shining enormous, with rays emitted as one sees from stars in old pictures. I thought the rays might be caused by my spectacles, so took them off. With my naked eye the rays were still there. It is surely seldom that one actually sees rays.

At last night's PCC meeting the Vicar talked unmitigated rot, and went so far as to say that one ought to pay no attention to the Diocesan Advisory Committee vetos. He had a friend, another vicar in the neighbourhood, who wanted to put up a shed in the churchyard, and was told by them not to; he did it, and good luck to him, etc. I said nothing because the Vicar was talking in general terms, but had he suggested that we at Alderley should ignore the Diocesan Committee over some specific case here, I would have spoken up. A. says that last Sunday in his sermon he spoke violently against Graham Sutherland's tapestry in Coventry Cathedral. Silly ass. So Graham is to him what Bartók was to me twenty-five years ago.

At the Reynolds Stone† party in London A. saw Lionel Esher out of the corner of an eye and tried to avoid him. But he put down his glass and crossed the room to talk. Desperately she thought, 'What am I to say about Jim's letter to him?'‡ But Lionel

---

* Francis Lennox-Boyd, 1909–44, elegant and artistic youngest of four brothers. Three died on active service.
† Reynolds Stone, 1909–79, designer, graphic engraver and printer.
‡ J.L.-M.'s letter contained somewhat intemperate criticism of Casson's apparent approval of architectural vandalism in Bath, of which Casson was official adviser to the City Council.

said, 'I have had the most charming letter from Jim. It couldn't
have been nicer. It's true I haven't been to Bath to see what has
happened there lately. I just felt I had to come to the rescue of
Casson.' A. mightily relieved to be on good terms with this
delightful friend and says to me, 'You've no idea what I have to go
through sometimes on your account.'

Thursday, 18th May

A very enjoyable opera party on Monday given by the Donaldsons.* Invited to the royal box. But the D. of Kent deciding to go
at the last minute we were given seats in the stalls instead – better
for seeing than the box – and ate in the intervals in the little
downstairs room under the box. Frankie said that King Edward
VII went night after night to the opera, and was in fact the last
monarch to be musical. He was apparently at Covent Garden two
nights before he died. The Baldwins and Pempy Reed[†] the other
guests. Conversation in the interval was fun. Bloggs said he wished
he could be moved by opera. If *Don Carlos* doesn't move him then
no opera will. He said he would like to see an opera on skates. I
said do you think the deathbed scene in *Otello* would turn out
well? Just the ticket, he said, This made me laugh during the next
act. Greatly though I enjoyed this splendid performance I was not
always concentrating as I should have been. Was thinking of my
novel. Treating the music like Nancy's manure.[‡]

Friday, 19th May

Went to see the Titian, *Diana and Actaeon*, in the National Gallery
and thought it an indifferent painting. I am not in favour of raising
over £1 million for this picture which does not belong to England
whereas the same amount of money might save part of Bath which

---

* John G.S. (Jack), b. 1907, and Frances (Frankie), b. 1907, Lord and Lady
Donaldson of Kingsbridge.
† Penelope (Pempy) Dudley Ward, m. 1948 Sir Carol Reed, film producer
and director who d. 1976.
‡ Nancy Mitford always boasted that she was unmusical and merely treated
memorable tunes as manure for the plots of novels in her mind.

essentially does. It was strange while crossing Boris Anrep's*
mosaic floor to look at Eddy Sackville sitting at an open piano in
one corner. Very good likeness too considering the large size of the
cubes. A good way of being immortalized – being walked on.

Jim Richards† lunched with me at his request. Nothing much to
say to him. He is portly and about to retire from editing the
Architectural Review after years and years. We gobbled at each other
benignly.

John Fowler dined at Brooks's, and J.K.-B. came. J.K.-B. rather
tiresome in taking umbrage when I mentioned that John F. was to
visit Montacute, he adopting the attitude that it was irksome his
work at Montacute about to be undone, whereas all that Fowler is
being asked is to suggest appropriate blinds to keep the light out.
I told J. that every house of the NT that I had arranged had already
been rearranged, every guidebook I had written had been rewrit-
ten or scrapped, and that I didn't mind in the least. In the nature
of things it has to be.

Johnnie Churchill telephoned during dinner to say he was at the
New Berkeley Hotel with Kay Hallé, 'on the crack'‡ he said, after
forty years. So next morning at 12 I went to the New Berkeley to
see Kay and Johnnie. He is enormous, but mentally the same as he
was when I first met him, the eternal adolescent. Kay has blonde
hair and her face still youthful and sweet. She showed me two
books about Sir Winston which she has had published in America.
She said that Martin Gilbert who has taken over Randolph's Life
of his father came upon a packet of passionate love letters written
by Sir Winston to Lady Goonie Churchill,§ Johnnie's mother. I
had often been told that Sir W. was in love with her, but at what
stage of their lives I don't know. Johnnie does not think he is
Winston's son.

---

* Boris Anrep, pre-eminent mosaicist of Westminster Cathedral and the
National Gallery.
† Sir James M. Richards, 1907–91, architectural editor of *The Times*, writer
and historian.
‡ An esoteric joke shared by the three of us, too harmless and silly to be
explained.
§ Lady Gwendoline (Goonie) Bertie, 1885–1941. Married 1908 Major John
Spencer-Churchill.

I have bought at Sotheby's for £45 a scrap of a letter of Byron, but without his signature; in fact it is only three lines, without date, having been cut from a page with scissors. Such is the scarcity or rather value of any word written by B.'s own hand.

Sunday, 21st May

Audrey wrote me that it was ten years ago Mama died on 15th May. And although I had remembered that it was this month I had forgotten the exact date. I shall never forget the occasion. She had been very ill and failing for months and therefore her death was not unexpected, but the suddenness took me by surprise. Dick telephoned one morning at breakfast to say she had faded out during the night. I was so stunned that I could not speak, and had to ring off and telephone again later. I never shall forgive myself that I was not there beside her when she went, for a year before when she was dying in Evesham hospital I held her by both hands and dragged her back to life. When she did die I failed for lack of courage to fulfil a promise I made to her. It was that when in her coffin she should not be given a shroud tied in a knot over the head like the village women. I could not bring myself to see her when she was dead. A. however did and assured me this had not happened. I pray that Mama has forgiven me.

Bamber Gascoigne's novel, *Murgatreud*, is out. Almost unreadable although by a great effort I did get through it. Schoolboyish and unmelodious. Allegorical, and unfeeling. Old Bartók to me. Yet I have no doubt that his contemporaries like it, judging by the reviews they have given it. Which once again indicates the gap between his generation and mine. And he so clever, good and nice.

John Cornforth and I went to Flaxley Abbey for the afternoon. I am to do articles on this house for *Country Life*. The set-up is extraordinary. Present owners, by name Mr F.B. Watkins, scrap-metal merchant and wife, bought it ten years ago from the Crawley-Boevey family. Mrs Watkins unpretentious, direct, has no wish to assert herself or be known by the county. He commonplace, equally diffident, is intensely interested in the abbatial remains to the exclusion of everything else. Both unashamedly ignorant, have put themselves absolutely in the hands of Oliver Messel* who has

---

* Oliver Messel, 1904–78, theatrical producer, decorator and artist.

become their God, an absent one for he has lived in the Bahamas for the past five years. Mrs W. adores him. Has blown-up photographs of him in different rooms, including her bedroom. Every stick of furniture bought by him, or what's more from him. Most of the contents come from Nymans, Oliver's old home. He has decorated the house, placed the furniture, laid out the garden canals. They do nothing without his consent and there are rooms which have the furniture stacked in the middle, awaiting his arrival to arrange it. When Oliver was over here six months ago for a serious operation Mrs Watkins spent two months in London visiting him daily at the London Clinic and bringing special food. She speaks of him with bated breath. His bedroom is reserved for him alone. She showed us a screen which he made her put beside her bed, thus hiding her favourite photograph of Oliver on a chest of drawers behind the screen. 'Such a pity I can't now see his photograph from my bed,' she complained. So I asked why she did not move the photograph to her bed table. The reply was that Oliver had put it on the chest of drawers. I liked and admired Mrs Watkins. There is nothing commonplace about her.

Wednesday, 24th May

Cecil Day-Lewis has died. After meeting him in Rome last year at the Keats celebrations I tried to read his verse, but couldn't. It has no music and no message for me, and seems dead, or rather something which has never been alive. A tall, rugged man, with a deeply lined and scarred face. He was then very tired and ill. Rosamond will be in a state because he was her lover, indeed the love of her life for years. Poor Ros who indulges in grief will be undergoing an orgy. Day-Lewis read my novel in its first stage before Chatto's returned it to me for excisions.

How immensely pleased I am that my novel was accepted last month. Had it not been I really believe I would have given up. As it is I am impelled to go on writing. Now coming to the end of James II. But already the book will be very long.*

---

* Ultimately published in 1983 as *The Last Stuarts*. It was rather short.

Thursday, 25th May

Of course Ros had reasons for feeling aggrieved. Day-Lewis had been living with her for years and let it be understood that he couldn't marry her because his wife didn't want a divorce. Then without so much as a thank-you he divorced his wife and married Jill Balcon.*

I may feel ill in the morning so that I creep about as fragile as pottery. By the afternoon I may feel as strong as leather and as pliable, and resistant to all buffettings.

Yesterday at 1.30 – A. being away in London – the whippets and I boarded the car and motored to Moccas [Herefordshire]. I am glad I made the effort because I have not visited the Scar since May 1962 when I scattered Mama's ashes there. Although it was not fine when we arrived – I was unsure of the way from Brobury – and speckling with rain, the place was as beautiful as I remembered. Indeed I can think of no area in the British Isles which is more beautiful. It is still unspoilt although there were two cars in the lane approaching the track up which I walked, and wheelmarks of cars which had lately driven up to the Scar. This indicates that the brutal public has discovered the sacred precincts. The precipitous cliff above the Wye, so steep that I have vertigo looking over the edge, down upon the swirling river, clear and crystal. The wonderful aged Spanish chestnuts and oaks, the curve of the grassy banks from Bredwardine, the flat meadow spattered with veteran trees like shaggy tea-cosies and the deer park rising beyond, the oblique glimpse in the left foreground of the red brick Court, all vindicated my decision of twenty years ago or more that this is the loveliest view of England I could ever expect to find. And it is England and not Wales, although on the Marches. And although I once took Mama to the Court and she had no connection with Moccas, yet the Baileys† came from Brecon and Herefordshire, and I could think of no place more worthy of her ashes. Standing on the turf I thought as hard as I could about her, remembering how much she enjoyed a jolly good view. The deathly silence was broken only by the distant purr of the river below and the exotic cackle of pheasants in the wood behind me. This is praying, I presume, this thinking intensely about and wishing, hoping for the

---

* Jill Balcon, actress and reciter, m. 1951 Cecil Day-Lewis.
† J.L.-M.'s mother's family.

peace and happiness of somebody very beloved who is dead and
when alive had no belief in a future survival whatsoever. The dogs
and I walked further into the wood along the very edge of the Scar
to a spot opposite the house before returning, they, the dogs,
gambolling blissful and uncaring over the turf. My mother would
like that although she was not enthusiastic about whippets. Of Fop
she remarked, 'He would look well on an inkstand.' I am glad I
went, and glad that I chose this place for her.

Monday, 29th May

On Friday by train to London. At Didcot Alan Pryce-Jones got
into my carriage and talked till Paddington. That was an unexpected treat. He said Penelope [Betjeman] with whom he had
been lunching thought J.B. would not be offered the Laureateship,
and Stephen Spender's* friends were lobbying for Spender. I said,
but Stephen has protested to the press that he would not accept, if
offered. Alan complained that all his contemporaries in England
were failing, as though those in the United States were flourishing.
And he named Robin MacDouall† gaga, Patrick Kinross in general
decline, sleeping all day and interested in nothing, John Betj.
shuffling like an octopus. He, Alan, is spry as ever, the eternal
Peter Pan. He will, I hope, last for ever.

St Phil. Neri Day at the Oratory, beginning with Solemn Mass.
A fine performance, and in the old style, Latin ritual which was
impressive. Yet I was strangely unmoved, no longer belonging to
this Church, in spite of theatricals at the high altar, the Cardinal
[John Heenan] doffing and donning his mitre, my friend Father
Michael Napier,‡ tall and distinguished declaiming, and censers
swinging. Went round to the dinner. All the guests already assembled. The first person I came upon was Adrian Jones§ to whom I

---

* Sir Stephen Spender, b. 1909, poet and man of letters.
† Robin MacDouall, slightly *manqué* figure, and Oxford contemporary.
Secretary of the Travellers' Club.
‡ Father Michael Napier, of the Congregation of Oratorians, an Order
introduced to England by Cardinal Newman in 1847.
§ Adrian Jones, an inspector of the Ancient Monuments Department of the
Ministry of Works. Grandson of Captain Adrian Jones, sculptor of *Victory in
her Chariot*, Hyde Park Corner.

hurriedly whispered, 'Do I genuflect, or is it no longer done?' 'Certainly, to the ground, *if* you are presented. They hate it now, but you must.' I was presented, and I did genuflect to the ground. In fact I heard my knee make a resounding crack on the floor-boards. The Cardinal tried to prevent me but I wouldn't be prevented. But I had no opportunity of kissing his ring. Couldn't find it. Don't think he wore one. He has charm. He said, 'You were on the Pope's Commission investigating the Chair? Was it St Peter's do you think?' I told him what he doubtless knew already, that it was ninth century, Charles the Bald's, and explained the radio-carbon test. He laughed, and said, 'A pity, but it's just as well our Faith does not have to depend upon such relics.' I thought he would be shocked if he knew of my lapse from *our* Faith. Dinner at two long tables against the long walls of the Refectory, the Cardinal and Father Napier at the top cross table. Grace, etc. Excellent dinner, with champagne which I don't like, served by men in some form of uniform. All most civilized. I sat next to Adrian and a young Oratorian, Father Sebastian Dilke. Adrian explained that the qualifications for joining the Oratorians used to be a personal income of £400 a year, which was more than the Foreign Office's. They are an educated lot of men. The evening took me back thirty years to such occasions as the Wiseman dinners with Mrs Belloc Lowndes. Although intelligent and aw-fully jolly these Catholics are unreal. There is a pretentious sexless-ness about these people, which is false, and makes for unease.

Kay Hallé with whom I had a date after dinner was out when I called at the New Berkeley Hotel. I was rather relieved, and went to Eardley's flat to bed, leaving her a note to telephone if she returned before midnight. At 11.30 she rang and talked till 12.15. I enjoyed it. She is sweet and most affectionate. She had lunched at Chequers; having known Ted Heath all his life, why I don't know, and finds him sympathetic and cosy to talk to which is surely exceptional. 'Oh how I love the English, and how beautiful England is,' Kay said.

Tuesday, 30th May

Caroline [Somerset] very funny about the D. of Beaufort's rage against Tony Snowdon who, having been invited to Badminton for the horse trials, refused because they bored him. The refusal (not the reason) was all right, and pleased the Bs. But two days before the trials he said he *was* coming which entailed much alteration of rooms and putting old ladies in the attics, etc. He infuriated the D. by saying that hunting was cruel, which the D. resolutely denied. Then he said, 'The competitors in the horse trials must be *terrified.*' 'Equestrians are never terrified,' the Duke said, 'Only cissies are terrified.' He began belabouring the fire with a poker. Princess Margaret wanting to calm his rage, said, 'Tony doesn't mean terrified really. He means nervous.' 'No, I don't. I mean terrified,' Tony insisted. Whereupon the Duke, completely out of temper, shouted as he banged away at the fireplace, bending the poker, 'Damn this fire, I tell you. Damn it, damn it!' Tony thereupon left that afternoon while the party were at the trials without saying goodbye.

We had the garden open on Sunday. A terrible day, iron-grey and pouring rain. Also we had forty American ladies to tea brought by Ian McCallum. Dreadful old women who pored over the house, poking at everything, reading our letters, wiping their lipstick on my face towel, but most appreciative, good-mannered and I suppose nice. They kept saying to me, 'Oh, I do so love your book.' 'Which one?' I asked. 'Oh, the one about the Prince Regent.' 'Oh, but I have never written about the Prince Regent.' 'Oh, but Ian was reading it to us in the coach as we came along. It was so beautiful.' A. says one ought to be flattered by this sort of gush. It nauseates me. One old brute in orange pursued me and made me at the umbrella's point give her a copy of *Another Self* and autograph it. 'What is your name?' I asked, pen in hand. 'April,' she said, 'just put April.' Obediently I wrote it. A. said I was a fool, I should have said I had no copies, but I think if it has given her any pleasure, why not? And anything to get rid of her.

The weather is utterly hellish, a driving wind which we have had for a month without intermission, and cold, cold.

Friday, 2nd June

Wednesday being a stinking afternoon I decided to make a dash for Badminton which is now open on Wednesdays in the summer. I wanted to see the portrait of the Countess of Albany which is reproduced in a book on Prince Charlie published in 1900. Caroline said it was no longer there. Having bought my ticket and passed through all the state rooms I saw no sign of it. In each room a 'lady' steps forward, says with a sweet, sugary smile, 'Good afternoon, this is the Dining Room. Such a pleasant room I always say. The portrait on the left of the fireplace is of Queen Henrietta Maria by Reynolds. On the right King George I by Holbein. Now this is such a pretty piece of needle-work. In the olden days they did these things so beautifully I always think,' and so on, maddening patter, and all wrong. At any rate in the last room there was the Duchess,[*] as usual, talking to people as she likes to do. I went up and said I am J.L.-M. Yes, I know, she said, very well, of course. And promptly introduced me to someone, 'Do you know Mr Milnes-Gaskell?' However when I told her what I was searching for, she dived under a rope and dragged me upstairs. At the top of the grand staircase was the portrait, quite small, rather dirty, and enchanting. The Princess Stolberg[†] sitting on a baroque chair, wearing feathers in her hair (perhaps, no, not when she was titular Princess of Wales, for she was never *de facto*), holding a domino, a dog bounding at her feet, a northern view, could it be France or the Low Countries, in the background? I was delighted at last to see this picture. I told the Duchess about Don Nicholas's collection and she asked if I would take her to see it. Said she was sure she would have been a Jacobite. Said she hated Cromwell more than Mr Wilson. That the Duke of Windsor reminded her of Prince Charlie, which was shrewd. She is a simple, yet not stupid woman, uneducated, pathetic and, I assume, gnawed by jealousies. Can't listen to what one says; no one over 50 can, and has to chatter. Is intensely shy.

Monday, 5th June

After years and years of fighting against it I now allow myself to look at the keys of my typewriter. So very stupid that I never did this before. It is quite absurd that at my age I should still discipline myself over something that does not matter. A naturally bad, fumbling typer, I have at last given way, and get on much better

---

[*] Lady Mary Cambridge (Teck), wife of 10th Duke of Beaufort who d. 1984.
[†] Louisa Princess of Stolberg, and Countess of Albany, 1753–1824. Married 1772 Prince Charles Edward Stuart, 'The Young Pretender'.

than before. I have been like Dadie Rylands in submitting myself
to unnecessary tests of endurance.

At Holy Communion yesterday I thought how I never read the
Gospels, seldom think about Christ, or analyse my relations with
God. Just accept Him in a muzzy way, don't regard Him as
anything beyond a vague spirit of good, never as a friend, never
study the written Word. In the evening at a wretched service in
Wotton Church for the unveiling of a memorial tablet to Sir
Alan Durand* the Archdeacon preached. He said: 'Bear in mind
that God never asks the impossible of you. Never in any circumstances.' But is this true? It strikes me he is always doing this very
thing. Then I thought how each generation interprets God as it
wants to. If we are to believe what each successive generation of
priests tells us that God is He would vary from century to century,
and thus contradict His enduring, unchanging nature as the years
go by. This makes nonsense of Him for He ought to be constant.
What a muddle the whole thing is.

Sachie Sitwell[†] and Georgia for the weekend. Sachie terribly
hurt and upset that thirteen publishers have refused his last book.
Whereas he says a university in Texas has paid him £24,000 for his
manuscript notebooks. Why, he complains, does no publisher take
his work? It doesn't make sense. Altogether this university has paid
the Sitwell family over £100,000 for their manuscripts.

This morning Sachie said no one had any idea how awful his
mother's[‡] disgrace was to him when he was a boy at Eton. The
headlines of the papers were splashed with the news. It has affected
him all his life. At an entertainment at Chelsea barracks at the time
Osbert was an officer there, a comedian made fun of the incident.
All the guardsmen in respect for Osbert remained dumb and did
not betray a flicker of amusement.

Laurie Lee[§] came to luncheon with his perfectly sweet and
beautiful wife, Cathy. Laurie much fatter than formerly and has

---

[*] Brigadier Sir Alan Durand, 3rd Bt., 1893–1971. He and Lady Durand lived
in Wotton-under-Edge, Glos.

[†] Sir Sacheverell Sitwell, 6th Bt., 1897–1988, poet and writer, and his wife
Georgia Doble who d. 1980.

[‡] In 1915 Lady Ida Sitwell was convicted of fraud and sent to prison for three
months.

[§] Laurie Lee, troubadour poet and author.

lost his youthful good looks. He brought with him my *Another Self* which he made me sign. It always embarrasses me to do this when I have not given the book. I wrote something to this effect on the flyleaf, and he scrutinized what I had written closely. Myopically.

Sachie is quite the sweetest fellow in the world, an angelic nature, and stories come tumbling out of his magpie's mind like treasure disgorged. You never know what disconnected jewels will next appear. Laurie Lee said to me that he revered Sachie far above Osbert and Edith, 'I put him at the apex of the triangle,' he said. I passed this on to Sachie, thinking it good for his morale.

Wednesday, 7th June

Stayed two nights with Eardley. On arrival at 16 West Halkin St. found him poring over the list of theatres and films. Couldn't decide on what to see. Had to telephone Desmond Shawe-Taylor who suggested *Klute*. Went. The subject a call-girl in New York. Very fine photography and a splendid actress, Fonda. But the scenario too horrid, the squalor, cruelty, physicality – what do I mean? – so unspeakably beastly and unsympathetic that I felt sick and at one moment thought I must leave the cinema. All the people in the audience looked like the people in the film, belonging to the same brutish world.

The sentimental indignation over the way the Duke of Windsor was treated, exhibited mostly by leftists and others who want to do away with the monarchy, is very hard lines on poor George VI. He never wanted to become King and consented only out of a sense of duty. People today who were not alive thirty-six years ago do not understand the very real distress caused by the affair and the total absence of anyone wishing to make political capital out of it then. The truth is that the majority of British people and all the Dominions would not have Mrs Simpson as Queen. Possibly in a similar circumstance today they would. But then, they would not. I think I realized that at the time, if reluctant to admit it, for I rebuked Harold Nicolson for being a party to hoofing the King off his throne. I was wrong. My indignation was caused by my being a believer in divine right. When the other night I heard a repeat performance on the radio of the King's voice during the abdication speech about 'the woman I love', I so well recalled the actual occasion. I was staying that night with Diana [Mosley] at Wootton

Lodge in Staffordshire. The tears poured down our cheeks as we sat spellbound.

Yesterday I lunched at the Travellers' with Hugh Montgomery-Massingberd* who is now editor of *Burke's Peerage and Landed Gentry*. With him his assistant, Andrew Wells,[†] who must be about 23. They were perfectly charming but so deferential and polite, the younger one calling me Sir, that I was put in a state of acute nervousness. I could hardly bear it I was made so shy. Eardley said it was nonsense. He may be right, but nonetheless such overt treatment makes me very uneasy: covert would be all right.

Saturday, 10th June

On Tuesday A. and I went to *Orfeo* at Covent Garden. About the most nostalgic music in the world. I was transported and although the drama of this early opera is static and abstract the scenario has tragic and poignant significance. The negress was very handsome and with her short hair made quite a passable boy lover to a feminine Eurydice in Elizabeth Vaughan.[‡] Returning to Eardley's flat found Duncan Grant[§] still there, having dined with E. He is very much on the spot, a roguish fellow, a kind of everlasting child whom all the world protects. But it is sad how old men with no one to look after them become very dirty and unkempt. His long, wispy, ratty hair most unattractive, his teeth decayed and green. Altogether an unsavoury old sight. One can talk to him as to a contemporary. When I said I found complete nakedness on the stage less exciting than partial nakedness he said, I don't agree.

Tuesday, 13th June

John Pope-Hennessy[¶] has invited me to join the organizing committee of the Byron Exhibition which he is to stage for the death anniversary in 1974. Very kind of him, and done because I put the

---

* Hugh Montgomery-Massingberd, b. 1946. Genealogist, writer and obituary editor of the *Daily Telegraph*.

[†] Andrew Wells, b. 1949, publisher and author.

[‡] Elizabeth Vaughan, soprano and operatic singer.

[§] Duncan Grant, 1885–1978, artist.

[¶] Sir John Pope-Hennessy, b. 1913. Director of the Victoria and Albert Museum, 1967–73, and director of the British Museum, 1974–6. Art historian.

suggestion to him for such an exhibition. O how I regret missing the ring.

Billa [Harrod]* stayed last weekend. A. was put out because Billa dared to criticize her food. I told A. it was a joke but she did not see it in this light. I admit Billa is often sharp but her show of being jealous of others whom she considers to be in competition with her is feigned.

On *Panorama* last night a film about conditions in Bangladesh. The Bangladeshis are utterly hopeless; the appalling state of the refugee Hindu camps, the corruption, the incompetence, the abysmal cruelty of the people, the over-population make one despair for the future of the world. I merely want to dismiss such matters from my mind which is of course funking. Yet what can one do? Such people ought not to exist. Yet they breed. These ghastly people are a sort of standing, or seething, pollution of the western world's perimeter, of the civilization that we have known. I can't stand orientals, their deceit and abominable cruelty.

Began last night in bed a book by Ziegler† on William IV. Extremely well written, and entertaining. I don't know who he is, but I am amazed by his good writing. Have just finished vol. 1 of *Phineas Finn*. Now this is not well written. Eminently readable nonetheless, and the characters firmly drawn. But style not good when one stops to analyse. I have begun this week writing on the Old Pretender chapter. There is not enough data to make my book interesting, I mean data as to everyday matters so as to bring out the characters.

Pat Gibson to whom I wrote last week informing him of the dilapidated condition of Northwick Park house which I visited, has answered. He confirms that the house belongs to a Cowdray syndicate; that he did not know the house to be of any interest, and is appalled to learn of its condition and will speak to his family about it. So agitation does sometimes have effect.

Wednesday, 14th June

A Mrs Pope wrote out of the blue, offering me letters written by my uncle Robert Bailey to her late husband, called Jim Pope, of

---

* Wilhelmine Cresswell, b. 1911. Married 1938 Sir Roy Harrod (d. 1978). Norfolk conservationist and founder of Norfolk Churches Trust.
† Philip Ziegler, b. 1929. Biographer.

the Indian Civil Service. She says Robert and William Leveson-Gower were her husband's best friends. She never met Robert for she married in 1923.

Fop looks rather mothy now, and exceedingly thin. I took him to the vet who said his scent glands were not functioning properly. He squeezed them, a horrid process, and lots of pus, evil-smelling, came forth. Last night sleeping on his armchair he breathed in a stertorous way which alarmed me. I went up to him and kissed his dear old snout. When he walks beside me he nuzzles the back of my leg to tell me he is there.

I almost shocked A. with the vehemence with which I said this morning that I would betray my best friend and go to any lengths short of murder if I thought he proposed desecrating the landscape or an old building.

Thursday, 15th June

To London for *Alcina* at the Festival Hall. I don't like opera performed in a concert hall with the singers dressed in evening clothes, gaping at each other, half acting, half not. Some fine Handelian music and the best airs sung by James Bowman, counter tenor. He gets most applause. When he begins to sing, and in recitative, the voice is raucous. You think this is not to be borne. Then you get acclimatized as the saying goes. This young man has tremendous force, and his manner is nonchalant, and off-hand. Yet when he is singing he is concentrating tremendously. I found the manner rather attractive. He was criticized at Aldeburgh last week for being 'self-indulgent'.

Friday, 16th June

Such quiet, unwonted quiet, last night that reading in bed I could hear the Bristol trains, a sound I associate with Wickhamford, when as a boy lying in bed I sometimes listened to the expresses on the Honeybourne-Evesham track, which conveyed to me romance and mystery and freedom for others when I was stuck at home, fretting. I suppose I pictured rich and beautiful young creatures in first-class carriages *en route* to my adolescent vision of paradise.

Sunday, 18th June

Today raining again and bitterly cold. Wearing an overcoat in church this morning. So was everyone else. The Savorys' niece,* the pretty one who sings and her husband who plays the piano, both recent university students, were at Communion. Always a surprise when the young go.

Peterborough of the *Daily Telegraph* telephoned. They had heard I had written a novel. Taken unawares I said, Yes I had, and it was due to come out towards the end of the year. But when asked what about I hedged. I can't bring myself to say, incest and sodomy. So I said, a simple romantic tale, as it were a story by Mrs Molesworth with a twist. Then added that if they wanted further particulars, apply to Chatto & Windus. For I don't know what their views are on advance publicity. A. says Grace will give notice when she reads it. But she won't, and probably can't read, like the majority of mankind. Oh dear.

Micky Renshaw is staying. A very good guest, easy, willing to be entertained or to sit and read, full of fun and chat of the wicked sort. But a deeply selfish man, and ruthless, we both think.

Thursday, 22nd June

On Sunday after lunching at the Cottage, Caroline [Somerset] took Micky and A. to the House at Badminton. I perhaps foolishly (A. said, with idiotic bashfulness) declined because I did not want the Duchess to think I was hovering around again. I now wish I had gone because they were taken upstairs. They saw the room the Queen always stays in. It is Queen Mary's old room, A. says rather pretty, in pale pastel shades, a large and beautiful Regency bed. Whereas the D. of Edinburgh's room next door is very small and his bed a sort of truckle bed, the narrowest thing you can imagine.

We have just returned from an expedition with Eardley to Arlington Court [near Barnstaple], really in order to see once more Woodrow and Newman [curators], whom we appointed twenty-five years ago and who have an affection for us. We found the place greatly improved since we left it, not a thing we often say, or feel. Beautifully kept inside and out, well arranged (by us), having lately had much money spent on it. Astonishing that this ordinary house filled with ordinary things should have proved so very

---

* Penelope Price-Jones, soprano, and Philip Martin, pianist.

popular. When the Trust first discussed whether the house should be opened to the public I was opposed to it. The reasons for its success are that there are few better houses in this area of Devon for holiday-makers to visit during bad weather when they can't spend an afternoon at the sea, and that it contains model ships, seashells and other junk which appeals.

Friday, 23rd June

A. in the car said that we owed more to Harold and Vita than almost any of our older, now dead friends. I said yes undoubtedly, and that I missed them more than any. A. said she owed what gardening credit she now enjoys entirely to Vita who taught her all she knows. I thought of what I owed to Harold. Yesterday afternoon Newman rushed at me with a copy of *Another Self*, asking me to sign what he, like everyone else, calls my autobiography. Now it is not strictly an autobiography, but autobiographical sketches, which I regret I did not make plain. In writing this book I was inspired by Harold's *Some People*. That little classic gave me an idea for mine, but not the model.

This morning I received a letter from Richard Stewart-Jones's* sister Elizabeth [Pulford], suggesting that I write a biography of Rick. She says he has become a legendary figure, and while there are people alive who knew him, a life ought to be written. I could not write it because Rick had no life that needs recording bookwise, although his was a remarkable personality, wayward, idealistic, generous to a fault, intuitively intelligent, philanthropic. I could not write a life of this Sir Galahad without discussing certain aspects which would not suit his family, I daresay. Elizabeth says that his tiresome widow has destroyed all his boyhood letters to his mother, that sweet woman.

Monday, 26th June

I wish people would not telephone. Why can't they write? The editor of the *Sunday Telegraph* rang, asking me to review a book of Ruskin's letters from Italy. I asked when he wanted it; he said immediately. So I said I couldn't, because I was busy with a book and reviews for *Books and Bookmen*. One must draw the line

---

* Richard Stewart-Jones, 1915–57. Conservationist who lived in Chelsea.

somewhere. Now had the man written to me I should have had time for reflection.

Ros has written me a touching letter about Cecil Day-Lewis. Says that he murdered her, held a pistol at her heart at point-blank range, and fired. He killed her creative powers. There is no self-pity in this letter, and I take back any imputations I may have made that she revels in self-mortification. This clearly was a terrible blow from which she is still reeling.

When Olive Lloyd-Baker took me round her collection [at Hardwicke Hall, Glos.] of farm implements and showed me terrible instruments like the breast-plough, flails and very heavy sickles which men wielded across acres of fields I thought, What a cissy I am. Furthermore what physical endurance these men must have had, up till my lifetime, because these antiquated instruments of torture have only lately been discarded. No men do such physical labour any more. Dockers do not lift heavy cargoes, but merely guide cranes. I daresay miners still hack with their hands, but on the whole people do not do much physical work of a heavy sort any more. Can this be right? I think the muscles ought to be stretched to the utmost. Mine seldom were and I might be a better man if they had been. Pious talk. However, while Olive was descanting on the beauty of these weapons of destruction and fingering a scythe with her horny finger, I took a sideways glance at her face. There was a masculine glint in her eye.

Last night went to Langley House, now belonging to a Major Scott-Ashe, grandson of the Squire Ashe whom Kilvert wrote about. This woolly old squire a similar type, bucolic and stupid, but good. Knows little about Kilvert. The house, square, mid-Georgian, a textbook squire's house of the Jane Austen sort, cannot have changed at all since Kilvert's day. All the dear old family portraits still hanging on the walls, and little or no change in the musty decoration – one supposes.

Wednesday, 28th June

On Sunday and Monday we had the garden open. Sunday a beastly day, nearly 400 people came. Monday a bit better but leaden, and cold, fewer. Very many persons told me ours was the most romantic garden they had visited. They came clutching the RHS journal with A.'s article on our garden in it.

At 4.30 she and I left, and motored to London for John Betj.'s film première on Australia, and dinner after. While having drinks at the bar of the cinema Tony Snowdon arrived, ran up to us and talked about Bath. Full of vitality and cheer. Then Princess Margaret arrived, followed by the Prince of Wales. I was taken aback not having expected such. Elizabeth Cavendish presented us one by one. Then Princess Margaret came up to Tony and, small though he is, she almost tiptoed to kiss his ear, and whisper. Tony said, 'You know Jim?' 'Yes,' she said, and moved away. After the film we went to Rules restaurant in Maiden Lane where John had hired an upstairs room, with a single table. We were a party of ten, including Princess Margaret, Prince Charles and Tony. I sat next to Mary Duchess of D. and a nice youngish man, whom only afterwards I learnt was Patrick Garland.* Opposite him sat the girl he is living with, a film star, placed next to the P. of W., on Elizabeth's right. Then Tony, then A. on John Betj.'s left, John, Princess M., John Drummond who had produced the film, the Duchess, me, Garland. I hardly spoke a word to the royals, but watched them closely. Prince Charles is very charming, and very polite, shook hands with us all and smiled. P.M. is far from charming, is cross, exacting, too sophisticated, and sharp. She is physically attractive in a bun-like way, with trussed-up bosom, and hair like two cottage loaves, one balancing on the other. She wore a beautiful sapphire and diamond brooch. She smoked continuously from a long holder, and did not talk to John once. Prince Charles at 11 asked Elizabeth if he might leave, for he had to motor to Portsmouth. He said he was tired, and looked worn out. E. patted his hand and said, 'Of course, love, Sir,' and beckoned to John. We all rose. He shook hands with us, Princess M. kissed him and Tony called out, 'Good-night, Charles.' 'Good-night, Tony.' E., who had taken her shoes off under the table, walked barefoot downstairs and into the street to see the P. off. She said to the driver, 'Mind you drive carefully.' P.M. while she was out of the room picked up E.'s shoes and put them on her plate. This annoyed Tony who said, 'It is unlucky, and I don't like it.' So P.M. took them off, put them on her chair, and walked to the window. A. said to me, 'You must go and talk to her,' but I knew she didn't want me to. She said she wanted to leave. Indeed

---

* Patrick Garland, b. 1935, film and theatre director.

it was time. Finally she induced Tony to take her, after E. had said that I would drive her in my Morris. Thank God I didn't have to. In following her, Tony made us all promise to come back to Kensington Palace. Which we debated. I did not want to go because I thought P.M. would not be pleased. The Duchess said to me as we left, 'Well!' – nothing further.

However we went to the palace since the Duchess accompanied us, and we knew she would not stay long. Tony met us in the courtyard and explained to me the architecture; what was Wren's work, what his. Their apartments were very well done by Tony in mock William Kent style. P.M. more gracious to me in her own house and took me into the dining-room. But I did not find conversation very easy or agreeable.

Friday, 30th June

Yesterday the Bernays' boy[*] who has bought Alderley Farm lunched. He came to show us his plans for the vast new range of cow-houses he proposes building in the valley behind the village. A. said he was so terribly nervous that he could barely eat and did not drink his coffee. I did not notice this and thought he put up a good show. It was nice of him to tell us of his proposals. We expressed our distress and apprehension lest this beautiful valley might be spoilt thereby. It is the approach road to take the milk containers and the electricity wires and poles which must be installed that chiefly worries us. I am glad to be on good terms with him. He is Harold's godson, and a civilized youth.

Then John Fowler with Peter Hood,[†] his slave, motored from London to see the garden, now beginning to look its best, and fullest. He in raptures, and gushing so much one cannot be sure what he really feels.

I dined at Combe Hay Manor at the invitation of Barbara Robertson[‡] and Christopher Chancellor to meet K. Clark, who is one of the Bath Preservation Trust vice-presidents. I expected the whole committee to be present. But we were only eight in all,

---

[*] R. Bernays, son of R.H. Bernays, MP, and godson of Harold Nicolson.
[†] Peter Hood worked with John Fowler at Colefax & Fowler, decorators.
[‡] Barbara (née Fry) Robertson, wife of Charles Robertson and one-time chairman of the Bath Preservation Trust.

including Oxley the director and Jean Pratt* the secretary. Others
were two Robertsons (our hosts), K., Christopher [Chancellor],
Lord Raglan,† and me. Lord R. is to raise a debate in the House of
Lords in the autumn. The purpose of this dinner was to consider
how to brief Lord R. I liked him, mid-forties, quite bald, but
good-looking, chiselled face, and sandy dundrearies which I don't
take to. He is well versed in the various planning acts of Parliament, and an intimate friend of Wayland Kennet.‡ I urged that the
first thing was to get the Ministry or some central, national body
to control, vet and approve what the Bath Council proposes to do
with every Bath building that we consider of importance. K. very
wisely said that a list of these could be made within a week, for in
the city centre nearly every building is important.

K. was treated like the sage he is. All deferred to his opinions
and when he spoke all stopped talking, and listened attentively. He
said to me before dinner that Christopher talked too much and
his wife talked at the same time; that he could hardly bear it, and
that Jane refused to accompany him for this reason. K. thought
Christopher's mind was failing, and he knew that his own powers
were failing. It has taken him three months to prepare a lecture
which we are going to hear him deliver at Ditchley next month.
He says, no more lectures for him. Life is too short.

Combe Hay is a splendid house, touching the church, and
commanding a lake below and a bank of trees beyond the lake,
extending to an open amphitheatre of fields. House has a late
Georgian front, good; side elevation very well contrived also
late eighteenth century, and back elevation early Georgian and
v. fine.

Saturday, 1st July

Exactly a year ago I restarted this diary, meaning to continue
for six months by hook or crook. And here we are. Diary has

---

* Jean Pratt, indefatigable honorary secretary of the Bath Preservation Trust.
† FitzRoy Somerset, 5th Lord Raglan, b. 1927. Founder of the Bath Society,
1977.
‡ Wayland Young, 2nd Lord Kennet of the Dene, b. 1923. Labour Party
spokesman on environmental affairs in House of Lords.

not turned out the kind I meant. It is too factual, too gossipy, too introspective which I disapprove of, and lacks, well, cognition.

Last night dining with the young Garnetts* at Bradley Court I talk with Michael Briggs. He says that K. Clark treats him with the utmost courtesy because he is a friend of his son Alan, and makes it plain that this is his sole reason for doing so. The politer K. is the more Michael realizes how much he disdains him. I don't suppose this is strictly true. Michael notices how much K. has aged lately. The cause is Jane of course and her making a fool of herself – a perpetual anxiety to K. He has already had trouble with Alan,† now installed in Saltwood Castle. It is the usual story when a father having made over property to his eldest son continues to live on the property – Gerry Wellington, David Crawford, the late Miki Sekers‡ are other examples. Alan has sold off a parcel of land for building, which is v. near the Castle and K.'s new bungalow. Hence – conflict.

On a walk round the hillside of Foxholes with the whippets the sun was shining on and the wind gently blowing the long grasses. These I saw as deep mauve and light blue, just as they are in the pictures of Impressionists. The mauve and white clovers in flower, their heads a tight bunch of honey-smelling, musty bobbles like those of a Victorian tablecloth or fringe. The smell very nostalgic and sweet. The dogs hate walking in the long grass fields for they cannot see where they are going and have to jump from time to time to get their bearings. It is as if I were wading through a dense jungle with the bushes waving above my head.

Called at Stouts Hill, Uley, because I shall include it in my *Country Life* article on Hardwicke and the Lloyd-Bakers. Such a pretty, early Gothick Revival house, with fireplaces of much fantasy and delicacy. But the whole place ruined by the school extensions and the usual horrors of institutionalism inside the rooms, and out.

---

* A. Garnett (Andy), entrepreneur, and his wife Polly Devlin, journalist and author.
† Hon. Alan Clark, b. 1928. MP, author and diarist.
‡ Sir Nicholas Sekers, textile weaver and entrepreneur immigrant from Hungary. Patron of the arts.

Monday, 3rd July

Dining at the Somersets sat next to George Weidenfeld.* For years I have harboured a very minute grievance against this man. He once asked me to edit a large book on European palaces, and I agreed with some reluctance, being in the middle of another book. Everything was settled, including advantageous terms, but nothing was signed. I heard no more. Then I discovered from Sachie that he had been asked and accepted. Tonight Weidenfeld was charming to me, and very interesting. Flattered me over St Peter's and the last book, and then suggested that I might write for him one on Bernini and his times – a good subject for a scholar. Asked me what I was now writing and said he would gladly accept the Stuarts. I said, 'But you haven't seen it, and you might hate it.' 'I will take it on trust,' he said. But will he, or rather would he? He is extremely well informed. Talked of the baroque and eighteenth-century popes. Knows each one. Then talked of Palestine and Israelis. Had strong views about the Israeli problem. Says he is a deeply sympathizing Jew but not a practising one. Has no belief. I did not suppose he had. He defended the Israelis' adoption of the Hebrew tongue. Caroline joined us at this stage and strongly disapproved, believing a new language a mistake. W. said, 'It is not exactly new. It has been the Jews' tongue for 3,000 years.' Dear C. rather confused.

Cecil [Beaton] was staying. Wearing red velvet and a red ribbony tie, most becoming. He is always very friendly to me. Also present Count Pucci, a charming man, designer. Very *bien*, quiet and interesting. Told me that his childhood was so sheltered, that he and his brothers were not allowed to drive in a motorcar before they were 18, nor to see other children, and were made to draw on their own resources. He says as a result he is extremely shy when meeting strangers socially, but not the least nervous in making speeches in the Senate or interviewing Prime Ministers.

Caroline spilt one glass of red wine over the table in the drawing-room. While talking to me she waved another full one round and round and over me. I edged away fearful that she would spill the second glass over my pale trousers.

---

* Sir George Weidenfeld, b. 1919. Chairman of Weidenfeld and Nicolson, publishers, created Lord Weidenfeld, 1976.

Denys Sutton[*] on the telephone told me he got into the same railway carriage as Julian Amery[†] yesterday, and talked with him from Brighton to London. Denys told how worried he and others were about Bath. Amery, who is now Minister of Environment, was astonished, thought Bath was quite safe, had not seen any of the letters in *The Times* published during the last two months, and said he would like to visit Bath. So I at once telephoned Christopher Chancellor who said he would speak to Sutton, and try to arrange a date.

Christopher said that K. Clark confided in him that Jane was a perpetual worry; that every time he went from home for a night he had to send her to a hospital.

Grace [housekeeper] yesterday was looking out of the kitchen window at A. and Cecil Beaton walking in the garden. I asked her if she knew who he was. When I told her it was Cecil Beaton, she said, 'He's the cook, isn't he?' Not exactly, I replied, but a famous photographer. 'But he cooks too,' she said. I don't suppose Cecil can boil an egg. She is a goose.

Friday, 7th July

Dining with the young Garnetts the other night was an American woman, far from young, rather raddled, dressed in trousers and a shirt like a bathing suit, exposing her stomach and navel. I found both s. and n. extremely unappetizing. When people look unattractive to me I can barely be polite to them, or rather I try to avoid speaking to them in order not to be impolite. For instance at the Droghedas' box on Tuesday Aidan Crawley[‡] was so ugly with a square jowl and bad teeth that I could not look at, far less speak to him. His wife Virginia Cowles[§] I had a long talk to during two intervals. With her large, handsome oval head framed in close dark hair she reminded me of some strong-minded Victorian

---

[*] Denys Sutton, b. 1917. Editor of *Apollo*. Art historian and dilettante.

[†] Rt. Hon. Julian Amery, b. 1919. Conservative statesman. Secretary of State for Air, 1960.

[‡] Aidan Crawley, 1908–93, chairman of London Weekend Television, 1967–71.

[§] Virginia Cowles, 1912–83, American journalist and writer. Married Aidan Crawley 1945.

woman of letters like George Eliot. She is very concise, opinionated and forceful. Speaking of the famous chess match between
America and Russia in Iceland, she said that chess was the greatest
game invented by man; that no task required greater intellect. I
said then it was a pity that such great intellects as the leading world
champions clearly had should not be harnessed to some more
useful occupation. She retorted that this was a puritanical attitude.
Chess in itself was a worthwhile objective.

The opera was *Traviata* with Caballé, the Spanish soprano.
Everyone present who knows about music, Joan, Garrett, Jimmie
Smith, Tony Gishford* and A., all said hers was a faultless performance. I was impressed by her complete control, but not by the
vibrating timbre of her voice. In this opera Verdi shows genius
when he makes Violetta in two most tragic episodes (one the
reading of the letter) speak the words in a sobbing voice to a
background of the softest, most heart-rending music imaginable.

Have been pondering over what someone said the other day:
that when one is awake at 3 a.m. then one sees life, and death, as
they truly are, in their stark, terrible, hopeless reality; that at all
other times of day, one sees these infinite things through rose-
tinted spectacles; that everyday life is the delusion, is the occupa-
tional opiate which deceives us into optimistic speculation.

Wednesday, 12th July

Ian McCallum told me he was furious with Christopher Chancellor for making a gaffe at his expense. At a meeting recently,
with Ian sitting beside him, Christopher announced that since he
had taken over the chairmanship of the Bath Preservation Trust
the Trust had made great progress; for when he took over it was
in great disrepute. Ian, who was the last chairman, is not pleased.
The same day at Sally Westminster's garden opening I made a
similar gaffe, as though the idea was put into my head by Ian's
story. A woman, vaguely familiar, approached me. Gayly I said,
'Well, this garden *is* a vast improvement on what was here before.'
She looked crestfallen, and said, 'Sally bought the place from us.'

---

* Anthony J. Gishford, 1908–75, chairman of the English Opera Group,
1960. Director of Boosey & Hawkes, 1951–7.

Speaking of gaffes Caroline told us that she took the Weiden-
felds round Badminton on Sunday. Lady Weidenfeld said to Caroline, 'Did it take you a long time to find such a beautiful house?'
Caroline told this to someone who promptly repeated it to Sir
George.

Dining with Eliza Wansbrough on Monday to meet the
Woodruffs.* He is enormous, but enormous, with a belly larger
than Percy Lubbock's. He either perches on the edge of a chair or
sofa, or lies right back, flat, with his face and belly in the air. His
wife is a sister of Lord Acton and my old acquaintance Peter
Acton, who had the next room to mine in Magdalen quadrangle,
and was uncommunicative, and clannish. I had a long talk with
Woodruff before dinner. He and his wife have been given on
separate occasions a copy of my *St Peter's*. 'Hard cheese,' I said, 'I
hope you have given one if not both away.' 'We can't very well,'
he said, 'because His Holiness has inscribed them.' He told me that
the Pope lately received a memorandum signed by over 700
French priests to the effect that the Pope ought in the interests of
democracy to blow up St Peter's church. He says there is one
cardinal with extreme left views who would certainly do so if he
were elected the next pope. 'Then he is an anarchist as well as an
iconoclast,' I said.

Woodruffs have a little great-nephew aged 5 living with them.
At school he has a friend, the grandson of James Laver.† The little
Laver boy said to the headmaster, 'Grandfather Laver, Uncle
Douglas and God are the cleverest men I know. That makes three,
doesn't it?'

We dined with the Denys Suttons at Westwood [Manor] on
Wednesday. Strange and not agreeable to be in Ted Lister's cherished house after so many years, and what's more with his furniture
still there. We sat in what was his dining-room, the Suttons eating
in what used to be the kitchen. Sitting on the armchairs with Ted's
needlework, which incidentally he always protected with case
covers, except when Queen Mary came to tea, I thought how Ted

---

* Douglas Woodruff, 1897–1978, chairman of Associated Catholic Newspapers and editor of *The Tablet*, 1936–67; and his wife the Hon. Marie
Immaculée Acton.
† James Laver, 1899–1975, keeper of the Department of Engravings, Victoria
and Albert Museum, 1938–59. Expert on uniforms and clothing.

would have fumed. Sutton is an extremely clever man, and impresses us immensely. He says that the Common Market is supported chiefly by people who have not travelled, whereas its opponents are people who know the Continent, and France in particular. Says it is unbelievable how quickly the political situation has changed for the worse here. Does not put it beyond likelihood that a minority of leftists will, just as the Bolsheviks did in Russia, infiltrate themselves, and that one day soon we shall wake up to the fact that all private bank accounts have been frozen, all export of possessions stopped, and we shall be enslaved like those behind the Iron Curtain. Thinks an immediate revolution probable, and an authoritarian government absolutely essential. George Weidenfeld said exactly the same thing a week ago.

For the past two lovely nights we have heard a thrush sitting in the large catalpa tree singing like an opera soprano to its mate in a nest nearby. It begins at 8.30, not before, when the sun starts setting. Its note is as fine as a nightingale's; it also imitates other birds' notes. What a wonderful thing it is, and something which one takes for granted. I no longer do, either because I am getting old or, more likely, because I see the possibility of all bird life becoming extinct within a short time. We are watching a flycatcher's nest on the terrace wall facing the garden. Three little fledgelings are so grown up that they perch on the edge of the nest. How the nest carries their weight and bulk is a mystery.

Monday, 17th July

Candida Lycett Green* told me that she asked Princess Margaret if she ever saw Crusty (by whom she meant Tommy) Lascelles who has an apartment in Kensington Palace. The reply was, 'No, never. Certainly not. He ruined my life.' Candida asked me what she meant. I said presumably she was referring to the question of her marriage with Peter Townsend, when Lascelles,† who was King George VI's Secretary, opposed it.

Coming in at the back door I saw on the ground a naked fledgling. A. noticed that it was still breathing, and asked me to kill

---

* Candida, daughter of Sir John Betjeman and wife of Rupert Lycett Green. Writer on the smaller houses and cottages.
† Sir Alan (Tommy) Lascelles, 1887–1981, Royal Secretary.

it. I said I couldn't. So she took it and bashed it on the paving and threw it in the bushes. I feel dreadfully ashamed of myself. She made no remark, but she must think me extremely wet, which I am.

Yesterday Mrs Pope came to tea bringing me the packet of letters written by my uncle Robert Bailey to her husband from 1907 till R.'s death in 1917. Though they were boys together at Eton and friends of a lifetime all Robert's letters from the first to the last begin My dear Pope, and end, Yours ever, Robert or R. Bailey. Their flavour is of another age, their brand of humour, somewhat academic, always correct, gentlemanly, a trifle pedantic. Curious dated words and expressions are used throughout, like 'topping', 'your minor' (meaning your younger brother), 'your people' (for parents), 'town' (for London) and 'now I must turn in' (meaning 'go to bed'). All references to his greatest friend, William Leveson-Gower, are to Leveson-Gower, never to William. I remember he did address him as William in his later letters. He and Robert learnt to shoe horses for the exercise, and took a farriers' examination – Dadie Rylands' Self-mortification again.

Saturday, 22nd July

At Oxford on my way to London on Wednesday to look up further inventories of James II's belongings, in the Bodleian. While waiting the customary hour and more for the MSS to be produced wandered round the town. Looked at no. 63 High Street in which I had lodgings for two years, and wondered whether my room had been on the first or second floor – think the second – when a round-faced jolly man pushing a bicycle into the door asked if I wanted anything. I thanked him and said, No, I was merely looking at the house where I lodged forty years ago and more. 'Good Lord!' he said, and laughed heartily as though it was the funniest joke he had ever heard. Then I realized the man may have been about 20. I was horrified by Oxford, so down-at-heel, filthy streets, shabby streets, undergraduates worse than shabby, hippy to a man, jeans, beards, bare feet, hair in the wrong places, stinking; the walls have slogans daubed on them 'Why are the workers penalized?' 'Fuck Sparrow!' etc. Crowded, steaming and beastly. Hideous, unsympathetic new buildings beyond the university town, and by the station a wilderness of a car park; the station demolished and replaced by sheds which look as though put up in the afternoon for a week's duration. Walked into Magdalen. Much the same. My rooms in College, Cloisters no. 6 ground floor, looked as lugubrious as ever. Peter Acton had no. 5 next door and I remember him standing at the entrance in the cloister grinning superciliously. Gardens well maintained in an urban fashion, corporation bedded-out flowers in regiments in the borders.

William Plomer* gave a lecture at the Royal Society of Literature. What he said did not have deep significance, but the way he quietly and humorously delivered the lecture was a work of art. In reading some funny passages from Kilvert he briefly stopped to laugh, but not uncontrollably, which much enhanced the audience's pleasure. Still he did not impart the message why Kilvert is such a superlative diarist, beyond his being a poor curate working in the country who noticed life's small contingencies. There is more than that to him. He was a prose poet, he looked at natural things and he saw deep meaning in little events. He understood human nature like a god and sympathized with simple people. But William has become a beautiful man with his white hair and sharp gentle features, and his beautiful manners.

A fascinating talk on the Third Programme last night about computers. The speaker said that within one generation a super-machine will exceed the intelligence of man. Whereas today the computer gives forth what man has fed into it, tomorrow the computer will create on its own. It may even decide that man must be eliminated, and will proceed to do it. Frankenstein's monster come true. The ultra-intelligent machine is not just a probability, but a certainty. Furthermore within fifty years man will live to be 1,000 – another reason why the machine may decide to eliminate this pullulating pest from the earth's surface. If these prognostications about the potentialities of the ultra machine are true, then I foresee that there will be no further need for man to have a brain and use it, and so he will deteriorate into a brute or rather an inferior machine himself. The creator will be eaten by the created.

Friday, 28th July

John Fowler staying two nights in Bath with his assistant, Peter Hood. I visited the Bath Assembly Rooms with them, also Mon-

---

* William Plomer, 1903–73, author.

tacute. Was pleased John agreed with me that the precious fabrics at Montacute are suffering shockingly from too much light, and that unless protected the Gothic tapestries will have faded within another twenty-five years so as to be fit for the dustbin. I cannot get the N. Trust to realize the importance of protecting their fabrics even if it means darkening the rooms to twilight. I summoned up my powers of generosity, which are difficult to muster, and gave John my 1570 copy of Palladio's *Quattro Libri*, with which he was delighted and touchingly grateful. He said he would leave it back to me, but I said, No, we are the same age. He said of course he would predecease me. One can never be sure. Anyway I did not want him to think I regarded his life as a poor one.

When Robert Cecil* lunched with me in London and we were talking about the Robinson boys, he complained that they refused to be confirmed. He is godfather to Nick. I asked if they were atheists. No, he said, but they do not think there is anyone qualified to give them instruction. Surely this is a trifle arrogant. He said the Robinsons were costermongers in the eighteenth century.

In my book I have got well underway with Prince Charlie, but find I am writing the familiar story of his Scottish flight. Just could not resist it. Since it has been told so often I fear my version will be redundant.

Sunday, 30th July

On Friday evening we motored to Ditchley to hear a lecture by K. Clark on the Universal Man. Very suave, very balanced and plenty of food for thought. No lecture by K. disappoints. He told me the other day that the preparation of this lecture had given him infinite pain, and it was the last he would deliver. So I am glad I heard it. The Universal Man is someone who gives fresh answers to the ancient, timeless question – Alberti was the first, Leonardo, Newton, Franklin and Jefferson followed. Lord Perth in giving thanks suggested that K. was one such himself. I think this may be so. A. said as we came away that everything this man has to say is worth pondering. An extraordinary Foundation this at Ditchley. Why we were invited I don't know. Most of the invited were

---

* Robert Cecil, Assistant Director of the Wallace Collection, London, d. 1994.

distinguished ambassadors, artists, dons, the Cheethams,* Adrian
Daintrey,† John Sparrow,‡ and countless others. Diana Cooper
came late into the marquee and stood myopically at the entrance.
We made her sit with us. She looks an ancient woman now, with
sunken eyes and taut skin. Said she was involved in yet another
motoring contretemps with the police. Her foot got stuck under
the clutch, mercifully not the accelerator. Asked her age, which is
80, she replied, 'A certain age.' They interpreted it as 70. She was
pleased. K. came up to me most graciously – he is always gracious.
Said he had come straight from Houghton, which is far larger than
Ditchley, and less beautiful. Does not like the state rooms being
on the piano nobile. My opinion of Houghton is the opposite of
his. I find Houghton perfection. Ditchley is spoilt by the iron
cages over the chimney-stacks. It is a pity too that the sculpture
figures with trumpets on the main front are set in front of
the chimney stacks, which make them invisible. I find the outside
of this house a little too stiff and gaunt, but the inside wonderful.
After an excellent supper we walked on the west terrace. A
mown lawn gives way to a field of cut hay which slopes down to
the lake. Nothing could be more serene on a fine, calm, warm
summer night, the air perfumed with sweet smells. Mrs Lancaster's
planting of hedges with statuary a masterpiece, more French than
English.

Last night we dined with Eny [Strutt]. Her nephew Guy Strutt§
the only other guest, a most intelligent, well-informed man. After
dinner he talked of mental disease as though he were a doctor.
Referring to his half-brother John Rayleigh¶ he said a curious fact
is that schizophrenics are nearly always tall and gangling as indeed
John is; whereas manic-depressives are stocky in physique. Why
this should be is not known. A. and I remarked that Mrs Mason,
our late housekeeper, was stocky, and certainly a manic-depressive.

---

* Sir Nicolas (John) Cheetham, b. 1910, and Lady Mabel Cheetham. He was
ambassador to Mexico, 1964–8.
† Adrian Daintrey, artist.
‡ John Sparrow, warden of All Souls College, Oxford, 1952–77. Born 1906,
d. 1992, man of letters and bibliophile.
§ Hon. Guy Strutt, b. 1921. Younger son of 4th Lord Rayleigh.
¶ John Strutt, 5th Lord Rayleigh, 1908–88.

Strutt said that mental disease was caused by chemical deficiencies or irregularities; that in taking blood from a schizophrenic and injecting it into a fly and giving that fly to a spider to eat, the spider will make an irregular, Heath Robinson web, and not one of the normal, regular pattern. He also asserted that doctors now make use of graphology in detecting whether patients are afflicted with mental disease and of what sort. This science taken more seriously on the Continent than in Britain. For example, he showed a specimen of his brother John's handwriting to a distinguished doctor who on the spot diagnosed his trouble as schizophrenia. Strutt also told a story of the late Duchess of Albany who at church found that her large bun was coming undone. After receiving communion she pinned the bun to the beard of a man praying in the pew behind her.

Thursday, 3rd August

Yesterday morning scanning *The Times* and reaching the obituary page I noticed the heading *Father I. Evans.** At first this meant nothing. On looking again I realised it was Illtud. A pang shot through. Then before reading the obit. turned to a paragraph on the opposite page about the tomatoes which have to be thrown into the sea because of the dock strike. Thus do the deaths of our dearest friends – not that Illtud was anything of the sort – affect us when we have passed the age of 60. I suppose it is God's kindly means of obscuring the yawning grave when we already have one foot in it. I immediately telephoned Eliza [Wansbrough] who knew and was dreadfully upset. Shall have supper with her tomorrow evening on my way home from Beckley.

Friday, 4th August

Motored to Beckley Park, so called. It is a small house, very high with at the back three square projecting garde-robe flues and a staircase, the latter a twisting spiral of oak treads carved underneath into soffits and the ends set squarely into the wall. Was perhaps built as a hunting lodge. You approach down a long, wooded lane, and it stands with feet on Otmoor. A most romantic, timeless old house like the end of a delicious dream, a harbour one longs to get

---

* Father Illtud Evans, OP. Intellectual Roman Catholic priest.

to. The shaded garden of clipped box pyramids and curlicues, and tight yew hedges. Semi-moated still. Red brick on a stone base. Inside, plastered walls studded with timber, ancient furniture and the general atmosphere reminding me of Westwood, Ted's house, *délabré* too as though it had just survived Cromwell's Civil War. The bedrooms looked very uncomfortable and before central heating was installed it must have been the coldest house in Oxfordshire. I liked the Feildings,* dedicated to the place, as to a delicate and precious child. They are threatened with a motorway 50 yards from their front door *and* a reservoir which will submerge not only Otmoor, the oldest moor in the world, but Beckley House as well. The view from the upstairs windows of a far-away fen-like landscape, uneventful, seemingly isolated, yet beastly Oxford suburbs but 2 miles off.

I then dined at Broughton Poggs with Eliza who is wretched about Illtud's death, and remorseful too. He had a stroke staying on Euboea island and died in an Athens hospital. Eliza feels sure the heat was too much for him and that he had probably drunk too much wine. She agreed he had become gross through eating, drinking and smoking too much. Now she regrets not having bought cigarettes for him towards the end of his month's visit to her, when convalescing. She said as fast as she filled the boxes he emptied them. I find this sort of thing in Catholic priests, which seems to be very common, particularly those in Orders – and he was a Dominican – distasteful. It is a contradiction of what the layman expects of a monk. But it is understandable because in monasteries they are starved.

Thursday, 10th August

The Duke of Beaufort told A. that he had received over fifty applications for the Badminton living; that the greater number of applicants were young clergymen, and the majority of these turned it down because the place was too dull, too easy and did not offer the challenge they wanted. I suppose this is encouraging. But why should lay priests want a challenge?

After church on Sunday our rector told me that, when he takes services at Hawkesbury to relieve the Hawkesbury rector on holiday, the congregation is never more than 4 persons, and the

---

* Mr and Mrs Percy Feilding, who retrieved, repaired and reinstated Beckley Park, and created the garden.

total population of Hawkesbury parish 1,000; whereas at Alderley
we righteous amount often to 10 (we were 11 today) out of a total
30 souls. How good we must be by comparison. The Rector says
it is a poor lookout for Hawkesbury Old Church, which is so
beautiful, and also so big.

Dining with Geoffrey Houghton-Brown.* He asked what my
novel was about for he had read the *Daily Telegraph* paragraph on
it. When I told him briefly he remarked caustically, 'Your friends
will say it is wishful thinking.' This alarms me. Will they really?

Cathy Lee† at luncheon on Sunday told me that every evening
Laurie goes to the Woolpack which is just above their cottage; and
returns at 11. She then has to give him dinner, having long before
that given the child its meal. He suffers from recurrent and acute
depressions, often self-induced. 'I tell him it is his own silly fault.
He takes Epanutin and other pills, regulating the doses according
to how he feels, and reacts.'

Just as I was boarding a bus opposite St Stephen's Hospital
yesterday Babs‡ rushed up, enfolded me in a voluminous embrace
on the pavement, jumped the queue, and followed me. I paid for
her ticket to the Green Park. We sat on the top deck for she is
a chain-smoker, all the daily workers silently reading their papers
or gazing into space – until we arrived. Babs without the least
concern or consideration for others talked at the top of her voice
a spate of highbrow stuff. She began with praise of A.'s article in
the RHS Journal and of her garden. I politely asked *sotto voce* what
book she was working on. 'The courtesans of Italy,' she bellowed.
'There is nothing, simply nothing I don't know about Italian
brothels,' she said. People looked over their newspapers at this
elderly British spinster. Then she rattled on about Aretino, how
permissive, yet how poetical he was. His descriptions of gardens
were so cerebral. And she proceeded to quote him for ten minutes.
I thought she was praising our garden at Alderley. I heard her
saying, 'Your pleached lime walks, your fanciful box hedges, your
topiary yew hedges. May we come again and enjoy the exquisite
calm and solace of your garden in the spring?' I said, 'Well, Babs,

---

* Geoffrey Houghton-Brown, 1903–93, dilettante and painter.
† Catherine Polge, m. 1950 Laurie Lee.
‡ Babs Johnson (*nom de plume* Georgina Masson), d. 1980. Writer and author
on gardens and buildings in Italy. Lived in Rome.

the garden is not up to much in the spring. You really ought to come next June.' 'What are you talking about?' she asked, 'I was quoting Aretino.' She must have thought me a fool. I don't care. English women writers can be terrible bores about their own books.

Monday, 14th August

Thursday afternoon Midi and I walked through the fields and back through the woods, getting torn to shreds by the briars. When I left her outside the Mount House Derick was setting off to Wotton in his mini-car. He threw me a word and I noticed how extremely red his face was and how bloodshot his eyes, and later remarked to A. how ill he looked. Indeed I talked to Midi about his health on our walk. She said his influenza last week made him tired and his temperature had fallen to well below normal. She did not seem unduly worried.

On Friday A. and I motored to Long Crichel for the weekend, the first for many a year. We enjoyed ourselves immensely. A. found Raymond [Mortimer] very gentle, unfrightening and sympathetic, always having been frightened of him before. Indeed he has mellowed. Desmond [Shawe-Taylor] excitable as though on the verge of discovering a new Maria Callas or Jussi Björling. Pat [Trevor-Roper]* our other host curiously silent and withdrawn, as it might be in awe of the others' superior intellects. But theirs are not superior. The real reason is that because Raymond and Desmond talk so much he cannot be bothered to compete unless his opinion is asked for. On the way we visited the garden at Cranborne Manor, that romantic house. Garden poetic like a missal illumination or a series of verdure tapestry panels. It is a wonderful place. We then visited the Anthony Hobsons† at Whitbury. Highly civilized pair, sharing our apprehensions about the world. And yesterday we lunched with the Reynolds Stones.

After luncheon Reynolds conducted us round his wilderness garden [Old Rectory, Litton Cheney, Dorset] from which he seeks exclusive inspiration. He neither wishes to nor can paint other

---

* Patrick Trevor-Roper, b. 1916. Ophthalmic surgeon and lecturer. A resident of Long Crichel House, Dorset.
† Anthony Hobson, b. 1921, bibliographic scholar, and Tania Vinogradoff his wife, who d. 1987.

places. The wilderness is beautiful, but uncontrolled, and I suppose even wildernesses need to be trimmed from time to time. But he will not have a fallen tree removed. Instead he allows it to remain a rustic archway covered with moss across a tangled path. Sylvia Townsend Warner* lunching. She asked if the Nat. Trust would accept her collection of china cats. What on earth can these be? I said I would have a look at them.

All the people we met this weekend were highly intelligent; all aesthetes. All deeply apprehensive about the dire threats to the land-scape, in fact to the whole earth. Yet not one of them has authority to help right matters. All must accept the devastating flood of spoliation. These people representing the highest standards of civilization are powerless to stop it. The flood is hastened by those who have the power, namely the vast mindless, faceless majority with no principles but personal greed.

On our return last night found a note from Midi which I did not open in a hurry, unpacking and putting things straight first. Then opened and read that Derick had died on Friday at 1 o'clock while we were setting out for Long Crichel. Poor Midi was in London for the day at a National Trust meeting. He was found dead at the garden gateway. I went round to the Mount House and met Midi and Bamber in the hall. At first both much moved, but Midi took me into the garden and walked and talked for ten minutes, very calm and controlled as I would have expected. Funeral to be at midday on Tuesday. I am putting off my journey to Scotland and A. telephoned Nancy in Versailles. She was going to ask if Nancy would mind her postponing her visit but N.'s voice so piteous, 'You are going to chuck, are you? I am dreadfully ill,' that A. could not bring herself to mention what she had intended to say.

Yesterday was A.'s birthday. I gave her a diamond eternity ring, one of my mother's.

Thursday, 17th August

On Monday to luncheon at Corsham [Court] for a meeting of the Methuen trustees with Robin [Fedden] and Fred Bishop†

---

* Sylvia Townsend Warner, 1893–1978, novelist.
† Sir Frederick Bishop, b. 1915. Secretary to Prime Minister, 1956–9; director-general of the National Trust, 1971–5.

representing the Nat. Trust. A strange position to find myself in, trustee of a large country house confronting NT officials. Paul Methuen's nephew John[*] present. He and Paul make thinly veiled attempts to be polite to one another. Paul growls and picks on every remark of the nephew. They are poles apart. Waves of mutual antipathy washing around the room. When I was leaving John met me getting into my car and said that his uncle did not know it, but he had fixed the settlement all right. By which I understood him to mean that when Paul re-settled the Estate's future he, John, made his solicitor insert a clause whereby he can bar the entail when he succeeds. An unwise thing to confide in me who am Paul's friend and only anxious to tie things up so that future heirs shall not dissipate the property.

I had to put off my departure at dawn on Thursday for Benbecula[†] on account of Derick's funeral. Had great trouble re-booking a seat for Wednesday. At funeral the church half full with relations, friends and villagers. While the congregation trooped out to the open grave I remained in the porch beside Quentin Crewe who was in his chair with an attendant. I cannot bear watching coffins being lowered into yawning holes. Then I helped the Rector clear up. Had to go back to the church door for the key and heard the jolly young sexton whistling while he shovelled earth with a hollow rattle upon the wooden lid; and thought how five days before I had watched the occupant drive his car at too spanking a pace into Wotton. Lunched with the Gascoignes after the service.

Stayed Tuesday night in London, arriving after dinner which I ate with a quarter-bottle of wine in the train, and was agreeably oiled. Left following morning, reaching Glasgow at noon. Waited for the Benbecula plane at 1 o'clock. Was piloted to the gangway, and at the door of the plane told that it could not land at Benbecula because of bad weather and was flying straight to Stornoway. What was I to do? Was told that to get from Storno-way to South Uist would take six or seven hours; then that there might be a plane flying tomorrow; and that there was no vacancy on the return flights of Saturday and Monday next. So reluctantly

---

[*] John Methuen, 6th Lord Methuen, b. 1925.
[†] J.L.-M.'s prearranged journey to the Outer Hebrides on the tracks of Prince Charles Edward Stuart.

decided I must return to London. Have sent my ticket back to the agents, begging them to get me off some cost of the journey.

Met old Tom* this afternoon out walking in the village and asked after his wife Mrs Gingle who has been operated on for cancer and whose case the Rector says is desperate. Tom said she was getting along nice, was at home now and was going off for a course of the radio, by which he meant radium treatment. Was he indifferent or being very stoical? I suppose the latter, just as Midi is. The Savorys said to me, 'It is their culture,' in referring to the guts and courage of the Gascoigne family.

Tom Gingle and Bill Raines belong to the true old Gloucester-shire type. There are few left who speak Gloucestershire. An old man I met at Slad the other day, did. When I asked for Laurie Lee's house he indicated, 'Ay, you'll find it under the Woolpack, yon-der.' Yonder is too good a word, too useful to be dispatched and made archaic. There is no alternative word as indicative. Yet it has gone with thee and thine, to our loss.

Saturday, 19th August

Went to talk with Joan Evans last evening. She visibly older in that she has developed that skinned look, taut and shiny face, straight falling hair like rain; but is as talkative as ever. Her chest rather more hollow and she has a tiresome, ticklish little cough. She told me her father was born in 1823, and her grandfather in 1781. That she hated Ivy Compton-Burnett ('That something, something woman,' she hissed) because Ivy made mischief between her and Margaret Jourdain, once a very great friend of Joan. Said she learnt more from Margaret in her young days than from any other person; and that Margaret's sister (the one who met Marie An-toinette at Versailles) left her, Joan, some treasures which Ivy claimed had been winkled out of the sister and ought to have gone to Margaret; that jealousy was the reason, but unjustified because 'my friendship with Margaret was entirely unemotional'. 'Then,' I asked, 'hers with Ivy was emotional?' 'Oh yes.' I could not follow up the subject. At any rate Joan expressed her hatred with venom in her eyes. I said I liked Ivy and Margaret immensely. The subject arose when Joan took me into her dining-room to show me for the

---

* Tom Gingle, formerly occasional help in garden at Alderley.

tenth time the porphyry head, a lovely thing bought in Italy by her brother Arthur Evans. Asked my advice what to do with it on her death. I could not well say, 'Leave it to me,' so I said, 'Don't, whatever you do, leave it to a museum.' 'Yes, I think I shall leave it to the Ashmolean.' 'Where it will be put in a cellar and be forgotten,' I added. She said, 'I would have left it to Margaret Whinney, only she is too old, quite 75.' Why does she ask me these things? Is it to tease?

Joan Evan's other great hate is Winston Churchill. She would not watch his funeral on television. She is almost the only person to agree with me that Winston Churchill was responsible for the widespread destruction of European works of art in that he refused to consider conditional surrender. Had he done so the war would have ended long before it did and before the nations sought to release their rage in needless carnage and destruction. Besides, Churchill so evidently enjoyed war that I could never like him. I merely acknowledge him, just as I acknowledge Genghis Khan, to have been great.

Joan showed me a drawing given her by Donald Milner* of the Pavillon de Flore of the Louvre, which is excellent. She greatly values the drawing and likes it for sentimental reasons. She told me she used to wait on a seat beneath the pavilion for a lover – 'perfectly respectable I need hardly assure you' – granted – 'It was a case of *l'amitié amoureuse*.' I dared not ask, was it a man?

Sunday, 20th August

Lunched with Miss Lloyd-Baker at Hardwicke. Could not refuse her request for advice. She has bought a nice little early nine-teenth-century yeoman's house at Moreton Valence just off the Hardwicke estate into which she may retire. Certainly she intends to alter it. Of course I am opposed to any structural alteration of an unspoilt building however humble. But I had to concede that to be made into a gent's residence this one required improvements. The living rooms are gloomy with small windows, and the south blank wall is at present stark and austere. The original staircase, simple but ingenious, is like a ladder. I tried to convey

---

* Donald Milner, d. 1993, artist in water-colours living in Wotton-under-Edge, Glos. Director of the Royal West of England Academy.

that when the gentry buy small houses fit for yeomen they usually spoil them, but I could not be too severe in her case. Yet she is bound to shelter behind my sanction if criticized for what she is about to do.

A. returned last night from Versailles. She had a perfectly ghastly week. Nancy crying with extreme pain; her sufferings terrible. She is so doped she does not remember how much dope she has taken. Has no nurse, only Hassan the young Moroccan servant. A. by dint of persuasion, finally threats, got N.'s consent to be flown in a stretcher to London next Wednesday for an operation by Dr Syriac. N. will regard this as a surrender no less ignominious than that of the French generals taken to Berlin. A. fears Nancy will never return to France. She was up with her the greater part of the nights and had to call the local doctor twice each night. There was absolutely nothing he could do but give her stronger drugs. A ghastly situation.

Monday, 21st August

Yesterday we lunched with Midi, Bamber and Christina. How lucky Midi is in these children. Veronica and William Plowden[*] also there before luncheon, with babies, all very scruffy, but so solicitous. Bamber told A. they would not leave their mother until they felt sure she was all right.

I made a gaffe. We were observing at the luncheon table how thin Christina was. Before I realized the liberty implied I remarked that she looked like a piece of chewed string. There was an ugly pause, and Bamber said with a wry laugh, 'I shall have to ask you to meet me behind the gasometer.' Christina flushed. A few minutes later I compared Christina's beauty with Veronica's, and said she resembled a Gothic Madonna, Veronica a sibyl by Burne-Jones. Whereupon, smiles all round – at least I think so. Later A. rebuked me for my string remark. She said it was the sort of thing no woman relishes even in jest. But I protested, in vain, that Christina was young enough to be my daughter. 'Never mind,' A. said. How touchy women are about their appearance, even

---

[*] Veronica Gascoigne, m. 1960 the Hon. William Plowden b. 1935, executive director of the UK Harkness Fellowship, New York.

modern girls who pay no heed whatever to conventional dress and make-up.

Tuesday, 22nd August

I do not often look at my body closely. I did so today in the glass. It is becoming like that of St Jerome in Old Masters, the old man's, bulging at the waist in a roll, elsewhere creased, dented and scrawny, like stretched elastic.

I motor to Marston in Lincolnshire to stay two nights with the Squarson, Henry Thorold.* He looks as Rory Cameron might look under torture: a profile like George III's and a stomach like George IV's. Is rather greedy and hogs his food. An enthusiast. Madly keen antiquarian. His passionate interests are architecture and genealogy. Knows Lincolnshire backwards, and all the families that ever were, they being to a man his relations. Is fervently right-wing and deplores all that I deplore. Is in fact a most sympathetic being. He motors around the country in a large old Bentley motor car and wears a dog-collar, an unexpected combination. Belongs to the school of Wyndham Ketton-Cremer† and Gyles Isham,‡ who is a close friend. Is one of the last county historian squires. Should be an archdeacon. Marston his house is the fragment of a once larger medieval mansion, reduced in size in Georgian times. Crammed with Thorold portraits. Henry has recently imported and set up a whole room from a family house, Burston near Dulverton, namely a 1699 plaster ceiling and wainscot, grained and painted with coats of arms, and over the fireplace a portrait of a country house, possibly Burston at that date.

Wednesday, 23rd August

All day motoring with Henry, principal objective being the Wyatt mausoleum at Brocklesby Park, a very delicate and wonderful

---

* Revd Henry Thorold, b. 1921, Squire of Marston Manor, Lincs. Chaplain General to the Forces and to King George VI. Lincs. county historian. Chaplain of Lancing College, 1949–68.
† R.W. Ketton-Cremer, 1906–69. Squire of Felbrigg Hall, Norfolk. County historian and man of letters.
‡ Sir Gyles Isham, 12th Bt., 1903–76, of Lamport Hall, Northants. Landowner, actor and connoisseur.

artefact on the lines of the Tivoli Temple of Vesta. Two things struck me as being wrong. One is that although an eye-catcher from the house, the entrance door and steps of the mausoleum are not centred on the house; the other is that the sarcophagi (stone) in the exedras are set behind the columns. This is clumsy. They ought to be behind the intercolumniations. I cannot understand why Wyatt did this. Perhaps when drunk and no one liked to say anything.

Thursday, 24th August

This morning Henry took me to Harlaxton Manor. I was last there in 1944 when Mrs Van der Elst* would not allow me access beyond the back regions, although she had sent for me. This time we penetrated the state rooms. And what a treat. I think it is the most remarkable Victorian country house I have ever seen. Never remember being so struck by a building before. It is nineteenth-century baroque revival. The great staircase is a *tour de force*, with cherubs scrambling over ceilings and swags in the round. This conception apparently Burn's[†] not Salvin's.[‡] There is much harking to Vanbrugh especially in the forecourt entrance pylons. Quality of all is superabundant strength. Great hall somewhat too narrow. The Jesuits have painted out the ceiling of the gallery which contained scenes of the gods disporting themselves. Frankly I have yet to see the painted ceiling which could turn my thoughts to lasciviousness. What a house! The sort of nineteenth-century architecture which thrills me. Bayons Manor is another, in the same county.

Sunday, 27th August

I asked Bamber if he would bid for me at a sale in a small house in Uley which he and Christina took me to on the preview day, I

---

[*] Rich lady crusader against capital punishment.
[†] William Burn, 1789–1870, Victorian architect of heavy derivative classical style with deviations to Scottish baronial.
[‡] Anthony Salvin, 1799–1881, domestic architect in styles ranging from castellar to Tudor to Georgian.

being away for the actual sale last week. I bid for an early twen-
tieth-century edition of Pepys's diary, up to £12. It fetched £20.
My other bid was up to £20 for three eighteenth-century vols. of
Warburton's translation of Virgil. They fetched £180. Prices as-
tronomical, a Dutch landscape fetching £40,000, bought of course
by a London dealer. It is no longer possible to pick up a bargain in
the country. Indeed I think it harder than in London, country sales
fetching higher prices than at Christie's and Sotheby's.

Monday, 28th August

Yesterday we had the Westmorlands* and Denys Suttons to luncheon. David told us he is chairman of the Commonwealth Games
Committee and has just returned from a hurried visit to Munich.
Said that the participators in the Olympic Games waiting at Munich all got on well and displayed no nationalistic animosities
whatever; that the political wire-pulling was directed from the
governments of the various African states, and the decision to
boycott Rhodesia was made by these governments; that when
announced in Munich the boycott caused surprise and embarrassment amongst the players of all nations. The Westmorlands are a
striking pair. He a fine fellow with exquisite manners. She, Jane,
one of the most beautiful women I have seen. It is almost *lèse-
majesté* to be in the same room with someone so divine.

Denys Sutton impresses me greatly. Has become distinguished in
his middle age, almost leonine, bushy hair like grey sunrays
through a cloud, and little spade beard. Suggests a mid-European
professor of Hebrew. His affability belies what I know from
second-hand information – his irritability and disagreeableness to
inferiors. But he has the mind of a stored art computer. By the flick
of a mental button can disgorge whatever information is required
within a second. Said to me, 'Now I have a good architectural
reviewer I shall send him all books on that subject. He can cope
with them all.' 'But,' I said, 'there is much architecture on which
he may be abysmally ignorant.' He answered, 'He only has to
know about the basic principles of the science and have general
knowledge.' Said that the young architectural historians were far

---

* David Fane, 15th Earl of Westmorland, 1924–93, and Jane Findlay his
wife.

better writers than the young pictorial historians for some reason. Instanced Watkin,* Mordaunt Crook,† Mark Girouard.‡ Said how bitchy the picture historians were. A young man sent a loathsome letter to one of his contributors, a rather diffident woman who had written on the de la Tour exhibition. She showed it to Denys in distress. Since the letter was written on Courtauld Institute paper he sent it to Anthony Blunt who gave the young man the stick. Denys will never publish anything of his again. He is devoting one whole number of *Apollo* to K. Clark. Agrees that K. is a *great* man.

Tuesday, 29th August

Mama's birthday. I think of her lying in bed, looking so pretty, with her blue eyes and a blue ribbon somewhere about her nightdress, those eyes twinkling with mischief as she tells the funniest story imaginable about someone she is fondest of. And whenever I dream of her she is utterly ageless.

Ursula Codrington§ after luncheon here yesterday told us that two years ago Leslie [L.P.] Hartley said 'It is awful that you have to work so hard for a living, and have absolutely no money of your own. I have got more money than I know what to do with. I want to make over to you enough to enable you to live comfortably for the rest of your life without working.' Ursula thanked him warmly and said she must think the offer over. After a week she wrote declining it because she did not want their friendship to be based on any sort of obligation. She told her great friend, the German professor, who said she was mad. She ought never to have declined. So Ursula wrote to Leslie again, saying she had now changed her mind, and if he hadn't already given the money to somebody else she would after all gratefully accept it. The reply

---

* David John Watkin, b. 1941. Fellow of Peterhouse, Cambridge, lecturer on history of art, and author of architectural books.
† Joe Mordaunt Crook, b. 1937. Professor of architectural history and author. Slade Professor of Fine Art, Oxford, 1979–80.
‡ Mark Girouard, b. 1931, writer and architectural historian, Slade Professor of Fine Art, Oxford, 1975–6.
§ Ursula Codrington, secretary and confidential friend of several well-known authors.

she received was cold. Leslie said he *had* in the meantime given the money to somebody else. Ursula said to me, 'So you see through my own folly I have lost both the money and my pride.'

A. said apropos my novel, 'It wouldn't have mattered if Bamber had written it because he is younger than you and does not live here in the country, leading a conventional life, sitting on the Wotton Planning Committee and the PCC.' But although I do these things I am not altogether a conventional person. This morning I received a postcard from John Sutcliffe* saying the book is marvellous and he is shortly submitting some sketches for the jacket.

Wednesday, 30th August

Listening to a double piano concerto by Poulenc† in bed this morning, I thought he is about the last composer whose music I can enjoy. Not so astringent as Stravinsky and less powerful, but melodious, polite and very French. Also whimsical. The rattling and discord are melodic. I met Poulenc twice with A. after the war. I even think he came to see us at Roquebrune – a very tall, ungainly, shapeless man, somewhat in the touselled build of de Gaulle, with the face of an elephant. He was extremely reticent and quiet, spoke little and not a word of English, which however he understood; and displayed a gentle irony.

Friday, 1st September

Yesterday being Audrey's birthday I took her to luncheon at the Bay Tree in Burford and on to Wickhamford to see the old Haineses. But before calling we walked into the orchard and talked to the gardener of the present owners of the manor. He said they were away and we might walk in the garden. We went into the church and both agreed it had been too tarted up. All the oak pews which used to be silvery grey are now varnished a black treacle. A blood-red un-fitted 'fitted carpet' covers the chancel. In our day the church very simple and slightly down at heel. I am so pleased with Reynolds [Stone] slate tablet I had put up to our parents. A beautiful thing worthy of the monuments in this old church. The

---

* John Sutcliffe, artist and designer of book jackets.
† François Poulenc, 1899–1963, French composer, disciple of Satie and friend of Cocteau. One of the musical group, *Les Six*.

garden much changed. Nice that an opening has been made in the trees the far side of the pond so that a distant view now had from the house across the field opposite and the hills beyond Broadway. Found in the spinney the dogs' cemetery. I had forgotten it. Little stones carved with the names and dates of the departed, with sentimental inscriptions and even poetry quotations, rather touching and what Vita would have called 'how'. The drain at the deep end of the pond still emitting the same clear, resonant note of falling subterranean water brought back ambivalent memories of adolescence. Peered through the windows of downstairs rooms, all pitch dark and melancholy. Commonplace furniture and subfusc stuff, quite without taste and the most ghastly glass door leading to the terrace. Hideous bedding-out, reds and yellows. In fact the house struck me as the most melancholy place imaginable. No wonder it was an unhappy one.

Beautiful sunny day and driving back across the Cotswolds the sky darkened behind a pitch-black cloud of the sinister sort, caused by stubble burning which takes place at this time of year all over the country. It destroys much animal and all insect life, little voles and spiders. Makes one sick. At Wickhamford all the elms dead, and every surviving tree has some disease. The pear trees, apple trees and prunus in the village gardens all dying. A sort of death pall has descended. What can be the meaning?

Tuesday, 5th September

Of course, whatever they say, the cause must be poison, in the shape of spray, or salt, or tar, or some artificial mortality-inducing, short-term chemical which farmers drown our earth with. And if that were not enough they have to burn what is left.

Penelope [Betjeman] came to luncheon and I took her to Hawkesbury to look at some derelict cottages. Which she liked but has already found something in Radnor which she wants more and has made a bid for. Truly I hope she does not come to live within a mile of us. I don't think I could bear it. I love her dearly but she is impossible to be with for longer than two hours at a stretch. No wonder John cannot endure. She bulldozes one, is utterly self-centred. She overwhelms, and overbears. Strange thing is she makes pitiable excuses for John always. Says he has to go to Scotland, or he has to stay in London for a film. She never admits that he prefers to be with Elizabeth, and is with Elizabeth the greater part of his spare time.

On arrival here a terrier – 'as good as gold' of course – two horse saddles, some sacks and paper parcels and a bale of straw tumble out of the boot of her car. In the hall she flings the straw on the floor for the dog to lie on. It promptly lifts its leg against the staircase.

Wednesday, 6th September

As we arrived at Laurie Lee's new house on Sunday, walking across a beastly path of concrete just below their picture window, poor A. again fell flat on her front. I could not prevent it for she was behind me. So quick it was. Mercifully she merely grazed, badly it is true, her two poor legs below the knees. No other hurt. She behaved wonderfully, appeared not even to be shaken, never said a word, merely dabbed TCP on the wounds and laughed whereas I just gaped with horror, and admiration: not helpful. I believe this accident shook me more than her. It is dreadful to see A., always so poised, so distinguished, thrown off her balance and laid low. Makes me realize how precious she is to me, more and more as the years whirl by, and dread ever losing her. She left this afternoon early for London and Venice. The place takes on a muted, veiled, crepuscular aspect. The two great-nephews came to tea with me. I gave Nick the water-colour sketch by David Cox which I promised him if he passed his exam. He has got a B grade for his art thesis on Cox, which is good. We were not shy, but I must talk all the time for the silences are not congenial. Of the two Henry may be the easier because he has a better social manner.

When this morning I remarked to Margery (for something to say), 'Isn't the Arab massacre of the Israeli Olympic men simply dreadful?' she said, 'Yes, I hardly feel safe going about these days,' a Françoise retort. As she never goes further from Alderley than Wotton I don't think she need worry unduly. To A.'s expressions of similar horror to her Mr, all he vouchsafed was 'No.'

Having watched the Trades Union Congress on the television I am more and more convinced that Communism must come to this country within twenty-five years. The sheer force of it can't be withstood.

I go to London tomorrow and the next day fly with Eardley to Vienna. I don't want to go much, and am sad without A., but as she said this afternoon in parting, 'It is your fault. And your choice.' It is true. I did think it a good plan six months ago.

Thursday, 21st September

Back from Austria last night. A. already gone to bed, having returned from Venice the evening before. Great welcome from both dogs who tore down the stairs and covered me with licks. Their welcome always heart-warming. Eardley and I had been in Austria for a fortnight almost. We flew together to Vienna, intending to stay in that capital several nights. But the one room we managed to book was dreadfully noisy and we were informed there were no single rooms to be had in the whole city, so left the next afternoon. It is difficult getting single rooms anywhere unless one is on a package tour. In Vienna I managed to pay two visits to the Picture Gallery and was amazed by the collection's breadth, depth, what you will. It vies with the Prado in universality and stature. Did these pictures come largely from the imperial family I wonder. We had the usual row at Avis in hiring our car, for they said we must pay at a higher rate than the London branch had informed E. The girl behind the counter finally said, in a fury of rage, 'Your car is a whale label.' 'Is a what?' we asked. She repeated the astonishing statement. 'Oh yes,' we cried joyfully and left for the country. This girl the only, the single disagreeable person we met throughout our tour.

We stayed three nights above the Danube at Emmersdorf, opposite Melk, in a tumbledown 'Edwardian' castle, Schloss Rothenhof. We called the estimable lady who owned the establishment Mrs Burnet Brown after the late successor to Miss Talbot[*] of Lacock Abbey whom she in some wise resembled. With E. as with friends of a lifetime one is constantly saying, 'That person reminds me of So-and-So.' The Danube by Melk magnificent, enormous, profound and passionate. It flows in strange eddies which for a long time I couldn't understand because the eddies were not over one particular irregularity of the river bed, but flowing with the river, as it were in moving dimples. I decided that since there were

---

[*] Matilda Talbot, 1871–1958, donor of Lacock Abbey and village, Wilts, to the National Trust on the understanding that Talbot descendants might live in part of the Abbey.

no shallows, these eddies occurred where the river was on an unusually steep declivity, and flowing faster than normal. I could have a love affair with this river, and end by hurling myself into its bosom. In walking alongside felt tempted to do this.

For five days or so we visited numerous churches and monasteries, nearly all of which I had seen previously. Top of these comes the monastic library of Altenburg with blue and yellow painted ceiling, and white and brown book bindings and far views from the windows over the crests of trees. Like sailing or flying at skimming level over an endless forest. There is a magic about Austria at this season of the year, the gardens swaying with sunflowers, the window boxes dripping with begonias and petunias. At Gmunden we stayed in the Park Hotel on the border of the lake. One day drove to Almsee, left the car and walked along the shore until we reached a *gasthof* and lunched deliciously. This lake utterly silent and fathomless, bounded at the far end by a wall of mountain. After a shower of rain on our return walk bubbles rose to the surface from the bottom of the lake. At first we thought they were caused by fish, then realized the cause must be springs.

For four nights we stayed at Kössen in the Tyrol at the *gasthof* called Zum Postillion, of a young Baron Niedermair-Altenburg. From here we walked each morning, always finding a stray *gasthof* to lunch in. The Baron would talk to us each evening after dinner over our white wine. He is a friend of Angus [Menzies] and George [Dix], is very handsome, reminding me of Jamesey P.-H. in his younger days. Intelligent and *racé*, and full of charm, yet somehow too splendid to be true.* On our walks E. and I talked about him as though we knew him intimately, in a game of make-believe. We speculated on his character, his life, his temperament, his tastes, girlfriends, his inclinations. We spoke of him as a brother, a son, a lover; whereas we did not even know his Christian name. He was scrupulously correct, polite, informative, and distant. I was charmed with his devotion to Austria; he spoke of 'her' as the most beautiful, most civilized, desirable 'person' in the world. He loathed the Germans who form the majority of the tourists to Kössen and his clients. Described their dishonesty, how they steal from the hotel bedrooms. One of his servants caught a guest in a bus about to

---

* Baron Niedermair-Altenburg turned out not to be a baron.

depart with a painted chair from the hotel. The Baron worked for six years in London learning to be an hotelier. He decided that England was not a fit country to adopt. It is, he assured us, unsettled; there are endless strikes, whereas in Austria there are no strikes. In Austria there is only one Union, there are not several as with us. The country is run by a very socialist government.

Saturday, 23rd September

A Dutch couple called at the door. The wife was the great-grand-niece of Brian Houghton Hodgson* who lived in our house for thirty years, dying in 1894, a man for whom we have a great regard. They own the portraits of Hodgson which are illustrated in his *Life*. Very nice, stuffy and fusty, and Dutch. It is extraordinary how often people call whose ancestors lived here. I am always delighted to show them round.

Yesterday spent at Stourhead with Graham [Stuart] Thomas and Kenneth Woodbridge. Woodbridge has taught me what is the trouble with this property. It should not be treated as a garden, but as a park. In other words Graham is a gardener, and a nursery gardener, and when he retires his place should be taken by a forester. The mistake recently made at Stourhead has been to plant isolated specimen trees instead of groves of prosaic trees, like willows, poplars, beeches, tulip-trees, in masses, not in spots. And I am sure those damned rhododendrons are a mistake and should be decimated if not eliminated altogether.

Tuesday, 26th September

Got a very sweet letter from Eardley today, saying I am the easiest person to be with because he never has to think before he talks, and can be as happy either talking or remaining silent. I have replied that I regard him as my familiar. Indeed it amazes me that I can be with him all day and every day for a fortnight and never tire of his company.

A. and I went blackberrying in the felled wood across Ozleworth Bottom. A lovely, still autumn day. The unaccustomed view from this side of the valley towards Alderley was, we both

---

* Brian Houghton Hodgson, 1800–94, Indian civil servant and collector of manuscripts, now in British Museum.

thought, more spectacular than the other way round, one reason being that both Alderley and Foxholes woods are still standing. When they are felled and replanted with conifers the valley will not be very special. How tragically perishable all this beauty is. When A. suggests blackberrying I don't want to go. Once out with my walking-stick pulling at the brambles, with the sweet-sour autumnal smells of crushed leaves and blackberries in my nostrils, all my childhood love of the country revives and becomes concentrated in this pursuit of far away. Surely no fruit is so economical, so tightly packed, so beady. The dogs get very bored hanging around.

To return to Austria. Eardley and I came by chance upon a house in which Beethoven spent the last winter of his life before going to Vienna to die. We were motoring to Krems and the Danube and passed through a village called Gneixendorf. A sign indicated a way to Beethoven's House. We debated whether it was worth stopping and looking for it. Decided it might be. Then passed it by without recognizing it. Retraced. Finally were directed to a smallish country house of about 1800. Not a proper show house, it belongs to a farmer's wife whose grandfather bought it in the 1850s or '60s. On the first floor are the composer's rooms in which he stayed with his nephew. There was the sitting-room, the walls painted in landscape scenes, very pretty. The bedroom with two adjacent beds which I thought must be of later date, but the farmer's wife assured us were his. From the windows a prominent view of Gottweig monastery on the hill across the Danube. The year of Beethoven's visit was 1826.

In Salzburg we visited Mozart's house, a very different establishment. This is a tourist shrine. Many visitors wandering around. First floor a gallery of posters and programmes, etc. But the top floor on which he was born is furnished more or less as it was, or supposed to be, when the family lived there, with M.'s own harpsichord. A few relics, two locks of hair. One seemed faded, unless it was his when he was a child. The other strong, dark brown. How pitiable hair is, so lonely it looks as though it is something left behind that ought to have been buried.

Friday, 29th September

A. says that old people get suspicious without reason. She has lately found that notes have been disappearing from her wallet, and suspicion flies at once to one person. It is nearly confirmed by her finding out from her bank in Wotton that another bank received from our milkman a £20 note with the consecutive number to two others of the same amount which she had in her wallet. So we are waiting to learn from the milkman by whom he was given this particular note.

The swallows were not only circling overhead two days ago, but diving at the nest over my bedroom window in the corner under the cornice (where they always nest) to feed the young we heard squeaking in anticipation. Surely this is very late in the season for such antics. Yet tonight there is no sign of swallows, old or young. I can hardly believe that nestlings of two days ago could so quickly be equipped to fly across the continent of Africa.

A. telephoned Nancy in hospital yesterday to arrange date for a visit. Nancy answered the telephone with the single word 'Cancer'. So it is, and she knows.

Saturday 30th September

Have lately spent several evenings talking to Joan Evans. She much enjoys a good gossip. But my! she is astringent and clever, and critical and intolerant of fools.

Joan told me the whole story of Rose Macaulay's love affair with Gerald O'Donovan. He was a renegade priest who ran away from the Beda College in Rome to marry Beryl Verschoyle. They had three children, one at least alive today. He met Rose during the first war and they had a passionate and lasting affair. The story in *The Sunday Times* of the flat being bombed and all the lover's letters being destroyed was entirely autobiographical. Rose was unworldly, indiscreet, impulsive, but intensely lovable as well as very clever indeed.

Joan is giving me – for my lifetime only – a huge Persian carpet for the library here, on condition that when I die or leave this house, I leave or give it to the National Trust. It is sewn up in a bundle and I am to call for it next week. I have not even seen it.

Joan talks very slowly, precisely, a little pedantically, and her stories are long drawn out. She does not want one to talk. This suits me on the whole because I go to listen to her, but it does not make for conversation, and often I want to interject.

We lunched with Diana [Westmorland] at Lyegrove. Only Julian present, looking pale. David Somerset who imitates her beautiful, slightly cracked, broken, sad but amusing voice, says 'Don't you think she is more of a lady than Diana Cooper?' I said – this was lunching at the Cottage – I had never thought of making the comparison, but I did think no one more *racée* than Diana W. Yes, he agreed, and nothing Diana W. said, no amount of four-letter words she might utter, would make any difference. Not that I have ever heard her utter one, but she does not the least mind what she does say. For instance before luncheon her charming grandson Burghie with a very pretty girl were at Lyegrove when we arrived. After they went Diana said, 'The Westmorlands are away for the weekend. These two are staying alone. Do you suppose they tuck up together after luncheon?' 'Yes,' I said, 'I hope so.' Julian said he thought not; it was surprising how little the young did go to bed with each other. I said I thought they were seldom out of bed together. Burghie has beautiful manners, like all Fanes, and unlike some children of friends in these parts.

Motoring to Cirencester this morning I noticed that at long last the old disused army camp at Beverstone is being dismantled. The result presumably of constant pressure by the Council for the Protection of Rural England. This after thirty years of disfigurement. Lunched with Prue and two boys, Ted being in Scotland. I was shown Henry's falcon which is dressed in the traditional jess and bells and held on his wrist with a leash, a splendid cruel creature. I said to Henry, 'It seems a pity one can never make friends with such as him.' 'No, but each has a healthy respect for the other. It is a partnership rather than a friendship.' A point of view I appreciate.

Tuesday, 3rd October

Little things which others take in their stride reduce me to a state verging on nervous collapse, viz: having to put across to the parish meeting last night the story of the proposed building of new cow-stalls on Alderley Farm. The meeting saw little harm in this huge disfigurement of a beautiful unspoilt valley of small scale, being concerned only with the possible smell of slurry which I rather like. I got through this all right. Next, facing the suspect this afternoon with the theft of a £20 note from A.'s bag, one of several which have disappeared over the months. We had proof from the bank and the milkman. Of course she was tearful, denied positively that she had taken others, or any object, which I knew was untrue, said that her husband would kill her and leave out of shame at what she had done, their children would disown her and the whole bloody lot would starve. She contradicted herself as all liars do, in saying first that she was so desperate that she was driven to steal the one note; and in the next breath denying that she had any debts or was in need of cash. Didn't know what had come over her, etc. I sat watching the agony across her face, the plausible gestures, the acute embarrassment, and disliked her. I merely said that I would not tell her husband or the police. Before the interview my heart beat a thousand miles an hour, and now I feel as though I had raced to Wotton and back, non-stop.

Had a letter from some art historians in New York – will I give them a photograph of my picture of St Peter's, because Ben Nicolson[*] told them he was sure I would. But I have no photograph and cannot get someone from Bristol to come all this way to take one. I saw Ben two days ago, looking lean, cadaverous and extremely scruffy. His friends are fond of him, but I dislike his political views, his beastliness to his wonderful mother and his narrow-ranging art historicism. I have no patience with art historians. Give me amateurs any day – and by amateurs I mean unpedantic lovers of art, not soulless machines, computers which tell the date of a picture or piece of furniture and its maker by rote.

Cecil Beaton was lunching with the Somersets on Sunday. He said that all writers should make money, no matter whether their books were good or bad, or were needed. I said there were too many books published and I felt very little sympathy with authors of unwanted books. They ought to do something else for a living, sweep streets or become bus conductors. I hastened to add, before he had time to say it himself, that I did *not* exclude any of the books I had written from this unwanted category, but that I had hitherto earned my living by other means and now had some private means; and was a damned *rentier* in fact.

Wednesday, 11th October

Yesterday A. and I set off with Micky Renshaw and Philip Dimmick[†] from Kyrenia [Cyprus] in Micky's small Morris van for

---

[*] Benedict Nicolson, 1914–78, art historian and editor of *Burlington Magazine*, 1947–78; son of Sir Harold Nicolson and the Hon. V. Sackville-West.
[†] Philip Dimmick, friend of Michael Renshaw.

Turkey. Took the car ferry from Nicosia to Mersin, a journey of eight hours. Between Silifke and the ancient city of Diocaesarea are several tomb structures. One of these standing alone, and another adjacent to an ordinary temple structure, are most unusual in being of two stages and orders, Doric below, Composite above. They are otherwise like garden temples. Both have pediments carved out of vast blocks of stone and rounded arches within. The roofs of both are formed of barrel vaults carrying massive stone tiles in two layers on either side the ridge. This is something which I do not remember ever having seen in antique architecture, unless it be the Temple of the Winds in Athens. The Temple of Zeus at Diocaesarea has Corinthian capitals said to be the earliest of that order known; certainly they look either archaic or decadent, perhaps Egyptian.

At Anamur we stayed in a motel, certainly the most disagreeable of any we stayed in during the trip. The rooms were filthy, with cockroaches scuttling across the floor. We had to surround our beds with insect powder. A cricket kept A. and me awake most of the night with its echoing chirp in the resonant room. The riviera road from Mersin to Side, or rather from Silifke to Antalya, the most beautiful I have seen. Long, long stretches as yet unspoilt. Vivid green pine trees, with strong resinous smell, descending to the steep sea, sometimes turquoise, sometimes sapphire. Empty golden beaches, where we stopped and bathed. The setting sun on the red rocks unforgettable. The range of Taurus mountains set back to the north as it were the Apennines behind Reggio. No words can describe this perhaps obvious beauty. The French and Italian rivieras must have looked like this 200 years ago, only they always had villas. Here none. Whatever the Turks build today is hideous and shabby, and unfinished. As we drove Micky sang, 'In the night of dirt and squalor / onward marched the beetle band / Chirping songs of expectation / as they bit the languid hand.' Anamur castle reaches the top of castles seen. The sea literally laps the corner towers. A mosque in the middle of the rampart. The outer walls crenellated. We climbed one tower of barrel-vaulted chambers supported on a central single round pillar containing the spiral staircase. This lovely place we had to ourselves at 9 a.m. before a charabanc of trippers from Glasgow arrived. Dear old Scotch bodies, mostly crippled and already very tired, sucking peppermints and loathing every moment.

Thursday, 12th October

The theatre at Side. It is the classical theatres here which amaze. So complete. This one has an open view from the crescent of seats towards the sea and mountains. I believe that originally there was always a back stage wall and the stage was covered with tarpaulin or its equivalent. Along each gangway the end seats have a claw leg. The vaulted lavatory in a semi-circle round a vast pier with niches for statues, very fine. Channels for flushing. The side ruins are somewhat spoilt by unsightly iron stanchions for wire-netting, as yet lacking, and iron pylons much in evidence. Amazement at the expenditure which the ancients lavished on public entertainment, cruel though it often was, and the great numbers inhabiting the packed cities, if these immense theatres are anything to go by. Here the outside of the theatre is two-tiered. The so-named Kaisersaal, or gymnasium, is the most baroque thing imaginable, concave-headed arches to the niches.

Aspendos theatre a barrack-like structure, unbeautiful, though astonishing because intact. I suspect as much Seljuk as ancient, and presumably the rectangular windows are Byzantine. The proscenium façade the most complete of any in the world, over-elaborate carved openings, with alternate pointed and elliptical heads. Theatre built into the hillside. We picnicked entirely alone in the auditorium. Perge theatre is even steeper if not larger. Here heaps of carved marble columns and entablatures crashed to the ground, presumably during earthquakes. The dreadful destruction of beautiful artefacts of yesterday contrasted with the survival of loathsome plastic products of today. Today is hell. At Perge theatre there is the only evidence of a barricade between the tormented wild beasts and the audience.

Side was not discovered until 1900 and the present town arose around the excavated ruins. In the heat of Saturday morning I was, as I thought, entirely alone until a dark, handsome head popped up from behind a fallen piece of masonry. It was that of young John Murray[*] who doubtless had been hoping he was the only pebble on the beach. We saluted each other guardedly, but respectfully, as English people do in foreign parts. The proscenium end of the theatre a tumble of masonry only kept from total collapse by the

---

[*] John Murray (VII), of the publishing house founded in 1768.

columns having fallen into the horizontal. Here as in the Lebanon the ancient columns have been used by subsequent builders and cut horizontally as a kind of binding. I can see one from my bedroom window in the little hotel in Pamphylia we stay in. The vast soffit of the imperial *loge* is one solid piece of marble on end and as it fell *in situ* on the right of the auditorium. The original setting of royal boxes like that at Covent Garden. A large roundel of carved bay leaves on the soffit, the entablature heavy with moulding.

The muezzin here sounds at 3.15 a.m. I dislike its nasal wail. Throughout Pamphylia [the region] the cotton is being picked. Large sacks of snow-white down bursting through the seams. Rows of parked lorries one behind another waiting along the roads to collect them.

During dinner at our hotel at Side an unrehearsed interlude. Three local musicians march in headed by a piper. Violinist holding instrument below his waist and sawing it; a drummer. For two hours the same rhythmic dance tune, waxing into a frenzy. All the diners get up and join in, no one quite touching hands but waving handkerchiefs. Men dancing to men, women to women. Then the waiters dance curiously crouched up, one to another and to the guests. It was like a ballet scene, absolutely spontaneous, gay and yet melancholy.

Sunday, 15th October

Termesso necessitated climbing a steep hill, we having motored several miles above sea level and left our car under a tree. On the way we gave a lift to the custodian who told us he walked to work daily 8 kilometres up this mountainside. Then we went on foot, following him, through a forest of stunted oaks. Up, up, up, no direction signs. We came to an avenue of dismantled tombs, desecrated by treasure-seekers and jumbled together, helter-skelter like fallen packs of cards. Only they are huge sarcophagi, the size of Santa Costanza's in Rome, made of stone with anthemia at the corner of the lids, and tremendously heavy. A sparse carved decoration and Greek lapidary inscriptions. Peering from the rocks and deciduous trees, at this height, and remote, they are mysterious, almost sinister. A most haunted spot. The ubiquitous theatre has a view to the left of a towering rock face, and to the right a glimpse of distant blue sea through a gorge. We walked back across what seemed a street with round holes in the middle. Actually the holes were the open oculi of domes to deep water cisterns below. Yet the walls and vaulting of these caverns have plaster surfaces painted yellow. We picnicked below the city.

Motored on to Pamalukke, in the dark. We noticed that the plastic covering over our luggage on the roof had become dislodged and was waving behind the car like a pennon. We said, 'Let's hope no luggage has gone with it.' On arrival at Hierapolis found that indeed poor Philip's bag had fallen off.

Our motel built round the hot waters of Hierapolis with totally unobstructed view of the valley below and distant mountains, Lear-like. Swim in the hot water, which is like molten lead, heavy and tiring to move in, but soothing to the skin. Calceolareous waters said by the ancients to be beneficial. In afternoon I motored with Philip to local towns in search of news of lost luggage. At the gendarmerie hopeless, conflicting reports of what might have happened, theories and suggestions advanced by fairly friendly officials. The most fatuous that we should be accompanied by a stray Turk to the nearest town, Dinar, and search every white car we might find parked in the streets. Happy-go-lucky idiots. Returned to motel and bathed in the pool in the dark. Curious sensation to step from icy air into hot water, and worse to walk wet into the night.

St Philip's martyrium here most interesting early Christian edifice. Ambulatory through eight corner piers, angled. Columns must have been within the arcade. The cross, or Chi-rho, over each arch. Must have carried a huge dome. Large square side chapels. Cannot find out date of these ruins. Fourth century, or more likely sixth. Name provoked inevitable ill-timed jests anent poor Philip's martyrdom.

Wednesday, 18th October

Ephesus again after several years, and not improved. This is a tourist's paradise, and so has become much spoilt. Also archaeologist's hay-making resort. I would advise visitors to Turkey to come here first, because of the city's great scale, giving an idea of what a large classical city was like; also the long streets contribute greatly to the atmosphere. But there has been far too much and indifferent restoration. Even street paving has been carelessly relaid, judging by the marks on individual stones made by the chariot wheels —

always to me a most moving and convincing reminder of the busy past – because the ruts are no longer consecutive. They don't coincide. What sacrilege to have shifted these, unless previous civilizations to ours have done it. Several temples, like Trajan's, have been restored in a contemptible way, so as to be out of scale. A pediment has been raised on some concrete stumps. Theatre, though enormous, too restored. Although the setting is much as it was, the magic of Ephesus has departed. In other words where archaeology comes first aesthetics come a bad second. Aphrodisias is comparatively isolated, and in its natural state. Nice to see a stork's nest on one of the highest columns, left unmolested. The best ruin is that of the little concert hall with marble-lined pit for orchestra, now a pond filled with croaking frogs.

Thursday, 19th October

Motoring from Kusadasi to Side made a very long day. Besides stormy and cold. Between Denizli and Dinar, driving beside the shallow, empty, sandy lake with steep mountain range the far side, we watched flying towards us in arrow formation a flock of large birds in migration. Stopped, got out and looked through glasses. They were storks, their long necks outstretched, calling hoarsely to one another. Ahead of the main body a vanguard of six to eight and in the rear six flying more slowly as though they were the veterans. The foremost group wheeled croakingly to the left as though to investigate the way, corrected their course and proceeded southwards, the others not having reconnoitred in obedient pursuit. Had they come from Holland?

Rosie Baldwin,[*] who was Rosie Rodd and lives at Kusadasi, is passionately endeavouring to arouse Turkish concern for the dwindling wild life of their country. They don't care a damn. Nor are they the very least interested in preserving the landscape, or old buildings. Rosie looks like an old madam. She is still the same warm-hearted gypsy, now married to an uneducated, bearded American with a past. Did something like smuggling which brought her into trouble. His livelihood is hiring a motor-boat to tourists. Rosie keeps an antique or boutique shop. Like many expatriates she extols in one breath the life she has chosen and the

---

[*] Rosemary (Rosie) Dove, m. first 1948 the Hon. Gustaf Rodd.

inhabitants; and in the next protests that she is frightened, declaring them villainous people. She is clearly homesick and unhappy, and presumably very poor. The last time I saw her she danced a tarantella on a restaurant table in Trastevere. A darling.

Turkish towns are detestable, noisy and shabby. The old parts are slummy, the modern parts hideous beyond belief, the buildings unfinished blocks of cement set in wildernesses of waste and filth.

Wednesday, 1st November

Last night went to Sadler's Wells to see *Jeptha*, Handel's opera; I think the last opera Handel wrote. Said to be a hotch-potch from previous works it nevertheless contains very many splendid arias and the music is divine. We enjoyed it greatly. Handel was evidently much concerned by the inexorability of fate and the dictates of ruthless gods. Yet in this case he makes Jeptha impose his own fate, or rather the fate of his daughter. It was not Jehovah who made the idiotic condition that the first person Jeptha should cast his eyes upon must be sacrificed, but Jeptha himself. In consequence it is difficult for the opera-goer to feel great emotion over the crisis, which is as unnecessary as it is ridiculous.

This morning I went to the V & A Neo-classical Exhibition. It is the best arranged of any exhibition I have ever seen. Wonderful exhibits wonderfully displayed in a series of rooms decorated, albeit in cardboard and makeshift stuffs, to suit the works of art they illustrate.

Quixotically I bought this morning in Crown Passage two silver medals – one of James II when D. of York, the other of Cardinal Henry of York when he succeeded his brother as *de jure* King of England. The first solid and splendidly cast. The second touchingly inscribed: '*Non desideriis hominum sed voluntate Dei.*'

Sunday, 5th November

Spent the last three days at Flaxley Abbey,* arriving tennish each morning, reading through manuscript papers, being given luncheon and tea. Am very beholden to these sweet people, particularly Mrs Watkins who is pure gold. No wonder Oliver [Messel] adores

---

* Flaxley Abbey, near Westbury-on-Severn, Glos. Ancient seat of Crawley-Boevey family.

her. She sits most of the day, like one of our whippets at home, on the bottom step of the front stairs whence she can control every situation by sheer benevolence and waiting for Oliver perhaps. Mr W. a bit of a pedant about the monastic history of Flaxley; takes me out of doors in the rain to prove some point he has made that a stone in the wall is monastic, or a foundation recently dug up reveals where the chapter house once stood. This sort of information leaves me rather cold.

Mrs Watkins asked me if I wanted scampi for luncheon. I said, No, I much preferred the homely food she cooked, like the steak and kidney pie of yesterday. Mr W. professed he was so glad I said this; he never ate shrimps since his mother once saw a human corpse washed ashore. It was swarming with them.

Wednesday, 8th November

That idiot Grace left this morning, on the best possible terms. Her reason for going solely that she cannot work with a thief about the place. Otherwise she was blissfully content here; loved her flat and her work. Silly though she is she suited us well. I have now to inform Margery of the reason for Grace's going. Grace had told Mr Margery whose reply was: 'The vif is mad. She ought to be shut up. When you give her a finger she takes an arm.' And to A. he said, 'One day I shall walk out on her.' A jolly look out. The awful thing for a man in his position – which I need not specify – but a man entirely dependent on his wife and with four children to boot, is that he cannot do it.

Poor Lady Berwick* has been killed in a motor smash, crossing the main road from the Mytton and Mermaid, where she had been dining with her best friend, to the Attingham Park gates. Christopher Wall† tells me she was 83, very lonely, with creeping arthritis and subject to bronchitis; that it was a mercy she had no pain and died quickly. I think fondly of her when I first met her and Lord Berwick before the war, discussing with them how to make over Attingham to the National Trust. She was then very beautiful, young middle-aged, stately, unhappy with her old

---

* Teresa Hudson, m. 1919 8th Lord Berwick of Attingham Park, Shropshire.
† Christopher Wall, b. 1929, National Trust regional representative for Mercia.

eccentric husband, wanting romance. I always admired her, but found her too much *grande dame*, too much the tragedy queen. After Lord B. died how she mourned!

Friday, 10th November

On Tuesday walked with the whippets to tea with the Sam Lloyds* at Bagpath. It took me under $1\frac{1}{2}$ hours, and I went the longer way by the Wotton road as far as Wortley, then the Ozleworth lane, past Ashcroft, because of the wet and mud in the fields. It was a dank afternoon, yet I loved the silence and the dripping loneliness. Poor Sam had a very bad fall from his horse in September while riding with his groom, below London Bridge in Ozleworth park. He was knocked unconscious and broke a leg. The groom yelled for help and was heard by Brenda Tomlinson at Brook Cottage. She put on her gumboots and ran to help. She gallantly remained with the prostrate Sam while the groom rode back to Bagpath, warned Peggy and telephoned for an ambulance. Great difficulty getting him on a hurdle to the ambulance at Ozleworth lodge. Brenda was very kind.

Peggy Lloyd told me over tea that she has arranged to be buried in Bagpath churchyard because there is a rule that a church cannot be declared redundant until thirty years have elapsed since the last body has been buried in the churchyard. She says they are longing to declare the church redundant, and therefore she had better be in no hurry to get underground. Sam merely laughed. I can't believe she has got it right. A. called for me in the car, and we drove home.

Yesterday, Grace having left us I said to Margery who was cleaning A.'s bathroom after breakfast, 'Well, Grace has gone.' 'Yes, isn't it a shame.' 'Perhaps you don't know why?' 'No, I'm sure I don't.' 'It was because of you,' I said.

This afternoon we motored to Uley and down a small lane to look at a hill called Cam Peaked Down, which the NT have asked me to inspect with a view to their buying. It is an outcrop of the Cotswold escarpment, and comes at the end of the adjoining Cam

Long Down. I walked along the top of the Long Down. It was a beautiful afternoon, quiet and crisp, with distant storm clouds like drawn purple curtains, but sunny where we were. Very clear views of Gloucester Cathedral tower and the Malverns beyond. But my! how built-up the Vale has become. Just below the Peaked Down a vast chimney of the Cam Flour Mills was belching white smoke – at least it wasn't black – and roaring, like Oldham factory machinery. As our neighbour Mrs Anthony says, we live in the suburbs now.

Monday, 13th November

On Saturday night dining with the Briggses at Midford (Castle) I sat next to Anthony Blond.* I had long heard of him yet was expecting a flaxen haired Nordic giant. He is a dark, saturnine dwarf. Jewish I presume although his nose turns upwards. He is stocky, stalwart, and was dressed in mauve velveteen. He is ill-mannered, evidently leftist, easy to talk to, unprepossessing and what else? Conversation began by him saying, 'I like strikes. The more strikes there are the more I admire the British working man.' I said, 'I dislike strikes and the more there are the more I despise the working man.' Pause. He said, 'I enjoy tipping. It gives me a sense of power.' I said, 'Tipping ought to be abolished. It corrupts the giver and the receiver, and is absurd.' Pause. He said, 'You seem to be a consistent Conservative. I like left-wingers.' I said, 'I loathe left-wingers. You strike me however as very inconsistent.' End of conversation. When we left at midnight we shook hands warmly. He said, 'I would publish any book of yours.' I said, 'You are very complimentary, but I am sure you wouldn't.' Odd thing is that I nearly sent him my novel and might have done if Chatto had turned it down.

Last night we dined with Eliza [Wansbrough] at Broughton Poggs. Father Gilbey† staying. He is well groomed and well dressed in clerical togs and a sort of mourning coat. He has a silver calling-card case in his pocket; is entertaining, likes heraldry and gossip. Is bright and good company. A. liked him although she doesn't care for many priests, whom she generally finds very badly

---

* Anthony Blond, publisher and author.
† Monsignor Alfred Gilbey, b. 1900, Roman Catholic priest and dignitary.

dressed, and often grubby. Father Gilbey is the only member of the Travellers' allowed to live in the club building.

Thursday, 16th November

Crossing the Mall yesterday afternoon I stood and watched a troop of the Life Guards pass by. The leading horse was a grey and the officer on him wore a maroon cloak spread across the horse's rump. Behind in lines of three all the other horses were black, each with white socks. The men's steel helmets glinted in the wintry sun. Scarlet plumes hung behind the casques; the men's cloaks were black. Each man carried an upright drawn sword. I thought I had never seen a more beautiful show. And underneath the pageantry the men blackguards no doubt. Of course we do relish as much colour and pageantry as we can get. It is puritanical and untruthful or self-deceptive to pretend otherwise.

One night in London, staying at Brooks's. Very comfortable. On descending to breakfast I see across the passage four dear, or horrible, old chars sitting at one of the games tables in the card room, having a good natter. Two others dusting the staircase in a desultory way, both with cigarettes dangling from their lower lips. I pointed this out, without saying a word, to Oliver Barnett,* who cast up his eyes. Dined the Tuesday evening alone with Raymond [Mortimer]. Asked him why he had not written his autobiography. Said he could not remember anything of interest told him in the past, and only trivia. I said trivia were often more interesting than the profundities of the great. The truth is that Raymond is at heart a modest man, without ambition and with no wish to strike attitudes.

I was to have seen Nancy [Mitford] by appointment on my return to the station but she had had a blood transfusion the previous day, and was not up to visitors. In a horrid way I was relieved for I dread seeing poor N. in her present state.

Yesterday morning went to the Abbey which, or rather the nave of which, was sealed off. Asked to be shown to the Dean's Verger's office. Verger was sitting in a grossly over-heated room off the south aisle, sneezing. I said, 'You have an awful cold.' He said it

---

* Sir Oliver Barnett, QC. b. 1907, Judge Advocate General of the Forces 1963–8.

was the chill of the nave. I thought it was the overheat of his nasty little cubby hole. I have known this verger by sight for years. Handsome – knows it – and dignified when heading canonical processions holy poker in hand. He allowed me to look at Mrs Boevy's tomb by Gibbs and showed me the Jerusalem Chamber, on condition that I did not refer to it in an article without first asking the permission of Dykes Bower, the Abbey architect. Then I went to St James's Palace through the Lord Chamberlain's entrance. Met by Oliver Millar* – always so polite and also dignified – and directed to the huge Queen Anne Room at the south-east corner of the palace, which he affirmed was the room in which James III was born. But I can't believe this. It is far too large, that is to say if the original birth-room corresponded with the dimensions of this one, which dates from the early 19th century after a fire.

Sunday, 19th November

Sarah [Churchill]† in the film on Chartwell told of her father's liking of cats, especially tortoiseshells. There has always to be one at Chartwell. Once Sir Winston scolded his and it ran away. He told his secretary to put up a notice announcing that if the cat would return it would be forgiven. Sarah used to accompany him on his walks round the estate. He enjoyed scratching the pigs' backs. He said to her, 'Dogs look up to man. Cats look down on man. But pigs accept him as one of themselves.'

Thursday, 23rd November

Have finished three articles on Flaxley Abbey and can now get down to my Stuart book again after nearly three months' interval, caused by going to Austria, to Turkey and this *Country Life* work. Terrible how these interruptions occur, or terrible that I allow them.

Joanie Harford came to sup with us last night. Said that her Mrs Ricketts produced a beautiful daughter by a neighbour in the nearby vicinity twenty-five years ago. Her husband was so angry

---

* Sir Oliver Millar, KCVO, b. 1923, director of the Royal Collections and surveyor of the Queen's Pictures, 1972–88.
† Sarah Spencer-Churchill, daughter of Sir Winston Churchill, actress. Married 1st, 1936, Vic Oliver, stage entertainer, and 2nd, 24th Lord Audley.

that to punish her, as he thought, he refused ever to sleep with her again. So he removed himself to the sitting-room where to this day he sleeps in great discomfort on two chairs. Mrs Ricketts remains in the marital bed, which is just what she always wanted, she told Joanie. The wages of sin are everlasting.

A letter from Debo that had Nancy not had the blood transfusion which weakened her temporarily last week she would have faded away. She has leukaemia amongst other cancers. Anthony Chaplin told A. that N.'s leukaemia was probably caused by excessive sun bathing. I think most likely for she used to go every year to the Lido where she sunned herself for days on end. I always knew sun bathing to be a mistake, and I wish A. had not overdone it as indeed she used to when living at Roquebrune.

The genius of Virginia Woolf strikes me each time I read one sentence of a letter or jotting of hers, often written in between bouts of madness or even during them. Which makes me question how mad anyone ever is. I am reading volume II of Quentin Bell's Life. Excellent. But I am tired of the Bloomsberries and their squalid little incestuous relationships. They were an inestimable lot really. During the greatest war of carnage known to civilization they played no part in relieving suffering. Neither V. Woolf nor L. Strachey once refers to the horrors of the war to which they deliberately blinded themselves. I believe they were right to be pacifists for that war was totally unjustifiable. But their bitchy conduct at Garsington enjoying the fleshpots of Lady Ottoline Morell* whom they all abused and mocked behind her back does not commend them. Lady O. was the most stalwart of the lot. I saw her but once, at a picture exhibition. She pranced, head in air and with flaring nostrils, into the gallery and out again like an ill-disposed rocking-horse.

Saturday, 25th November

I lose battles all along the line. The Rural District Council has decided – I knew of course that they would – to allow the erection of an enormous cow factory in the Ozleworth valley behind this village, in spite of the valley being within the AONB which stands for Area of Outstanding Natural Beauty. These designations mean

---

* Lady Ottoline Cavendish-Bentinck, 1873–1938, m. 1902 Philip Morell. Bloomsbury hostess.

absolutely nothing. There is always a reason, venal or financial –
same thing – for the local authority to give way. Beauty of
landscape is absolutely at a discount in England and the world. Let
us face it. The most beautiful country of northern Europe in my
youth will before I am dead be irredeemably ruined, damned and
finished. Within one lifetime – it is a terrifying thought; and since
it coincides with my lifetime I feel fractionally responsible.

Sunday, 26th November

Stir-up Sunday. I remember the thrill of hearing the first words of
today's collect when I was a child, the evocation of scrumptious
Christmas pudding.

   Poor old Fop who has been ill these past weeks and had a serious
operation ten days ago, the removal of his scent glands, had to
return to the vet yesterday because of a leakage. His absence causes
a great blank in our little lives here. In bed last night I thought,
one *must* love, no matter whether one's love is returned. If it is, so
much the better. One should not expect it to be. Dogs certainly
depend on us. This is why they are important for the sake of our
character if for no other reason. For if they don't love us we must
not cease to love them.

Thursday, 30th November

St Andrew's day, on which Bonnie Prince Charlie successively
disgraced himself by getting drunk; and finally so disgustingly
drunk that his wife decided he was no longer to be borne and
flounced off to a convent, and thence with her lover, Alfieri. And
over fifty years ago I was wont to sit on the wall beside the Slough
road, wearing a scug cap, striped blue and white, and cheer the
Oppidans in their match against the Tugs at the Field Game. I used
to wonder how the perspiring mass, steaming beneath me, could
be so tough, so brave, so splendid.

Friday, 1st December

Compton Mackenzie* has died, having just missed reaching 90. I
spent forty-eight hours or so with him. He was writing a lightning
book about the National Trust, some twenty years ago. Various

---

* Sir Compton Mackenzie, 1883–1972, prolific author.

members of the Trust staff conducted him round specific areas. I
was deputed to meet him at the Swan, Bibury, and take him over
from Humphrey ap Evans. He had clearly fallen for Humphrey,
spoke to him and about him with affection and admiration. We
dined at the Swan and found dining there also by chance Barbara
Rothschild* and Rex Warner.† Anyway we had an uproarious
evening. His memory was prodigious. There was no one he had
met once whom he did not vividly remember. He was at Magdalen with my uncle Robert and spoke warmly of him, as
everyone who knew him did. (The late Dean of Westminster,
Donne, said the same complimentary things about him to me.)
The next night we stayed at the Shakespeare Hotel, Stratford. He
said before we got there that he had stayed in the hotel as a boy of
10 when one of his parents, I think the mother, was acting. He had
never been there since. He described the room he then slept in,
called, he thought Sir John Fastolph, at the end of a certain long
passage, which you approached this way and that. He wanted to
see if the room was still there. It was, and with the same title,
exactly as he described after an interval of fifty years or so. He was
very jolly with me, and friendly. We talked of George Lloyd and
mutual friends. I never saw him again. I wish I had.

Sunday, 3rd December

Before lunching with Peggy Willis‡ at Radway we went to see the
Grange, Radway, which I have always wished to see, as a specimen of early neo-Gothic architecture by Sanderson Miller. Very
disappointing in this regard, for what S. Miller did was to add some
thin trimmings of little beauty or substance. They are mere
scratchings at the surface of a dear old Elizabethan house. Inside
too his rooms, if they are his in being classical, not Gothic, are
feeble in the extreme. Nevertheless the house has charm, a spooky
charm. Its setting is divine, under Edgehill, the park sweeping in a
sickle away and upwards, with the tower, 'true rust of The Barons'

---

* Barbara, d. 1992, daughter of St John Hutchinson, KC, and first wife of 3rd
Lord Rothschild.
† Rex Warner, b. 1905, author, poet and university professor.
‡ Margaret Anne (Peggy), daughter of T. Walker, m. 1930 Philip Dunne of
Gatley Park, Herefordshire.

Wars', on the skyline. The house however full of fascinating pictures and furniture. I noticed one portrait of Sir Francis Dashwood in monk's tonsure, quaffing from a glass of wine. Also a conversation piece painting of Dashwoods, nice until I looked closely into it. I liked best the owner, rugged and handsome Mrs Starkey who kept saying, 'Lees-Milne, Lees-Milne, what does that remind me of?' 'My father,' I suggested, 'and hunting here with the Warwickshire [Hounds] and Harry Gwyer* who lived in Peggy's house next door.' I said to her, 'Have you been here long?' 'No,' she said, 'forty years' – a retort one could receive only from someone mock modest like her, for she meant that all these family possessions were inherited, even if the house was not.

Sitting next to Peggy Willis I wondered how she managed with only one hand, and that her left, all her life; so beautiful a woman she must have been, with two if not more husbands and beaux galore. She is very civilized and sympathetic. The Donaldsons and Sitwells to lunch, a lovely gathering on a winter's day.

Saturday, 9th December

As I left Eardley's flat this morning I was struggling to fold up my new collapsible umbrella. I said, 'Of all the things I hate most I hate gadgets.' He said he did too. 'Only Eddy [Sackville] loved them. Nothing gave him greater satisfaction than to buy a hat which would turn into a stove.'

Then carrying my smallish bag with my evening clothes therein, and my torn old sack with books for the London Library, I walked off briskly into the bright sunshine. For the past five days it has poured. Hence my new umbrella because I have lost, or I hope only mislaid, Papa's umbrella, which I would not lose for the world, having found myself by mistake with one belonging to another member of Brooks's (Lord Spencer). Took a bus at Hyde Park Corner to the Green Park for three new pennies. The black conductor very friendly because it is Saturday and the streets are comparatively empty and people are normal again and behaving like human beings and not animals as they do during rush hours. Said, 'This is Green Park, Mister,' pointing to what I knew forty

---

* Harry Gwyer (Mrs), a hard-going lady side-saddler, famed in the Warwickshire Hunt in the 1920s.

years before he was born. As I leapt off the bus like a gazelle I gave
him a gracious smile. Walked to Maggs bookshop, thinking since
it is a fine day and as Xmas is coming and I ought to be buying
presents for other people I shall instead buy myself that autograph
letter of Wordsworth for £200. Maggs shop shut. Walked to
Brooks's to enquire about my umbrella. Shut. To St George's
Bookshop to buy John Kenworthy-Brown's new book on French
furniture. Shut. To the London Library to get a book about the
Cardinal Duke. Book out. To the British Museum reading room.
Open. Hurray, and empty, hurray again. Went to the Reserved
Book department and was told to fill in a form for my already
ordered book. Waited half an hour. Returned to the desk and
said affably, 'If the books I wrote for are not here, that may mean
my letter has not arrived, Xmas rush and all, just tell me and I will
fill in another entry and wait another two hours.' 'Can't do
that', they said, 'it's Saturday.' 'So I see,' I said, 'on Saturday
London goes to sleep.' He shrugged his shoulders. I returned
fuming to my place. And thought shall I clear off, and go home.
Began putting on my overcoat, when lo! two books arrived. They
contained Pope Benedict XIV's letters and I scanned the index
for references to the Cardinal Duke. There were dozens. I went
through every one and learnt more about the Cardinal from these
references than from any other source. It is clear as day that he
was, poor man, homosexual. He had infatuations for young, handsome clerics. The Pope was surprised. Thought there was nothing
criminal in it. Nor was there. I doubt bed very much. Not at all I
should say. But his old father was very upset, and gave the lover the
sack. There were sulks, non-speakers and the Cardinal flounced off
twice. The father said I never want to see you again, and when the
son left, wept and begged his return. Not one word is mentioned
about love, or sex. Yet there it is, and no book has suggested it that
I am aware of it, until muck-raker Milne comes along. It all started
with Raymond apprising me of a disparaging remark in Mrs
Thrale's diary about the Cardinal's footman leaning too closely
over the Cardinal's chair, which might lead to other clues.

Monday, 11th December

At *Rigoletto* in the royal box, as the guests of Burnet (Pavitt), we
were six on Friday. I have never been among so few before. Nice

it was. Colly Clark, K.'s daughter, one of them. She talks very much, is sharp, but intelligent and likeable. Having accorded my book – always 'your book' as though I have written but one – *Another Self* praise she asked me point-blank whether it was true. Will people ask me if *Heretics in Love* or *St Peter's* is true? Maud Russell was there. When she told me she hated bathing in private swimming pools but preferred public to private beaches I expressed surprise. 'After all,' I said, 'you are the most exclusive woman I know. And the most fastidious.' She did not look pleased, so I added that I admired both qualities.

At luncheon yesterday Isabel Briggs said that in one of his prefaces Henry James tells how at dinner a neighbour began a story about a friend. 'Stop!' James cried, 'Don't tell me another word', and practically stuffed her mouth. It gave him the key to one of his greatest novels. Michael Astor said that last week he was bidding for Victoriana at Sotheby's Belgravia store. He got so excited, so carried away that he started bidding against himself. Determined to get some object he heard the auctioneer say, '£10, £10 is now bid.' Michael said, '£15!' The auctioneer picking up his bid said, '£15. Any offer over £15?' 'Yes,' Michael shouted, '£20!'

With reprehensible extravagance I have sent Maggs a cheque of £200 for a wonderful autograph letter of Wordsworth. On the strength of a cheque unexpectedly received from some bonds I have. The joyous reward of wickedness far exceeds that of righteousness.

Friday, 15th December

Audrey said rather pathetically while lunching here that Elaine complains about her always talking of the past. But I told Audrey, the present isn't much catch and there isn't a future. So why not?

John [Kenworthy-Browne]'s criticism is always sound. I have told him he is a sort of young sage. He has read the *Heretics* and says that the end is confusing. He is right. J. who cannot always decide what is the right course for him to take knows what others should take, and when and how they go wrong. He would be a splendid proof-reader, like Eddie Marsh, for he pinpoints errors and queries ambiguities. That is a very valuable gift. In fact he is an extremely perceptive person, because he is super-sensitive.

I stayed Tuesday night at Chatsworth for the committee at Sudbury yesterday. Only Debo and Pam [Jackson] there. Woman

[Pam] stayed one extra night because of my coming which flattered. It was fun the three of us gossiping. They told me their
grandfather Gibson Bowles, after their grandmother's death, had
an affair with his children's governess. The governess left and was
established elsewhere. She produced four illegitimate children for
him. They cannot understand why he did not marry her, for he
was a widower and she was everything that could be desired. It was
not snobbishness. Lady Redesdale remembered the governess leaving suddenly. She as a child was very upset. Then years later she
met the governess on a London pavement wheeling a perambu-
lator with curly headed babies in it. One of the illegitimate grandchildren is a well-known commentator on the BBC and interviewed
Nancy, her first cousin once removed. They got on very well and
N. told her how they were related. She had not known. Debo and
Woman think it the more strange of Gibson Bowles not to have
married the governess because he was illegitimate and never knew
who his mother was. He suffered much accordingly. His father
Milner Gibson, MP subsequently married and Gibson was brought
up with his half-brothers. His step-mother used to say to guests,
'These are my children and this is Tommy Bowles. And if you are
not nice to him you need not stay in my house.' The remark did
not however make the boy feel at ease.

Sunday, 17th December

Last night a young man, doctor of history I think from Liverpool
University, came for the night. He is writing a book about Princess
Winnie [Winaretta de Polignac]. Came to see A. not me, and plied
her with questions. Sensitive, intelligent and earnest. Not handsome, but a fine face, and very long, white, nervous fingers.
Pronounces Italian, Itarlian and holds his fork in that ungainly way
as though it were a dangerous instrument. Kept saying things like,
'Did the Princess really know Lady Diana Cooper, Lady Cunard,
Lady Colefax, Miss Rosamond Lehmann?' We almost felt apo-
logetic for knowing them ourselves and all the others he mentioned, and finally A. said, 'You see the circle was small. All these
people knew each other.' One wonders how he can and what he
will make of such a circle. How can he, born towards the end of
the war, and living in a genteel villa in the outskirts of Liverpool,
have a clue? But then how can anyone writing about a past age and

a circle of society which he has never been in, have a clue? It is audacity to write about anyone from the past. One can never know what their jokes were, their sophisticated nuances. One will take seriously what they laughed at and will laugh at what they felt seriously about.

Tuesday, 19th December

Audrey rang up on Sunday to say that Tony Stevens* had died during the night. She was with him in the hospital the afternoon before and he seemed better. He had sudden heart failure. The first she knew was the village policeman calling at 9.30. I am dreadfully sorry for poor Audrey, yet I can feel no sorrow for T.S. I long ago ceased to dislike – no that is not true – to hate him, which I did for a long time. But I could not come to like him. He was a bounder, and boring, quite apart from his dreadful failings in the past. Yet he was an object of pity, a failure, and like most people I suppose he had his pride. Audrey whom I went to see at Moor Wood yesterday said he always intended to slip away. He has devised his body to the hospital to be dissected. Audrey said feelingly that she could not leave him like that without a prayer or two, and she has got the parson from Windrush whom she is fond of to say a few. All rather pathetic. I ask myself do they have him in a coffin in these circumstances, or merely on a slab in the mortuary under a sheet. The mind boggles over the grisly prospect. What finally happens in cases of this sort? Do they sever the head like a fish's so as to make the corpse more anonymous? Or what? Poor Audrey must be pondering these unmentionable things in her head, and heart.

Yesterday she was like a pathetic little old hen that has received an injury and cannot make out what has happened to it. Clucking, darting about, and talking, talking nineteen words to the dozen.

Friday, 22nd December

Leslie Hartley's death has saddened me. He had a winning quality, and an affectionate manner. Ursula [Codrington] said there was no one she enjoyed being alone with more. You could say anything

---

* Tony Stevens, J.L.-M.'s sister Audrey's second husband whom she married during the war.

to him. She tried to get him to ask me to dine alone with him, but too late. It never came off. And he would not wish to offend A. by asking me without her. He wrote me a very sweet letter about *Another Self*. Ursula gave him my novel to read in its early form. He did not write to me about it, but told her it was well written, but could not be published because of the subject.

Wednesday, 27th December

It is interesting that the classless classes can never thank. This Christmas I have given £2 apiece to the dustman, milkman, postman and paper deliverer, for which no word of acknowledgement has come my way. They accept the gratuity as a matter of right. It isn't a right, but if one did not give, then the dustman would empty the dustbins on the drive, the paper deliverer would deliver the wrong newspaper. Actually in fairness to her the newspaper lady is sweet; so are the postmen, and so may be the dustmen whom I do not know. No doubt they don't consider they get enough. Even so they do not thank.

Caroline came yesterday before luncheon bringing her mother Daphne Fielding. The latter embraced me on the doorstep on coming and going. I was touched. Yet I hardly know her, having met her about three times in all. Is it meant to say, you are a friend of Caroline, so I accept you as one of mine? Very nice anyway. She is a kind-hearted, extroverted, twentyish beauty, with a mind. I asked her as a great friend of Diana Petre* to suggest that Diana does not mention her sister Sally by name in Diana's forthcoming book on their mother, for we know Sally is sensitive about her parentage and would hate it, yet is too proud to say so. Daphne agreed.

Lunching with the Gascoignes at the Mount House Midi said how topsyturvy the world is in the following respect. Whereas her son-in-law Will Plowden, descendant of one of the oldest families in Great Britain, sends his children to be educated at a comprehensive school in Battersea, where they have learnt to speak like cockneys and behave like yahoos, Charles Tomlinson, whose parents are working-class folk in Stoke-on-Trent, sends his daughters

---

* Diana Petre (Mrs), novelist. Author of *The Secret Orchard of Roger Ackerley*, 1975.

to Westonbirt, the smartest girls' school in the land. Now it isn't as though a comprehensive in Battersea educates better than say, Winchester or Westonbirt. It is a case of deliberate downgrading of children, of which I disapprove. I don't suppose the education at Westonbirt is highly academic, but it is from all reports pretty good. The Tomlinsons are right to wish to upgrade. Will Plowden told A. that he is a member of the Think Tank (for which he has largely to thank Eton), in fact has left the London School of Economics for this important purpose, which is a full-time job. William Rees-Mogg is another member. We went to a champagne supper last night at Ston Easton;* terrible din, crowds of known and unknown. But we found the John Jolliffes† to talk to. John introduced us to his uncle Oxford who looks a million and is years younger than us. Has white hair *à la brosse* and horny hands caked with earth, and is learned and very Catholic. Told us he possesses Mary Queen of Scots' veil and other Stuart objects left to his ancestor Sir John Hippesley by the Cardinal of York for being kind to the Cardinal when he was in misfortune and penury.

Saturday, 30th December

The Rector said on Christmas morning, 'When I have ploughed through services at Alderley, Tresham and Hillesley I am going to bed with [I didn't know what he was going to say], a large, a LARGE, Jim, bottle of port and my pipe.' Ploughed through!

We are having the shortest days now. By 4 it is too dark to read by daylight. I love it, the drawing of curtains, lighting of fires and back to the cosy womb. So long as we don't have social engagements I am as happy here as the days are short and the evenings long. Today I have finished the section on the Cardinal of York. I have the final section on the Countess of Albany ahead. Then I shall have finished, or rather finished getting the Stuarts down on paper – before tackling the polishing, the typing, the pruning, the correcting of publisher's corrections, the retyping, the prefacing, the acknowledging, the illustrating, the jacketing, the indexing

---

* Ston Easton Park, Som. (*c.* 1750), where the Rees-Moggses were then living. It has a Georgian bathroom.
† Hon. John Jolliffe, b. 1935, biographer and reviewer, and the Hon. Victoria Eden his wife.

and the whole seemingly endless appendiculating which every book, other than a novel, calls for.

Index